英语国际人

MW01273689

英语畅谈

青春文化50主题

50 Topics On
Youth Culture

刘佳静　Jessica Robertson　Liz Carter 著

外文出版社
FOREIGN LANGUAGES PRESS

Forword

The purpose of this book is to provide young students of English with a text that addresses not only grammatical concerns but also practical ones. The topics of this book are designed to address the needs and interests of the younger generation. Some of the topics include blogs, Google and infomania, for the technology-inclined. Those who are thinking about starting their careers might find the topics on interviews or headhunting interesting. There are also topics on social life, such as dating and nightlife. The lessons in this book are intended to give readers practice with the English vocabulary and grammar needed to discuss topics that have direct applications in their daily lives.

Dialogue

Every chapter contains 5 dialogues, often between a Chinese person and a foreigner or between two foreigners, about the chapter's topic. The style of speech is colloquial and idiomatic appropriate for everyday conversation. By reading these dialogues out loud, the reader may develop a sense for the flow of English conversation and how spoken English may differ from written English.

Background Reading

Each chapter also contains background reading. This section provides useful information about the chapter's topic that both elaborates on the discussion in the dialogue and enables the reader to have a firmer grasp of the situation. While the dialogue will provide the reader with the linguistic tools to better express his or her opinions, the background reading will provide the reader with more detailed information or a broader contextual perspective on the topic.

Exercise

The exercises will enable the reader to learn grammatical points, idioms, and conventions of speech more effectively and thoroughly. Through these exercises, readers will be encouraged to express their own opinions on the topic in English as well as to demonstrate their understanding of other prevalent opinions. Overall, the diversity of the exercises encourages a well-rounded approach to studying the language and understanding the topic.

Acknowledgements

I would like to thank my two co-authors, Jessica Robertson and Liz Carter; not only are they my favorite students, they are also my greatest friends. I am also grateful to Ms. Cai Qing of the Foreign Languages Press; she has given us enormous encouragement and support. I would like to thank our editors Li Yuan and Wang Huan for giving us so many invaluable suggestions, and finally, I must thank my roommate Zou Yin and my classmate Wang Minyuan; without their help this book would never have been possible.

Liu Jiajing

前　言

本书兼顾语法学习和实际应用，是为学英语的年轻人量身定做的。书中的话题力求满足年轻人的兴趣和需要。一些话题，包括博客、Google 和资讯癖等与科技有关；初涉职场的人会发现面试或猎头这样的话题很有意思；也有关于社交生活的话题，比如约会和夜生活等。本书旨在让读者大量运用口语中常用的词汇和语法。

对话

每一个主题包括 5 篇对话，这些对话都针对某个话题，通常是在一个中国人和一个外国人或两个外国人之间展开。对话的风格既通俗又地道——很适合日常对话。如果你大声朗读这些对话，你会对英文对话的语流产生语感，也会体会出英语口语和书面语有哪些不同。

背景阅读

每一篇对话后都有背景阅读。这个部分提供了关于这个话题的有用的信息，不仅详细介绍了对话中的议题，而且可以使读者加深对话题的了解。如果说对话可以给读者提供语言上的帮助以表达自己观点的话，那么背景阅读则给读者提供了关于这个话题的更详尽的信息或更广泛的视角。

练习

练习可以使读者更有效、更全面地学习语法点、习语和口语中的一些固定表达法。通过这些练习，读者们会更乐于用英语表达他们针对此话题的看法，陈述他们对于其它流行说法的见解。总之，练习的多样性有利于读者全面地学习语言和理解话题。

感谢

感谢我的两个合作者 Jessica Robertson 和 Liz Carter，她们不仅是我最喜欢的学生，也是我最好的朋友；感谢外文出版社的蔡菁女士，她给了我们巨大的鼓励和支持；感谢编辑李湲和王欢，她们给我们提供了大量宝贵的建议；感谢我的室友邹隐和我的同学王敏媛，本书得以面世，也离不开她们的帮助。

刘佳静

学习指南

....

　　巧学活用本书能达到以一当十的效果，你至少可以做以下练习：

语音练习： 选取你最感兴趣的课文，尽力模仿录音中的语音语调，把自己的朗读录下来和录音比较，找出差距反复模仿，直到乱真。

口语练习： 利用书中对话做两人对练，或者和录音对练。就书中的主题换一个论点或谈话思路进行开放式对话创作。

听力练习： 利用随书的 MP3 录音做精听和泛听练习。常用的内容精听，即反复听直到听懂每一个字并能流利跟读为止；其他内容泛听，能听懂大意并基本能跟读即可。

听写练习： 听写能力表现在做课堂笔记和讲座笔记、会议记录等。利用本书 MP3 可以做听写练习，反复听写直到没有错误为止。

语汇练习： 利用书中的词汇表，并摘录课文中精彩实用的句型或用法，建立自己的主题词汇库。

翻译练习： 利用书中句型和对话做汉译英或英译汉练习，口译或笔译均可。

　　你可以根据自己的英语水平、工作需要和学习习惯将各种方法融会贯通，形成最适合自己的学习方法。当然，如果仅限于书本，再多的练习也只是纸上谈兵。如果你有找人开练的强烈愿望并付诸行动，离你的学习目标也就不远了。

Contents
目　录

英语畅谈
青春文化50主题

50 Topics On
Youth Culture

1. Career Planning

职业规划

Dialogue

A: How's the job search going?

B: I've had two interviews, but both companies are really good, so I'm having a really hard time deciding. I'd love to hear what you think.

A: Sure, what's the story?

B: The first one is a big, pretty well-known American company; the job there is in software design. The other company is smaller, and it's not very well-known but it's growing fast. At that one I'd be doing tech sales.

A: Isn't your degree in computers? Why would they hire you for a sales position?

B: I also took a bunch of econ classes at school, and I did an internship in marketing, so I guess they think I'm the right one for the job because I've got a better understanding of marketing than someone with a pure tech background, and a stronger background in IT than someone who just did marketing.

A: What about the benefits? That's a really important thing to pay attention to when you're looking for a job.

B: Well, the salary at the American company is pretty good and more stable, and the benefits are good too. At the smaller company the salary fluctuates more. I mean, salespeople's salaries are always on the low end, and there aren't benefits aside from health insurance. The commission is where you really earn your money.

A: Well this is an entry-level job; you're not going to make a ton on commission right away. But I think people actually perform best under pressure. You should also consider the fact that at the big company there are a lot of people and a lot of departments, with each person working on their own particular, specialized part, so there aren't a lot of opportunities to develop new skills. At the small company, on the other hand, you'll probably have to do everything yourself a lot of the time. It may be busy, but you'll grow so quickly, and you'll really feel like you've accomplished something.

B: That's a good point. Also, I'm really outgoing, I like meeting different kinds of people, you know? That's the kind of personality you have to have to be a good salesperson. I'm not like some of my classmates—they're much more shy, so they're well-suited for computer engineering jobs.

A: Personality is crucial! The sales job also lets you take advantage of the opportunity to do some networking—and that's incredibly important for your future career development.

B: I hadn't even thought of that. But I just think if you don't take the risk when you're young, you'll regret it when you're old. Since there's no absolute standard of good or bad where work is concerned, I think I just have to listen to my heart, and choose the job that I'll enjoy.

A: Well said. The most important thing is which one you're more interested in—it doesn't matter how great a job looks on paper if you don't enjoy it. Good luck!

对 话

A: 你的工作找得怎么样了？

B: 已经通过了两家公司的面谈。都很不错，让我举棋不定，正想听听你的意见。

A: 好，说说看。

B: 第一个是一家比较有名的美国大公司，让我去做软件设计；另一个是一家不太有名但发展很快的小公司，让我去做技术销售。

A: 你的专业不是计算机吗？他们怎么会让你做销售呢？

B: 因为我在大学选修了很多经济学方面的课程，还参加过销售实习，所以他们觉得我比单纯做技术的人更懂市场营销，比单纯做销售的人有更强的 IT 背景，因此认定我是合适的人选。

A: 那么这两家公司的待遇都如何呢？这是找工作时一定要考虑的因素啊。

B: 怎么说呢，美国公司的收入不错，也很稳定，员工福利也很优厚；小公司的收入弹性很大，销售人员的基本工资较低，收入主要来源于佣金，除了医疗保险之外基本没有其他福利。

A: 你刚参加工作，不可能马上赚到大笔的佣金。不过，我觉得人在压力之下更容易出成绩。你想，大公司人多部门多，每个人从事的都是专业化的、局部的工作，缺少锻炼综合能力的机会。而在小公司呢，常常是一人身兼数职，忙是忙，但工作能力能迅速提高，更容易获得成就感。

B: 我也这么想。再说，我这人很外向，喜欢跟不同的人打交道，这性格就很适合做销售。不像有些同学个性内向，不善言谈，做 IT 工程师就很适合他们。

A: 性格决定命运嘛！你还可以利用做销售的机会建立人际关系网，这对今后事业的发展非常重要。

B: 嗯，这点我还真没想到。我只是觉得年轻时不拼一拼，老了会后悔的！既然工作的好坏没有绝对的标准，我就决定听从自己的心愿，选择自己喜欢的工作。

A: 说得好！兴趣才是恒久的原动力。一个你并不喜欢的工作看上去再好也没有意义。祝你好运！

How to Choose the Career That's Right for You? 怎样选择适合自己的职业?

Choose What You Love 择己所爱

If you're doing a job that you like, work itself can give you a feeling of satisfaction, and your career can also be a lot of fun. Interest is the best guide and the source of success; it's simply logical that there is a connection between liking your job and being successful at it. When you're planning your career, it's important to remember to consider your own strengths and value your own interests, and you will choose a career that you will love.

从事一项你所喜欢的工作,工作本身就能给你一种满足感,你的职业生涯也会从此变得妙趣横生。兴趣是最好的老师,是成功之母。可想而知,兴趣与成功机率有一定的相关性。在设计自己的职业生涯时,务必注意:考虑自己的特点,珍惜自己的兴趣,选择自己喜欢的职业。

Choose What You're Good at 择己所长

Any profession needs people who have mastered certain skills and possess certain qualifcations. No one can master everything in just one lifetime, so when you're choosing a career, choose what you're good at, and you'll benefit from bringing your strengths into full play. Think carefully about how you compare with other people, and choose a profession that doesn't conflict with your strengths, but instead makes the best use of them.

任何职业都要求从业者掌握一定的技能,具备一定的条件。而一个人一生中不能将所有技能都全部掌握。所以你必须在进行职业选择时择己所长,从而有利于发挥自己的优势。充分分析别人与自己,不要选择与自己的优势有冲突的职业,而要尽量充分利用自己的优势。

Choose a Career That's in Demand 择世所需

Society's needs are always evolving; old opportunities are constantly disappearing and new ones are constantly being created. Yesterday's hot commodity might be replaced tomorrow by something that no one saw coming. So when you're planning your career, try to figure out what society needs, and choose what's in demand.

社会的需求不断演化着,旧的需求不断消失,新的需求不断产生。昨天的抢手货或许会在明天被一些尚不为人知的东西所取代。所以在设计你自己的职业生涯时,一定要分析社会需求,择世所需。

Choose What's Profitable 择己所利

Your ultimate goal when choosing a career is to find something that will make you happy, but your happiness will probably be influenced by your income too. A sensible choice of career orientation considers what's valuable from society's point of view and from your own. So when you make your choice, look for something that combines prestige and a good salary with the other variables that are important to you. That way you'll end up with a career that's most beneficial to you.

选择职业的终极目标在于追求个人幸福,而你的收入很可能会影响到你的幸福。明智的职业选择应该同时考虑到社会观念和个人意向。所以当你做职业方向的选择的时候,应该考虑到工作的社会地位和收入,以及在其它方面对你都很重要的职业。这样你就会成功地找到对你最有利的工作。

Exercises 练习

Answer these questions.

1. What factors does a person usually want to consider when looking for a job?
2. What makes up the bulk of a salesperson's salary?
3. What kind of work do you think suits outgoing people?

Translate these sentences into English.
1. 能谋得一份高收入的工作是所有求职者的梦想。
2. 那家公司的收入不错，也很稳定，员工福利也很优厚。
3. 销售人员的基本工资较低，收入主要来源于佣金。
4. 兴趣是最好的老师，也是成功的源泉。
5. 不同性格的人适合做不同的工作。
6. 选择职业的终极目标在于追求个人幸福。
7. 我一直对在跨国投资银行工作感兴趣。

Complete the following paragraph with these words or phrases.

considering   about   relations   journalism   skills   thinking

When you're __1__ about possible careers, think broadly. In addition to __2__ what you're good at, you should consider what is important to you. You can use your __3__ in computers, public __4__, science, graphic design, __5__ and more to make a difference on an issue that you really care __6__.

 Answers 答案

Translate these sentences into English.

1. Landing a well-paid job is something all job seekers dream of.
2. The salary at that company is pretty good and more stable, and the benefits are good too.
3. Salespeople's salaries are always on the low end; the commission is where they really earn their money.
4. Interest is the best guide and the source of success.
5. People with different kinds of personalities are best suited for different kinds of work.
6. Your ultimate goal when choosing a career is to find something that will make you happy.
7. I've always been interested in working for an international investment bank.

Complete the following paragraph with these words or phrases.

1. thinking   2. considering   3. skills   4. relations
5. journalism   6. about

词 汇 表	
interview	面试
well-known	有名的
software design	软件设计
tech sales	技术销售
degree	学位
a bunch of	一些
internship	实习
benefits	福利
pay attention to	注意
stable	稳定
fluctuate	波动，变动
aside from	除了
insurance	保险
commission	佣金
entry-level	初级的
outgoing	外向的
well-suited	适合的
crucial	最重要的
regret	后悔
absolute	绝对的
on paper	表面上
profession	职业
evolve	演化
constantly	不断地
sensible	明智的；合理的

2. Career Success and the Pursuit of Happiness

成功事业与快乐生活

Dialogue

A： I got an offere of promotion last week.

B： That's great! Congratulations!

A： I didn't take it—actually I quit my job altogether.

B： What? How come?

A： I never wanted to be an accountant. When I took that job five years ago it was only going to be a temporary thing, to pay off my college loans, but then I got stuck. I never liked working there but I never got around to quitting, because the salary and benefits were really good and it was safe, you know? When they offered me the promotion I realized that if I accepted the job I would really be accepting that this was what I was going to do until I retired. I don't want to spend my life doing a job I don't even like, so I decided that now is the time to find something I enjoy, before I have a family to support.

B： Wow, that's really brave.

A： Well maybe I would have been really successful, but what is success worth if you're not happy?

B： That's so true. Career success doesn't necessarily equal happiness. I think whether the two go together depends on who's defining success. Like if you're a really successful lawyer, but you never really wanted to be a lawyer, you did it just because your parents wanted you to, then you're not going to be happy.

A： You should always follow your heart, and decide for yourself what success means. That's what my mom did. She's a local politician, which she loves, and she's really good at it too. People have told her she should run for higher office, and she considered it, but in the end she decided not to.

B： Why not?

A： The reason she ran for office in the first place is that she loves our town and she wants to

6

make it an even better place to live. If she ran for state legislature her work wouldn't affect our town as directly, and also she'd have to move to the state capital, so she wouldn't even get to live there any more!

B： So even though getting elected on the state or even national level might be objectively considered more successful, she doesn't want to do it because she wouldn't be as happy.

A： Exactly. Like you were saying, there are different definitions of success. For my mom, being successful means making a real difference in our town, and the best way she can do that is by staying where she is.

B： Sounds like she's really found her niche. I hope you can find a job that you love that much!

A： I hope so too!

对 话

A： 上个星期，我接到了升职的通知。

B： 太好了！祝贺你！

A： 但是我没有接受，而且我辞职了。

B： 什么？你为什么这样做？

A： 我从来都不想做一个会计师，当我5年前开始做这个工作的时候，我只是想临时做一段时间，为了还我上大学的贷款，但是后来就离不开了。虽然我从来都不喜欢那儿的工作，但是也从来没想过辞职。因为你知道，那儿的收入和福利实在是不错，而且很有保证。但是当他们要给我升职时，我才意识到，如果我接受这个机会，我可能就要做这个工作一直到退休了。我不愿意用一生的时间做一个我不喜欢的工作，所以我觉得在我要供养家庭以前，现在正是我找一个自己喜欢的工作的时候了。

B： 哇！你真勇敢！

A： 尽管接受这次升职可能会让我的事业更成功，但是如果你不快乐，事业成功有什么用呢？

B： 是的。事业成功真的不等于生活快乐。我觉得这两者是否合一取决于你对成功的定义是什么。如果你是一个特别成功的律师，但是你根本不想做律师，当律师仅仅是你父母的期望，你当然不会快乐。

A： 我妈妈说，你应该总是听从内心的安排，自己来决定成功是什么。她是个地方议员，她喜欢做这个工作，而且做得非常好。别人说她应该竞选更高的职位，她也考虑过，但是最后她放弃了。

B： 她为什么不呢？

A： 她做这个工作首先是因为她特别喜欢我们的小镇，她希望把这个地方变得更好，更适宜人们生活。如果她竞选到更高的职位，到州议会去工作的话，她的工作就不能直接影响到我们的小镇了，同时我们也得搬到州首府，她甚至都不能住在镇上了。

B： 所以尽管被选为州议员或国会议员会被认为是非常成功的表现，她也不愿意，因为那不会使她快乐。

A： 是的。就像你说的，成功有不同的定义。对我妈妈来说，成功意味着给我们的小镇带来真实的变化，而实现这种变化的最好的方法就是留在那里继续工作。

B： 听起来她真正找到了适合自己的位置。我希望你也能找到自己喜欢做的工作。

A： 我也希望！

How Does Happiness Cause Career Success? 快乐生活如何能带来事业成功?

We all know that success can make you happier, but can happiness make you more successful? A new study says it can. A team of researchers at the University of California Riverside surveyed the results from 250 existing studies on the topic and found that happier people tended to have higher incomes and more fulfilling marriages, and to be healthier and even live longer. But none of this is surprising; what's surprising is that they found that happiness can be the cause, not just the result, of all of these things!

我们都知道成功会让你更快乐,但是快乐会让你更成功吗?一项新的调查表明是可以的。一组研究人员在加州大学河滨分校调查了250个关于这个题目的已有的研究结果,发现感到更快乐的人更容易拥有较高的收入和充实的婚姻,也更健康和长寿。但是这些并不令人吃惊,令人吃惊的是他们发现快乐是以上这些方面的原因,而不仅是结果。

Happier people are more energetic, creative and productive on the job, and they get along better with their co-workers. The personal confidence that goes along with happiness can impress bosses, clients and potential employers. Happiness and confidence make people more outgoing, which in turn can help them build connections later on in their career. Happy people are more likely to actively pursue their goals by taking risks and challenging themselves, and they're better at coping when things don't go as planned. Therefore, happy people are more likely to be hired and promoted, and they're also more likely to seek out success on their own.

更快乐的人更有精力和创造性,工作更有效,和同事相处得也更融洽。个人的自信和快乐会给老板、客户和潜在的雇主留下印象。快乐和自信会使人更友好,帮助他们在以后的工作中与人建立联系。快乐的人常常会冒险或挑战自己来主动追求他们的目标,如果事情不像计划中那样发展,他们也会处理得更好。因此,快乐的人很容易被雇用和提升,而且他们也容易从自己身上寻找成功。

Happiness can make you more successful, and then success can make you happier still, but how do you start the cycle? It doesn't take much. By simply approaching things with a more positive attitude, rather than expecting things to fail and focusing on the problems, your mood will improve right off the bat. Of course you don't want to ignore problems, but if you're optimistic that they can be solved then you're much more likely to find a solution. You can also make your day better just by smiling more, and those smiles will probably make the people around you happier too. When it comes to everyday life, simply choosing to be happier is a good way to start.

快乐会使你更成功,成功也会使你更快乐,但是怎么开始这个循环呢?这并不需要很多,仅仅用一个更积极的态度做事情,而不是担心事情失败而只看问题,你的情绪会自觉地得到改善。当然,你并不想忽视问题,但是如果你很乐观,就很容易找到解决问题的办法。仅仅多笑几次就能使你的日子更好过,还有这些笑容也会使你周围的人更快乐。在日常生活中,简单地选择更快乐就是一个很好的开始。

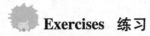 **Exercises** 练习

Answer these questions.

1. What is your definition of success?
2. Will you quit a promising job if you're not interested in it?

Translate these sentences into English.

1. 我没有接受这次升职的机会，而且我辞职了。
2. 那家公司的收入和福利实在是不错，而且很有保证。
3. 每个人都应该找到适合自己的定位。
4. 生活得更快乐的人更有精力和创造性，工作更有效，和同事相处得也更融洽。
5. 快乐的人很容易被雇用和提升，而且他们也容易从自己身上寻找成功。
6. 快乐会使你更成功，成功也会使你更快乐。
7. 如果工作中毫无乐趣可言，事业成功也就没有意义。

Complete the following paragraph with these words or phrases.

evidence   career   once   love   successful   priority   cycle

All the __1__ shows that success and happiness form a self-perpetuating __2__. So when you're starting your __3__, thinking about what will make you happy should be your first __4__. As Nobel Peace Prize winner Albert Schweitzer __5__ said, "Success is not the key to happiness. Happiness is the key to success. If you __6__ what you are doing, you will be __7__."

 Answers 答案

Translate these sentences into English.

1. I didn't take the promotion, and I quit my job altogether.
2. The salary and benefits in that company are really good and it is safe.
3. Everyone should find their niche.
4. Happier people are more energetic, creative and productive on the job, and they get along better with their co-workers.
5. Happy people are more likely to be hired and promoted, and they're also more likely to seek out success on their own.
6. Happiness can make you more successful, and success can also make you happier.
7. Career success is not worth the hard work unless it is an enjoyable experience.

Complete the following paragraph with these words or phrases.

1. evidence 2. cycle 3. career 4. priority
5. once 6. love 7. successful

词 汇 表

quit	辞职
accountant	会计师
temporary	临时的
loan	贷款
retire	退休
worth	值得
politician	政治家
legislature	立法机关
affect	影响
elect	选举
objectively	客观地
niche	定位
survey	调查
fulfilling	满足
energetic	精力充沛的
creative	有创造力的
productive	有效的
client	客户
outgoing	友好的
pursue	追求
risk	冒险
challenge	挑战
cycle	循环
mood	心情
optimistic	乐观的

3. Headhunting

猎　头

Dialogue

A： I heard that you recently changed jobs, and you got a good raise, right? Congratulations!

B： Thanks! I think the new job will be much more satisfying.

A： How did you find this job?

B： Now that's the really interesting part, this time I wasn't looking for a job, there was actually a job looking for me!

A： But how did your new company find you and know that you'd be good for the job?

B： They weren't the ones who came looking for me, at least not directly: it was a headhunting company.

A： What's a headhunting company?

B： It's a company that is paid by employers to find (in other words, to hunt for) qualified candidates for the job that the employer wants to fill.

A： So how do headhunting companies find talented people?

B： Most headhunting companies start building a pool of people as soon as they are founded, so once they have the client company's hiring requirements, they can start by searching within their own database of qualified people. Large companies are willing to pay the headhunters for this service because they've already done the work of recruiting people, so it's more efficient than if the company's own human resource department were to do it.

A： So you're in their army of qualified people!

B： Maybe, maybe not. If the client requires someone with very specific qualifications, the headhunter might have to go looking outside of their database. Because of this, headhunting companies are getting more and more specialized. For instance, there are some headhunting companies that are specifically for IT or consulting, among other things.

A： How did the headhunters get in contact with you?

B： I'm the same as the other candidates: we all unexpectedly got phone calls from the headhunter. While on the phone they'll give you a brief description of the job, pay, and benefits, and figure out whether you might be inclined to change jobs. The headhunters can also arrange interviews for the client company.

A: If the client company is willing to hire a headhunter to devote so much energy to looking for job candidates, it shows the client company must really have high standards for the position!

B: I was actually really surprised, I wasn't doing high level management; I was just a tech person, but I was still hunted down by them.

A: Don't be so modest, you were always the backbone of the tech department of your old company, I'm sure you made quite a name for yourself! But I remember you told me you had a three year contract with your former company. Since you quit before your contract came to term, did you have to pay them for breaking it?

B: Yeah, but my new company put forward the money.

A: Wow! I really envy you! I'm going to try to think of a way to attract the notice of these headhunting companies.

对 话

A: 听说你最近跳槽了，收入还增加了不少，是吗？恭喜恭喜啊！
B: 谢谢，我觉得新工作会更让人满意。
A: 你是怎么找到这个工作的呢？
B: 说起来很有意思，这次不是我找工作，而是工作来找我。
A: 可是你的新公司怎么找到你而且知道你一定适合他们的工作呢？
B: 不是他们来找我的，至少不是他们直接找我，而是猎头公司。
A: 什么是猎头公司？
B: 就是收雇主的钱并替他们去找他们想要的适合某个工作的有资格的人。
A: 那么，猎头公司怎么寻找人才呢？
B: 猎头公司的专业就在于它从成立伊始就要建立自己的人才库，这样一旦接到客户公司的招聘要求，他们便可以在自己的人才库中搜索相关人才。很多大公司愿意出重金请猎头公司找人，因为猎头公司已经做了一部分招聘工作，这比他们自己的人力资源部门招聘的效率高。
A: 这么说，你也在他们的人才库中了！
B: 可能是，也可能不是，如果客户需要有明确要求的人才，他们也得再出去找。因为这个，现在的猎头公司也越分越细了，比如有专门的 IT 猎头公司和咨询猎头公司等等。
A: 猎头是怎么联系你的呢？
B: 我和其他候选人一样，都是突然接到他们的电话，他们在电话中会大致介绍一下新工作的性质和福利待遇，弄清楚这些候选人是否有跳槽意向。猎头还会为他们的客户公司安排面试。
A: 客户公司愿意雇用猎头这么费尽心机地去找人，可见，那个公司对这个职位的要求真的是很高啊！
B: 所以我很意外，我并不是做管理的高层，只是一个技术人员，也被他们猎到了。
A: 你别谦虚了，你在原来的公司一直都是技术骨干，不出名才怪呢！但是我记得你告诉过我你和那家公司签了 3 年的合同，合同没到期你就辞职了，是不是要赔给他们违约金啊？
B: 是的，但是这些钱是我的新公司为我出的。
A: 太羡慕你了！我也要想办法引起猎头公司的注意！

How Do Headhunters Find Talented People? 猎头怎样找到人才?

After WWII, America and Europe searched for the scientists they needed from Germany and other countries. It was like they were hunting in the woods. They had professional companies everywhere helping them choose between outstanding talented people. The word "headhunting" came to be used to mean looking for qualified people. Headhunters help top-notch companies find the qualified candidates that they need.

二战以后, 欧美一些国家从德国等国家寻找自己需要的科学家, 就像丛林狩猎一样, 派专业公司到处帮他们物色优秀的人才。"猎头"这个词就被借用成为猎寻人才。猎头帮助优秀的企业找到他们所需要的合格人才。

What kind of people can become "hunted"? Headhunting companies in China give the general impression that they only search for talented people, and really put a big emphasis on four main qualities: the first is English ability; the second is length of experience and outstanding accomplishment; the third is strong education and credentials; and the fourth is solid work ethics.

什么样的人才可能成为"猎物"呢? 中国的猎头公司的普遍反映是, 他们替企业斟选人才, 通常讲究四大基本素质: 一是英语能力; 二是工作年限较长和业绩突出; 三是相当的学历和证书; 四是良好的职业道德。

Headhunters are understandably unwilling to reveal their methods. However, one source claimed that if he had one name and extension number, within a matter of hours he would have a good idea of who everyone in the department is and what they do. Here's how he did it: 1. If, for example, the original contact is unavailable, a colleague will answer the phone and happily divulge their own name. By a simple process of deduction, it is then easy to work out that person's position in the company; if people are sitting in adjacent desks, the chances are that they are in similar roles. 2. With clever questioning; the headhunter can navigate around the rest of the department and quickly compile a list of names and likely job roles. This information then can be stored for future reference. 3. Any name a headhunter comes across is written down and put on record. This process has been made much easier with the now widespread use of e-mail, which indicates a person's name, employer and even the department they work in. 4. Anyone contributing to an online newsgroup with informed, specialist opinion may well become the target of a headhunter.

可以理解, 猎头们不愿透露自己的方法。然而, 一种说法是, 如果他有一个名字和分机号码, 在几个小时内, 他就能搞清楚这个部门里的每个人, 以及他们都做什么。猎头们是这样做的: 1. 如果本来想找的人不在, 那么他的同事就会接电话, 而且很高兴地透露他们的名字。经过简单的推论, 猎头很容易得出这个人在公司里的职位。如果他们的桌子相邻, 那他们很可能是相似的职位。2. 问几个聪明的问题, 猎头可以弄清楚部门里的其他人, 并很快汇编成一张工作角色的清单。他们可以保存这些信息, 以备将来参考。3. 猎头看到任何人的名字都会写下来并存入记录。电子邮件的发明使这个过程更容易, 因为从邮件地址能看出一个人的名字、雇主甚至他工作的部门。4. 那些消息灵通的、有专家观点的、并且给在线新闻组投稿的人很容易成为猎头的目标。

Exercises 练习

Answer these questions.

1. What are headhunters?
2. How do headhunters usually contact the candidates?
3. What kind of people can be "hunted"?

Translate these sentences into English.

1. 我和这家公司签了 3 年的合同。
2. 猎头看到任何人的名字都会写下来并存入记录。
3. 从邮件地址能看出一个人的名字、雇主甚至他工作的部门。
4. 猎头帮助优秀的企业找到企业需要的合格人才。
5. 很多大公司愿意出重金请猎头公司找人，因为猎头公司已经做了一部分招聘工作。
6. 那些消息灵通的、有专家观点的人很容易成为猎头的目标。

Complete the following paragraph with these words or phrases.

in fact   move   however   target   persuade   fed   location

Some headhunters usually   1   people who are happy in their job and not looking to   2 .   3 , an Achilles heel can usually be found that allows the headhunter to   4   them that they might   5   want to change jobs. It may be that they are   6   up with the company, that they want more money, or that they want a change of   7 .

 Answers 答案

Translate these sentences into English.

1. I have a three year contract with this company.
2. Any name a headhunter comes across is written down and put on record.
3. A person's email address often indicates their name, employer and even the department they work in.
4. Headhunters help top-notch companies find the qualified people that they need.
5. Large companies are willing to pay the headhunters for this service because they've already done the work of recruiting people.
6. Anyone with informed, specialist opinion may well become the target of a headhunter.

Complete the following paragraph with these words or phrases.

1. target   2. move   3. however   4. persuade
5. in fact   6. fed   7. location

词 汇 表	
raise	提升；增加
satisfying	令人满意的
directly	直接
relatively	相当地；比较地
position	职位
talented	天才的；有才能的
professional	专业
found	建立
qualified	有资格的
recruit	招聘
human resource	人力资源
department	部门
consulting	咨询
contact	接触；联系
brief	简单的
description	描述
figure out	想出；领会
inclined	倾向于…的
arrange	安排
modest	谦虚的
backbone	骨干
contract	合同
envy	羡慕；妒忌
prominent	杰出的；突出的

13

Work 工作

4. Interviews

面 试

Dialogue

A: Recently I've been interviewing at a bunch of different companies, and I've discovered that the interview process at some companies is very different from when I first went looking for work.

B: What do you mean?

A: Before, interviewers would only ask a few questions that were directly related to work, but now interviews are much more complicated and involved. A couple of companies even made all of the interviewees play a game together. When the game had finished, some people were told that they did not suit this kind of work. The reason was that during the course of the game, those people showed that they didn't have team spirit.

B: Well, most companies these days really place an emphasis on teamwork, so even if the job applicant has really great abilities, if they don't work well with others, they aren't valuable to the company.

A: Still, interviewers often ask a few questions that I think are completely personal. For instance, "What kind of person do you think you are? What do you think your greatest weakness is? How can you deal with it? " I find these kinds of questions really hard to answer.

B: But these "personal questions" are actually very closely related to work. The point of the first question is to see whether your values are in line with the company's values. And the second question? Well, if you don't know your own weaknesses, then it shows you don't really understand yourself very well. How can a person who doesn't understand himself or herself understand other people and the work environment?

A: I see what you're saying. But that's not all: an increasingly number of interviews are also "situational", like, "What would you do if...?" These kinds of questions.

B: They ask these questions to make the job applicants provide practical examples of how they would tackle particular situations.

A: Right, and because I already have a few years of work experience, I was better qualified to answer the situational questions, and I think that was a big part of the reason why I was hired by the company in the end.

B: Congratulations! Have you noticed any other interesting changes?

A: Although interviews have gotten tougher and tougher, and the standards for applicants have gotten higher and higher, the atmosphere in interviews has actually gotten more and more relaxed. Most companies' interviewers sit on the same sofa as the interviewees, and speak to them as if chatting. They don't make people feel the least bit nervous.

B: They probably just want interviewees to relax, so they can open up and do as much talking as possible. Some people also say that this new informality also reflects the decreasing importance attached to hierarchy within organizations.

A: Yeah, interviews are increasingly becoming a conversation between equals.

对 话

A: 我最近去了好多家公司面试，发现现在一些公司的面试跟我第一次找工作时的面试真是大不一样啊！

B: 为什么这样说呢？

A: 以前，面试官只会问一些和工作有直接关系的问题，但是现在的面试很复杂、参与性很强。有的公司让所有的求职者一起做游戏，游戏完了以后有的人就被告知不适合这个工作，原因是在游戏的过程中，那些人表现出没有团队合作精神。

B: 是的，现在的公司大多都非常重视团队合作精神，所以即使应聘者的工作能力很强，如果不善于同别人合作，也不能为公司所用。

A: 还有，面试官常常会问一些我觉得完全是个人的问题。比如说，"你觉得自己是个什么样的人？你觉得自己最大的弱点是什么？怎样规避？"这些问题让我很难回答。

B: 这些"个人问题"实际上和工作有很大关系。第一个问题，他们是在考查你的价值观是否与公司的价值观相符。第二个问题，如果你连自己的弱点都不知道，那说明你对自己了解得不够清楚，一个连自己都不了解的人，怎么去了解别人和工作环境呢？

A: 我明白你说的，但这还不是全部。还有越来越多的面试采用"情景式"，就是"如果……你会怎么办？"之类的问题。

B: 他们这样问的目的是让求职者举出实际事例，说明自己如何处理某些特定情况。

A: 是的，因为我已经有了几年的工作经验，所以回答这些问题比较有优势，我觉得这是我最后被这家公司录用的重要原因。

B: 祝贺你！你还发现了别的有意思的不同吗？

A: 虽然面试越来越严格，对求职者的要求越来越高，但是面试的气氛却越来越轻松了，大部分公司的面试官和求职者都坐在沙发上，好像聊天儿一样谈话，让人感到一点儿也不拘谨。

B: 没错，他们就是想让求职者放松，尽可能地畅所欲言。也有人说，这种不拘礼节的新形式还反映出，在公司内部，等级观念越来越淡了。

A: 是啊！面试越来越成为平级之间的对话了。

Background Reading 背景阅读

Interview Process 面试方式

Interviews are used by most companies to hire for every category of staff they employ. They believe that, of all the selection tools available, interviews have the most influence on their appointment decisions.

大部分公司在雇用每个部门的员工时都采用面试。同时，他们也认为，在选择雇员的所有途径中，面试对于决定是否录用影响最大。

People-centered Interviews 人性化的面试

Nowadays, many companies' interviews are more people-centered, as shown in the following areas: before conducting interviews, some companies take all applicants on a tour of the work environment, and give them small gifts bearing the company logo, then finally begin the formal interview. There are also some companies who, whether or not the applicant's interview is successful, will pay for his or her transportation and even lodging in order to thank them for their interest in the company.

目前很多公司的面试都非常人性化，这主要表现在以下几个方面：有的公司会在面试之前带所有的求职者参观公司的工作环境，向求职者赠送印有该公司 logo 的小纪念品，然后才开始正式的面试。更有一些公司，不管求职者是否面试成功，都会付给他们来参加面试的交通费甚至住宿费，以感谢求职者对公司的关注。

High Level Technology 高科技手段

Some companies have already brought high level technology into the interview process: candidates can expect many interview panels to include at least one member who participates by means of video conferencing technology from another site or even overseas.

有的公司在面试中已经加入了高科技手段：求职者可以看到，面试小组中至少有一名成员是通过视频会议技术在外地甚至在海外参与面试。

Leaderless Group Discussion 无领导小组讨论

Leaderless Group Discussion is a comparatively open method of evaluating the more qualified job applicants. Within a set amount of time, with established questions and background information, it allows those being assessed to have a debate and put forward their opinions within a small group. The purpose of leaderless group discussion is to determine the teamwork abilities, leadership abilities, communication skills, debating skills, and decision making skills of the job applicants. At the same time it allows the applicants a chance to express their unique personality traits, like self-confidence, sense of responsibility, flexibility, emotional stability and ability to work well in a group. In this fashion, the evaluators can have a deeper understanding of their job applicants.

无领导小组讨论是一种较开放的人才测评方式，是指一组被评价者在既定时间内、既定背景下围绕指定问题展开讨论，并得出小组意见。无领导小组讨论的目的是考查被评价者的组织协调能力、领导能力、人际交往能力、辩论说服能力以及决策能力；同时表现被评价者在自信心、责任感、灵活性、情绪稳定性及团队精神等方面的个性特点和风格，从而能对被评价者有更深入的了解。

Exercises 练习

Answer these questions.

1. Why do most companies value team spirit?
2. During the interview, why do interviewers often ask some personal questions?
3. Why has the atmosphere in interviews become more relaxed?

Translate these sentences into English.

1. 每一个求职者都将被问及事先确定的相同问题。
2. 虽然面试日益严格，但其方式却越来越不拘礼节。
3. 现在的公司大多都非常重视团队合作精神。
4. 面试官常常会问一些"个人"问题。
5. 大部分公司在雇用每个部门的员工时都采用面试。
6. 在选择雇员的所有途径中，面试对于决定是否录用影响最大。
7. 胜任一个工作往往不仅取决于智力也取决于性格。

Complete the following paragraph with these words or phrases.

applicants rise intimidating unfamiliar relief role stressful

Interviews can be a __1__ time. New interview methods can be __2__: for instance, the leaderless group discussion may be __3__ to some job __4__. However, the increase of people-centered interviews can be a __5__ for some veteran job applicants. Though questions can be of all kinds, personal questions are on the __6__ and may play a key __7__ in the evaluation of candidates.

 Answers 答案

Translate these sentences into English.

1. Each candidate will be asked the same predetermined questions.
2. Despite their increasing rigor, interviews are generally becoming a lot less formal.
3. Most companies these days really place an emphasis on team spirit.
4. Interviewers often ask a few "personal" questions.
5. Interviews are used by most companies for every category of staff they employ.
6. Of all the selection tools available, interviews have the most influence on their appointment decisions.
7. Success in a job depends often as much on personality as on intelligence.

Complete the following paragraph with these words or phrases.

1. stressful   2. intimidating   3. unfamiliar   4. applicants
5. relief   6. rise   7. role

词 汇 表

be related to
和…有关
complicated
复杂的
team spirit
团队精神
emphasis
强调；重点
weakness
弱点
deal with
解决；处理
prove
证明
reasonable
合理的
interviewee
求职者
applicant
申请人
practical
实际的
tackle
解决
respect
方面
hire
雇用
atmosphere
气氛
informality
非正式
hierarchy
等级制度
staff
员工
appointment
任命；委任
lodging
住所
participate
参加
video conference
视频会议
comparatively
相当地
assess
评价；评估
debate
辩论

5. Gender Discrimination

性别歧视

Dialogue

A: Do you think our society has already achieved true gender equality?

B: I think we've made a lot of progress. Women can do all the things men can do nowadays. In a lot of work units, there are about equal numbers of women and men. Many of the things that women traditionally did, like cooking, cleaning, and taking care of the children, now tend to be shared more equally between husband and wife.

A: Everything you've said is true, but I think there are many instances of men and women still being unequal in our society. For instance, many women who are recent college graduates experience gender discrimination when they start looking for jobs.

B: Really? Do companies reject them because they're women? Or is there some other reason?

A: Yes, some companies do reject them simply because they're women. Actually, I myself have experienced this kind of thing. Two years ago, when I was looking for work, I applied for a job as a website editor. I like this kind of work; my major in college also really suited this kind of work. I even had an internship at that same company, and my boss really liked me. But in the end, they still rejected me.

B: I think you would make a really good website editor too! What reason did they give for rejecting you?

A: They made it sound like it was for my own good. They said, this kind of work is really hard, you have to work overtime a lot, and when something big happens, you have to work all through the night. You're a girl, and for you this kind of work is not only tiring, but also if you have to go home in the middle of the night it's not too safe... I said, this is no problem for me, I'm willing to do overtime and night shifts for a job I like. In the end they still said, very politely, we still want a man.

B: Wow, that is blatant gender discrimination. I guess you had no choice.

A: Exactly. Although I found an even better job later on, what if my whole life I never had the opportunity to be a website editor? I'd still be really disappointed right now. So I really hope that this kind of thing won't happen again to other people. But even today, gender discrimination is still prevalent.

B: I've also seen it clearly stated in the hiring information for a few companies that they only wanted male applicants, and a few even preferred male undergraduate students over female graduate students. In this respect, it seems we have a long way to go before we achieve equality between men and women.

A: I wish that day would arrive a little quicker! But right now there are people calling for legislation to ensure female college students can have equal employment opportunities, and I sure hope they succeed!

B: I hope so too!

对 话

A: 你觉得我们的社会做到真正的男女平等了吗？

B: 我觉得有很大的进步。现在男人可以做的事情，女人都可以做。在许多工作单位，男女比例也差不多达到了平衡。传统观念认为应该由女人做的事情，像做饭、做家务、照顾孩子等等，现在也都由丈夫和妻子双方共同分担了。

A: 你说的都是事实，但我觉得在社会上，还有很多男女不平等的现象。比如说，最近是大学生毕业找工作的高峰期，很多女大学生在找工作的过程中都受到了性别歧视。

B: 是吗？用人单位因为她们是女性而拒绝她们吗？还是有别的原因？

A: 是的，有些是完全的性别歧视。其实，我自己也有这样的经历。两年前，我找工作的时候，去了一家网站应聘，职位是网络编辑，我很喜欢这个工作，我的专业也很适合这个工作，我还在那儿实习过，我的上司也很喜欢我。可是，后来，他们还是拒绝了我。

B: 我也觉得你真的很适合做个网络编辑！他们拒绝你的理由是什么呢？

A: 他们的理由听起来是为了我好。他们说，做这个工作很辛苦，常常要加班，有大事件发生的时候，还得值夜班，你是个女孩子，对你来说，这样的工作不仅很累，而且你一个人半夜回家不太安全……我说，这些对我来说都没问题，我愿意为了我喜欢的工作加班和值夜班。他们最后委婉的说：我们还是想要一个男生。

B: 这简直就是公然的性别歧视！我觉得你没有选择。

A: 是的，虽然我后来也找到了一份更好的工作，但是可能我一辈子都没机会做网络编辑了，到现在我都很失望！所以我真的不希望这样的事情再发生在别人的身上。可是到了今天，性别歧视依然存在。

B: 我也曾经看过，一些公司的招聘信息上明确要求只要男性；还有一些公司宁可要男的本科生也不要女研究生。在这个方面，我们还需要走很长的路才能达到真正的男女平等。

A: 但愿这一天能快点儿来！现在已经有一些人呼吁通过立法来保障女大学生能拥有平等的就业机会，希望他们能成功！

B: 我也希望！

Gender Discrimination in the Employment Process 就业中的性别歧视

70% of female college students believe that men and women are not treated equally in the employment process. The greatest obstacle female college students face in the employment process is gender discrimination.

70% 的女大学生认为在求职过程中存在男女不平等。女大学生就业中面临的最大困难是性别歧视。

The main instances of gender discrimination cited by female students include, "work units clearly stating they only want male applicants", "if the position requires business trips or training in other places, they tend to employ men", "during interviews, they directly advise women to seek other work", "a few law firms clearly state that they only want men during their recruitment process", etc. Sometimes they ask female interviewees questions that are clearly sexist, like, "Do you know that a lawyer's work is hard, and you won't be able to take care of your home?", "Do you have a boyfriend?" and "This position will require frequent business trips and overtime, do you think that a lady would be suited to it?" etc.

学生列举的歧视女生的现象主要包括："招聘单位明确写明只招男生"、"如职位需要频繁出差或外地培训等时，就倾向于录用男生"、"在面试时直接建议女生另求它职"、"一些律师事务所在招聘要求中明确指出只要男生"等。有时候，他们会问女大学生们一些带有明显性别倾向的问题，如"你是否知道从事律师行业会比较辛苦，无法顾家?"、"你有男朋友吗?"和"我们这个职位会经常要求出差和加班，你认为由一位女士来从事合适吗?"等等。

Gender discrimination during the employment process is not only harmful to individual female college students; it also encourages the idea that "studying well is not as good as marrying well". Equally seriously, this kind of gender discrimination is a contradiction of egalitarian values, misallocates labor, and wastes human talent.

就业中的性别歧视，不仅不利于女大学生的学习和生活，还可能助长部分学生"学得好不如嫁得好"的观念。更严重的是，这种性别歧视破坏了社会的公平原则，使得劳动力资源配置出现扭曲，造成人力资源的浪费。

Some experts have said that while looking for work, women should understand companies that discriminate on the basis of gender. These companies are only concerned with finding employees that can be most valuable to the companies, and when they choose to hire a woman they have to consider the financial losses incurred by maternity leave, the possibility that she might pay more and more attention to her household, and whether or not she can go out alone on business trips. This kind of discrimination may not be malicious, but may in fact seem reasonable from the company's point of view. However, these concerns are based on stereotypes which are often unfair, and in many countries such as the US, employment discrimination on the basis of gender is illegal.

有专家表示，女性就业的时候要理解有性别偏见的企业。这些公司只想找到能为公司创造最大价值的员工。如果他们选择了女性，她们就得考虑女性生育期给公司带来的财务损失，女性在工作和家庭的平衡方面可能会越来越偏向家庭，以及是否能独自出差等问题。这种歧视可能不是恶意的，但实际上它的合理性是从公司的角度出发的。然而，这些忧虑都是建立在不公平的成见的基础上的。在很多国家，比如美国，招聘中的性别歧视是不合法的。

Exercises 练习

Answer these questions.
1. Have you ever experienced gender discrimination?
2. What would you do if you faced gender discrimination?
3. Do you agree with the view "studying well is not as good as marrying well"? Why?

Translate these sentences into English.
1. 很多女性在找工作的过程中都受到了性别歧视。
2. 家务应该由夫妻双方共同分担。
3. 我在那个公司实习了一个月。
4. 我常常加班和值夜班。
5. 相貌、身高、性别、婚姻状况是很多用人单位的几大"歧视因素"。
6. "学得好不如嫁得好。"
7. 男生们在找工作时通常会占上风。

Complete the following paragraph with these words or phrases.

> respondents   frustrations   rest assured   cutthroat
> fresh graduate   discrimination   exist

If your education or experience is only average, or if you are not a ___1___ , get ready for the ___2___ of the job market. But ___3___ , you are just one of the millions to face ___4___ in China's ___5___ job market. About 85 percent of the 3,424 ___6___ covered by a survey in 10 big cities, including Beijing and Shanghai, said discrimination in work and employment did ___7___ .

 Answers 答案

Translate these sentences into English.
1. Many women face gender discrimination when looking for a job.
2. Housework should be shared equally between husband and wife.
3. I had a one-month internship at that company.
4. I always work overtime and night shifts.
5. Discrimination may be based on appearance, height, gender or marital status.
6. "Studying well is not as good as marrying well."
7. Male students often have the upper hand during the job hunt.

Complete the following paragraph with these words or phrases.
1. fresh graduate   2. frustrations   3. rest assured   4. discrimination
5. cutthroat   6. respondents   7. exist

词 汇 表

achieve
　　　　达到；做到
gender equality
　　　　男女平等
unit
　　　　　　单位
instance
　　　　例子；实例
discrimination
　　　　　　歧视
reject
　　　　拒绝；抵制
website
　　　　　　网站
editor
　　　　　　编辑
overtime
　　　　　加班时间
night shift
　　　　　　夜班
prevalent
　　　流行的；普遍的
legislation
　　　　立法；法律
ensure
　　　　　　保证
obstacle
　　　　　　障碍
cite
　　　　　　引用
business trip
　　　　　　出差
sexist
　　　　性别歧视的
egalitarian
　　　　平等主义的
labor force
　　　　　劳动力
incur
　　　　招致；惹起
maternity
　　　　　产妇的
household
　　　一家人；家庭
malicious
　　　　　恶意的
fresh graduate
　　　　应届毕业生
rest assured
　　　　　放心

21

6. How to Meet Your Mate

认识方式

Dialogue

A： Hi! How was your date last night?

B： Ahem... It was fun, but I'm not sure yet if I like the guy. We'll just have to wait and see.

A： Man, I feel like it's been forever since I've been on a date, but you go on dates all the time! How do you meet the guys you date?

B： Well, on weekends I go out to the bars with a few friends. If I see a cute guy, I go up and chat with him a while. If he can hold up his end of a conversation, maybe I'll hang out with him a while longer, and if there's good music playing, maybe we'll dance. If I'm still interested at the end of the night, I'll ask for his number or give him mine. If at any point I decide he's just not my type, I can walk away.

A： That sounds good in theory, but the bar scene has never worked for me. It seems like whenever I go out to bars I get hit on by a bunch of real jerks, the kind who only have one thing on their mind.

B： Yeah, there is the danger of that. I still come in contact with plenty of sketchy guys. There doesn't seem to be any way of avoiding them, no matter how you go about it.

A： I don't know, I think the bar scene has more sketchy guys than anywhere else. Are there other places where you've met cool guys in the past?

B： Well, actually a friend of mine was telling me about how she met her boyfriend. She said she started taking an aerobics class at her local gym and not only did she meet new friends who shared the same interest in fitness as her, she also met a really nice guy.

A： Really? Well, I'm not really into aerobics and fitness, so I don't know if that would work for me.

B： I don't think you have to be into fitness, really. It could be any kind of club or group. If you like singing, camping, playing sports, reading, volunteering or anything else, I'm sure there's a club for it. Plus, with the guys you meet this way, you already know you have something in common! I've been thinking about joining a backpacking group myself. I like to get out of the city more and do some hiking. It's just an extra bonus that while I do that I can be on the lookout for a potential boyfriend, kill two birds with one stone.

A： Sounds like fun, but I'm really a city girl at heart, and also pretty busy. I just don't think I have time to join a club or group. I think I'll have a go at the old-fashioned method, and ask my friends to introduce me to some of their friends.

B： Well, let me know how it works out! I gotta run, I have a bus to catch.

A： See ya!

对 话

A： 嗨！你昨天晚上的约会怎么样？

B： 很好玩儿，但是我不确定自己是否喜欢那个男孩。我们还要再等等看。

A： 我很久都没有约会了，但是你好像一直在约会！你是怎么找到这些男孩的？

B： 嗯，周末的时候我会跟一些朋友去酒吧。如果我看见一个不错的家伙，我就会主动跟他聊一会儿。如果他很健谈，那我就多和他待一会儿，如果音乐很好，我们就会跳舞。到了分开的时候，如果我还对他有兴趣，我就会要他的电话号码，或是给他我的号码。如果在这个过程中，我发现他有一点儿不适合我，我就离开。

A： 听起来是不错，但是我觉得我在酒吧里那样做就没有用。不管我什么时候去酒吧，那些对我感兴趣的人看起来都是不太可靠、不怎么样的人，他们的脑子里只有一件事情，那就是出来寻开心。

B： 是的，有那样的危险。我也会遇到一些变态男。不管你怎么做，也避免不了遇到这样的人。

A： 我不知道，我觉得酒吧里不三不四的人比别的地方多。以前，你在别的地方遇到过好男孩吗？

B： 嗯，我的一个朋友告诉过我她是怎样遇到她的男朋友的。她说，她在当地的健身房里开始上健美操的课，在那儿，她不仅认识了很多和她一样对健身感兴趣的朋友，也遇到了一个非常好的男人。

A： 真的吗？不过我对有氧运动和健身不感兴趣，所以我不知道这样的情况对我适合不适合。

B： 我觉得你不一定要去跳健美操。你可以去参加任何一个俱乐部或者兴趣小组。如果你喜欢唱歌、野营、运动、读书、做志愿者或者任何其他的活动，我觉得都有这样的俱乐部。还有，通过这种方式认识的男人，你已经知道你们有共同点了！我在考虑参加一个背包客俱乐部。我喜欢到城市外面徒步走一走。我还可以同时找一找未来的男朋友——这是一箭双雕。

A： 听起来很有意思，但我骨子里真的是一个城市女孩，除此以外，我还特别忙。我觉得我根本没有时间去参加俱乐部或兴趣小组。我觉得我会试一试那个老套的办法，让我的朋友给我介绍一些她们的朋友。

B： 好，到时候告诉我这个办法是怎么起作用的。我要走了，要赶公共汽车。

A： 再见！祝你好运！

Background Reading 背景阅读

City Nightlife 城市夜生活

Many people meet each other at bars, clubs, and restaurants during the evening or night. This "scene" is called nightlife. The bigger and more cosmopolitan the city is, the better the nightlife is, because there are more interesting bars, clubs, and restaurants. Singles who want to meet people often do so by enjoying a city's nightlife, because they can do it in their free time, with friends, in a relaxing atmosphere.

许多人在晚上和夜间的酒吧、俱乐部和饭馆里认识对方。这种情形被称为夜生活。城市越大、越国际化，夜生活就越丰富，因为这样的城市里有更多、更有意思的酒吧、俱乐部和饭馆。想寻找异性的单身人士经常享受夜生活，因为他们可以在业余时间，跟朋友一起，享受轻松的气氛。

Problems with City Nightlife 城市夜生活带来的问题

Some singles don't like looking for a partner in bars or clubs. There are many reasons for this: you are less likely to meet people looking for long-term relationships, and more likely to find people looking for one-night stands and less serious relationships. Also, some singles prefer to spend their evenings quietly at home, alone or with a few friends, rather than in noisy bars and clubs with lots of people. Every person has his or her own preference, and the bar scene is not right for everyone.

一些单身人士不喜欢在酒吧和俱乐部寻找异性朋友。有如下几个原因：在酒吧里，找不到可以维持长期关系的异性，很可能你找到的人只想发生一夜情，而并不认真地看待相互之间的关系；还有，比起喧闹的酒吧和一大堆人，一些单身人士更喜欢晚上静静地待在家里或者跟几个朋友在一起；各人的喜好不同，所以酒吧生活并不适合每一个人。

Clubs and Organizations 俱乐部和各种组织

Many people meet potential partners or dates through involvement in clubs and organizations. There are many types of clubs, where you can meet both partners and friends, including outing clubs, chess clubs, flower arranging clubs, etc. You can also join an organization that exists to bring together people sharing a common cultural background or religious beliefs. Finally, there are also organizations dedicated to serving a specific purpose for the community or nation. By spending time volunteering with this kind of organization, you not only increase your chance of finding a good match, but you're doing something beneficial to society as well!

很多人通过俱乐部和组织认识他们未来的伴侣或约会对象。俱乐部有很多种，你可以在那儿认识约会对象和普通朋友，包括户外俱乐部、象棋俱乐部、插花俱乐部等等。你也可以参加一些有共同的文化和宗教背景的组织。此外，还有一些特别服务于社区或国家的组织。在这种组织里做志愿工作不仅有利于你寻找合适的伴侣，对社会来说也是一件好事！

Where Do Singles Meet? 单身人士在哪儿相遇？

The Forbes Magazine Online Survey shows that the top places singles meet include a friend's house (13%), parties (12%), bars (12%), church (8%), online (7%), work (6%), school (6%), grocery stores (5%), while walking their dog (5%), the gym (5%), charity events (4%), weddings (4%), funerals (3%), sporting events (2%), on the street (2%), in the park (1%), conferences (1%), and concerts (1%).

《福布斯》杂志在线调查显示单身人士们最有可能相遇的地方是：朋友家（13%），晚会（12%），酒吧（12%），教堂（8%），线上（7%），工作（6%），学校（6%），杂货店（5%），遛狗时（5%），健身房（5%），慈善事业（4%），婚礼（4%），葬礼（3%），运动会（2%），街上（2%），公园（1%），会议（1%），音乐会（1%）。

Exercises 练习

Answer these questions.

1. What is city nightlife?
2. Why do some people dislike the "bar scene"?
3. What are some of the most popular places to meet other singles?

Translate these sentences into English.

1. 单身人士经常在共同的朋友家里认识。
2. 单身人士可以通过婚介服务或网络互相认识。
3. 很多人在酒吧或俱乐部中享受夜生活的时候认识了他们的另一半。
4. 如果你不喜欢在酒吧找异性朋友，还有很多别的方式。
5. 参加俱乐部或组织的人会在很多方面受益。
6. 各人的喜好不同，所以酒吧生活并不适合每一个人。
7. 我骨子里是一个城市女孩。

Complete the following paragraph with these words or phrases.

lasting speed dating drastic be yourself special someone involves

Some singles go to __1__ measures to find potential partners, like __2__ or even television dating shows. However, the best way to find that __3__ is by doing something you enjoy that also __4__ meeting lots of new people. If you're doing something fun, you're more likely to just __5__, and that way if you do meet someone you'll already be on your way to a __6__ relationship.

 # Answers 答案

Translate these sentences into English.

1. Singles often meet at a mutual friend's house.
2. Singles can meet each other through dating services and websites.
3. Many people meet partners at bars or clubs while enjoying their city's nightlife.
4. If you don't like the bar scene, there are still many ways to meet people.
5. People who join clubs or organizations benefit in many ways.
6. Every person has his or her own preference, and the bar scene is not right for everyone.
7. I'm really a city girl at heart.

Complete the following paragraph with these words or phrases.

1. drastic 2. speed dating 3. special someone 4. involves
5. be yourself 6. lasting

词 汇 表

date	约会对象
chat	聊天
turn out	发现，出现
hang out	消磨时间
(cell) number	（手机）号码
at any point	随时
work for me	适合我
a bunch of	一群
jerk	不好的男人
sketchy	不三不四的
avoid	避免
gym	健身房
fitness	健康
camping	野营
volunteer	参加志愿活动
hike	徒步旅行
nice	善良，好
be into	对…感兴趣
be on the lookout for	寻找
potential	潜在的
kills two birds with one stone	一举两得
have a go at	试试
cosmopolitan	国际化的
dedicated	献身的

7. Dating Woes

交友的困难

A: Guess who I ran into the other day?

B: Who?

A: My ex-girlfriend. It was really awkward—we haven't seen each other since we broke up two months ago.

B: I know what you mean—the same thing happened with me and my ex-girlfriend, except it was even worse. When I saw her for the first time after we broke up she was making out with her new boyfriend.

A: Dude, that's rough. You've been broken up with her for a year already, right?

B: Yeah, and lately I've been thinking it would be nice to be in a relationship again, but I just can't seem to meet women who are girlfriend material.

A: Me too! I've been trying to get back into the dating scene lately but I just can't seem to meet any cool girls!

B: Maybe we've been going about it the wrong way. What have you been doing?

A: Well, I've just asked a few friends to introduce me to their friends. They set up a few blind dates, but the girls, well, I dunno... I just didn't feel any spark.

B: I know what you mean. I did meet this one girl at work, and we went out on a few dates. She was really sweet, we had great conversations, and she was pretty too. In the end, she was a nice enough girl, but I just didn't feel anything for her.

A: It's good that you ended it if there wasn't really anything there. No reason to waste time in a dead-end relationship. But that must have been awkward when you ended it if you still had to see her every day at work!

B: Actually the breakup was totally mutual. As it turns out she wasn't crazy about me either. I guess some people just don't click. The two of us are actually pretty good friends now,

26

but I still haven't found a girlfriend.

A： So have you been getting your friends to introduce you to people? Going on blind dates?

B： Oh, I never go on blind dates. I like to see for myself whether I have the potential to like someone before I go out on a date. Otherwise I might end up wasting a whole evening with someone excruciatingly boring or something. Like my mom always used to say to my older sister, "You have to kiss a lot of frogs to find your prince!" But personally I'd like to avoid as much frog-kissing as possible.

A： Haha, me too, but it seems like there's no other way!

B： Yeah, it's probably inevitable. But one can always hope!

对 话

A： 你猜我那天碰见谁了?

B： 谁啊?

A： 我的前女友,我很尴尬——自从两个月以前我们分手后就没见过面。

B： 我明白你的意思,我和我的前女友也是这样,而且更糟糕。我们分手以后,我第一次看见她的时候,她正和她的新男友在接吻呢。

A： 天,真糟糕。你和她分手已经一年了吧?

B： 是的,所以最近我一直在想,如果能再谈一次恋爱,那该多好啊! 但是我好像找不到合适的女孩。

A： 我也是,我最近试着回到谈恋爱时的情形,但是我找不到好女孩!

B： 可能我们的方式不对。你是怎么做的?

A： 嗯,我让我的朋友给我介绍他们的朋友。他们举行了几次"陌生约会",但是,来参加约会的女孩,我对她们一点儿感觉都没有。

B： 我明白你的意思。我在工作中也遇到了一个女孩,我们约会过几次。她很可爱,我们聊得很开心,而且她也很漂亮。总之,她是一个足够好的女孩,但我就是对她不来电。

A： 如果你真的对对方没什么感觉,那么你们结束关系真的是一件好事。没有理由为了这样一个没有结局的关系浪费时间。但是你们结束关系的时候一定很尴尬,因为你们工作的时候每天都会见面!

B： 实际上,我们双方都想分手,反正她对我也不来电。我觉得有些人第一次见面就知道彼此不合适。现在我们是很好的朋友,而我还在找女朋友。

A： 你也在见朋友的朋友吗? 一直在"陌生约会"?

B： 我从来不参加"陌生约会"。我想自己去找,看看我在约会之前还有没有可能喜欢上一个人? 要不然我可能会一整个晚上都浪费在一些无聊至极的人身上了。就像我妈妈对我姐姐说的:"在找到王子前,你可能得亲吻许多只青蛙!"但是我想尽可能避免这种情况。

A： 哈哈,我也是,但是好像没有别的办法。

B： 很可能是这样。但是一个人总可以有希望!

Background Reading 背景阅读

The Inertia of Long-term Relationships 长期恋爱关系的惰性

Many people stay in long-term relationships even though they aren't happy anymore. This is partially because they don't want to hurt their partner, and partially out of fear of re-entering the dating scene. Many people would rather stay in a mediocre relationship than risk not having one at all. This reluctance to leave an unsatisfying relationship is self-defeating, however, because it keeps both people in the relationship from finding more suitable partners and living more meaningful, satisfied lives.

虽然很多人对自己的另一半没有感觉了，但是他们仍然维持着恋爱关系。他们这样做的一个原因是他们不想伤害对方，另一方面是因为他们害怕再次进入与人约会的状态。比起冒险以后什么都得不到，他们宁愿维持平庸的、没有激情的关系。然而，勉强维持一段不美满的关系会弄巧成拙，因为这使双方都不能找到更合适的对象，过更有意义、更满意的生活。

The Frog Prince Story 青蛙王子的故事

The story of the Frog Prince was originally German, but has spread throughout the West. In the most popular version, a princess reluctantly befriends a frog, who begs her to kiss him. When she finally does, he transforms into a handsome prince. Many people will often cite this story to encourage women who encounter romantic troubles, saying "You have to kiss a lot of frogs to find your prince!" This has a double meaning: first, you will probably go on a lot of bad dates before you find Mr. Right. And second, you should give everyone a chance because even someone who seems like a frog could turn out to be a prince!

青蛙王子的故事来源于德国，但是广泛流传于西方国家。最流行的版本是，一个公主勉强和青蛙做了朋友，青蛙请求公主吻它一下，公主吻了它以后，它马上变成了一个英俊的王子。当女人们遇到恋爱问题的时候，人们就会引用这个故事来鼓励她们说："在遇到真正的王子前，你得亲吻很多只青蛙。"这个故事有两重意思：首先，在你找到理想人选之前，你可能要和很多不合适的人交往；第二，你应该给每个人机会，因为尽管有的人看起来像只青蛙，但是他有可能变成王子。

Trouble Finding Someone Special 找个特别的人不容易

There are many different obstacles to finding that special someone. Living in a rural area or not having access to transportation can restrict your opportunities to meet new people. Also, having particular religious beliefs or cultural traditions that you would like a potential partner to share can narrow down your field of possibilities. Personal qualities can also have a limiting effect: being shy and averse to meeting new people can make finding partners difficult.

想找到一个特别的人有很多不同的障碍。住在农村或者没有交通手段就会使你认识陌生人的机会减少。还有，如果你希望你的另一半和你一样有特定的宗教信仰或者文化传统，可能的人选又减少了。个人性格也会起到限制作用：害羞和不愿结交新朋友也会使寻找另一半变得很难。

Dating Services 约会服务

According to statistics, 48% of American men and 53% of all American women have used some kind of dating service. These kinds of services can range from more traditional matchmaking services to the increasingly popular speed dating, to telephone and online dating services. These services are especially popular among those who encounter problems mentioned above, such as living in a rural area (because you can meet new people even if they live far away) or requiring potential partners to share specific religious or cultural common ground (because you can request matches with these characteristics at the outset).

根据统计，48% 的美国男人和 53% 的美国女人使用过一些约会服务。这些服务包括传统的媒人介绍，也包括现在越来越流行的快速约会，电话和在线约会。这些服务在上面提到的那些想寻找特别的异性，又有很多麻烦的人中很流行，比如说，住在农村的人（因为即使他们住得很远，人们仍然可以结识陌生人），或者要求对方跟自己有共同信仰或文化背景的人（因为你从一开始就可以要求对方和你有共同点）。

Exercises 练习

Answer these questions.

1. Why might it be a bad idea to stay in a long-term relationship?
2. What are some things that could make it hard for a person to meet other singles?
3. Why is it better to "kiss a lot of frogs"?

Translate these sentences into English.

1. 他是一个足够好的男人，但我就是对他不来电。
2. 如果你们之间没有火花，那就应该分手。
3. 长时间的恋爱以后再回到约会时的状态很难。
4. 找到一个好男人很难，在遇到王子之前，你得亲吻很多只青蛙。
5. 害羞和不愿结交新朋友也会使寻找另一半变得比较难。
6. 诚实地面对自己，你就一定会找到你等待的人。
7. 我们友好地分手了。

Complete the following paragraph with these words or phrases.

> into   yourself   lesson   give people a chance   hurting
> surefire

One famous line from Shakespeare is a good ___1___ for singles who are looking for a partner："To thine own self be true," or in other words, "Be true to ___2___ ." The only ___3___ way to find someone to love is if you're always yourself when you meet new people. Also, you should ___4___ , but don't waste your time if you're not really ___5___ them. Finally, if you're in a relationship, don't let your fear of ___6___ the other person keep you from breaking up if you're unhappy.

 Answers 答案

Translate these sentences into English.

1. He was a nice enough guy, but I just didn't feel anything for him.
2. If you don't feel any spark, maybe you should break up.
3. Getting back into the dating scene after a long-term relationship can be hard.
4. Finding a good guy can be hard, but you just have to keep kissing frogs until you find your prince!
5. Being shy and averse to meeting new people can make it a little harder to find that special someone.
6. Be true to yourself and you're sure to find the person you've been waiting for.
7. We broke up amicably.

Complete the following paragraph with these words or phrases.

1. lesson   2. yourself   3. surefire   4. give people a chance
5. into   6. hurting

词 汇 表	
relationship	关系
seem to	好像；似乎
material	材料
scene	场景；状态
introduce	给…介绍
blind dates	陌生约会
spark	火花
treat	请…吃饭
gentleman	绅士
awkward	尴尬
mutual	相互的
click	（一见面就）合得来
potential	可能性
excruciatingly	极度地
boring	无聊的
inertia	惰性
partially	部分地
mediocre	平庸的
reluctance	勉强
spread	传播
transform	改变；变成
obstacle	障碍
rural	农村的
restrict	限制
religious	宗教的

8. Thinking About Your Future Spouse

未来伴侣的标准

Dialogue

A: Oh hey, long time no see! What's new? How's the love life?

B: It's kind of frustrating. My circle of friends is too small, and it's hard to find a boyfriend when there's nobody who suits me in my immediate circle.

A: What a coincidence: I went to this lecture just yesterday that was all about how to find a suitable partner.

B: Really? How was it? Was it useful?

A: The person who gave the lecture was a really beautiful young woman. The way she was dressed was extremely attractive but also very mature, and she was extremely well-spoken. Her speech was so interesting and funny that even the girls wanted her to be our girlfriend!

B: Well of course smart, beautiful, confident women like that aren't gonna have a problem finding a partner!

A: She was also wise far beyond her years. She said that even before she was 20 years old she had already realized that finding a suitable partner is one of the most important things in a person's life. She said, if you don't like your school, work or even your friends, you can change them. It's only your spouse with whom you will spend your whole life, whom you can't change at the drop of a hat.

B: Hmm, I totally agree—that's one of the reasons I still don't have a boyfriend, because I'm waiting for the guy who's really right for me. What else did she say?

A: She said that even at such a young age she decided she was going to find someone who would make her completely satisfied for the rest of her life. First, she set a few conditions for her future spouse; for example, her future husband definitely had to support her

30

decision to work. Also, she would have to find someone who she thought had a sense of humor and was interesting to talk to. Then she started to go about looking for suitable men who met these conditions.

B: Those seem like very practical criteria. Did she find someone in the end?

A: She did. She told us that she had already been married eight years, and in those eight years her husband had been very loving and supportive of her. Afterwards she turned and asked us what our most important requirement was in picking a spouse. Some people said that money was the most important condition, others said personality; some people said looks were the most important. I think intelligence is the most important! What are your standards?

B: Well... I haven't really thought about it.

A: Well get to it, start thinking about it! If you don't even have standards, how can you look for someone?

对 话

A: 嗨! 好久不见了, 有什么新情况吗? 爱情生活怎么样?

B: 真让人失望, 我的生活圈子太小了, 身边没有合适的人, 所以找不到男朋友。

A: 真巧, 昨天我听了一个很有意思的讲座, 讲的就是如何去找适合你的爱人。

B: 是吗? 讲得怎么样? 有用吗?

A: 给我们做讲座的是一个年轻漂亮的女士。她的衣着打扮精致迷人, 言谈举止优雅得体, 看起来很成熟, 说起话来又幽默有趣, 连我们这些女孩子都想找她做女朋友。

B: 聪明、漂亮又自信的女人当然不愁找不到爱人了!

A: 不, 她的智慧远远超过她的年龄。她在不到 20 岁的时候就意识到找一个合适的爱人是人一生中最重要的事情之一, 她说, 你的学校、工作甚至朋友等等, 如果你不喜欢, 你都可以换。唯有你的爱人, 你要跟他度过一生的时间, 不会轻易地换来换去。

B: 我完全同意这个看法, 所以到今天还没有男朋友, 因为我一直在等适合我的人出现。她还说了什么?

A: 她说即使她那么年轻, 她也决定要找一个让自己十分满意的人共度一生。首先, 她给自己未来的爱人列了几个条件, 比如说她未来的丈夫一定要支持她的工作; 还有, 她要找到一个她觉得有幽默感、说话有意思的人。然后她就开始按照这些条件一步一步地去圈定合适人选了。

B: 这些是很实际的标准啊! 最后她找到了吗?

A: 是的。她告诉我们她已经结婚 8 年了, 在这 8 年中, 她丈夫确实很爱她、很支持她。然后她还分别问了我们在选择爱人时最重要的条件是什么, 有人说经济条件最重要, 有人说性格最重要, 有人说长相最重要, 我觉得智商最重要, 哈哈! 你的标准是什么?

B: 这个……, 我还真没想过。

A: 赶快想一想吧! 你连标准都没有, 怎么去找呢?

Standards for Future Spouse 未来伴侣的标准

You can tell a lot about a woman from what kind of husband she says she wants; it shows what is important to her. The standards for potential partners often cited by single women cover a wide range of attributes. Some examples include: 1. He must be respectful to all women. 2. He must be considerate. 3. He must not have a temper. 4. He must be totally dependable. 5. He must have a good job and a good salary. 6. He must be self-confident. 7. He must not smoke or be an alcoholic. 8. He must be forgiving. 9. He must have a good sense of humor. 10. He must be able to cook.

你可以从一个女人想要什么样的丈夫看出她自己是什么样的人，这能显示出对她来说重要的东西是什么。单身女子为未来伴侣所列的标准包括很多品质。比如说：1. 尊敬所有的女性。2. 通情达理。3. 好脾气。4. 可以完全依靠。5. 工作好，收入高。6. 有自信。7. 不抽烟、不酗酒。8. 宽容大度。9. 幽默。10. 会做饭。

Methods of Meeting 约会方式

According to an international survey, when it came to meeting that special someone, a majority of respondents preferred to rely on friends for introductions. The country whose singles had the most favorable opinion of the Internet as a hunting ground was Portugal, where about half the surveyed men and women opted to find people online. Men and women preferred different methods of meeting someone in certain cases. For instance, thirty percent of Spanish men, but very few Spanish women, admitted to looking for love online. In France, 40 percent of men but only 10 percent of women went to parties, bars and clubs to meet someone. But one French statistic had no gender gap: both men and women rated looks as more important than their counterparts in other countries.

一项国际调查显示：在约会问题上，大多数受访者说他们更喜欢靠朋友介绍。葡萄牙人最热中于网上求偶，有一半受访的葡萄牙人选择网上寻求意中人。在某种情况下，男人和女人喜欢不同的见面方式。比如说，30% 的西班牙男士选择网恋，西班牙女士则不喜欢如此。在法国，40% 的男士喜欢在聚会时或在酒吧和俱乐部与异性碰面，选择这种方式的女性只有 10%。但法国的异性之间有一个共同特点：与其他国家的人相比，法国人无论男性还是女性，都更注重对方的相貌。

First Impressions 第一印象

When it comes to first impressions, a majority of men polled said beauty was more important than brains, while women put a sense of humor at the top of their list. Physical attraction was the top priority for men in France, Brazil, Greece, Japan and Britain. But while 40 percent of Portuguese men rated intelligence over looks in a first encounter, no Australian men did so. In the United States and Canada, humor was considered the most important trait by both men and women.

对于第一印象，大多数受调查的男性说女人的美貌比智商更重要，而女性则把男性的幽默感列于首位。法国、巴西、希腊、日本和英国的男士认为异性的容貌最重要；而 40% 的葡萄牙男士认为，第一次约会，女性的智商比美貌更重要，但澳大利亚男士并不这么认为。在加拿大和美国，无论男士还是女士都认为对方的幽默感最重要。

Exercises 练习

Answer these questions.

1. Do you think it's a good idea to set standards for your future spouse? Why or why not?
2. What are your standards for a potential spouse?
3. What would you do if your current boyfriend or girlfriend didn't meet your standards?

Translate these sentences into English.

1. 我的生活圈子太小了。
2. 她打扮得很迷人，并且很成熟。
3. 她的智慧远远超过她的年龄。
4. 找到一个合适的爱人是人一生中最重要的事情之一。
5. 她给自己未来的爱人列了几个条件。
6. 你选择爱人时最重要的条件什么？
7. 现在，很多年轻人都热中于网上求偶。

Complete the following paragraph with these words or phrases.

| prefer   catch   tickles   once   knowing   intelligence   humor |

When it comes to romance, women __1__ someone who __2__ their funny bone, while men opt for those who __3__ their eye. Good looks, __4__, and a sense of __5__ are all important but the most important thing is __6__ what you want. __7__ you know what you want; you can go out and get it!

 Answers 答案

Translate these sentences into English.

1. My circle of friends is too small.
2. The way she was dressed was attractive but also very mature.
3. She was wise far beyond her years.
4. Finding a suitable partner is one of the most important things in a person's life.
5. She set a few conditions for her future spouse.
6. What is your most important requirement in picking a spouse?
7. Nowadays, the Internet is a popular hunting ground among young people looking for love.

Complete the following paragraph with these words or phrases.

1. prefer   2. tickles   3. catch   4. intelligence
5. humor   6. knowing   7. Once

词 汇 表

immediate
最接近的
suitable
合适的
done up
打扮
extremely
极其
mature
成熟的
attractive
迷人的
wise
明智的
support
支持
personality
性格
looks
外表
intelligence
智商
attribute
特征；品质
temper
脾气
dependable
可依靠的
counterpart
对应的人或物
majority
大部分
sense of humor
幽默感
priority
优先权
rate . . . over
认为…更重要
encounter
遭遇
trait
品质；性格
tickle
逗乐；使愉快
opt
选择；决定

9. Being Proactive

主动出击

A： I followed your advice and set a few standards for picking my future spouse. But what good do standards do if you're still single and alone?

B： Don't worry! Once you've decided on a few of your most important standards it's much easier to find the person who's right for you! But you have to go out looking for them— if you're just sitting around waiting for someone to come chase you, then all of your standards will be meaningless.

A： Then what should I do? Will it come to taking out a "looking for Mr. Right" ad in the newspaper, and showing off my deepest soul for all the world to see? I don't wanna do that.

B： You don't necessarily have to put out an ad; if you know what kind of person you want you can go look for them yourself. First, you should expand your circle of friends. One way is to participate as much as possible in social activities like dances, parties, foreign language clubs, and so on. These are all good places to meet strangers.

A： I've tried these methods. But I'm a little shy in these kinds of situations so it's hard to get people to notice me. And I always feel embarrassed going after someone myself, because if they're not interested it might make them really uncomfortable.

B： Ok, well there are plenty of other options. You definitely have a few really close female friends, right? You should get a group together and do something fun, like go hiking or out to sing karaoke. Every time you get together you all bring your male friends, and maybe you'll find someone you like among the guys your friends bring along. If your friends are single too they can check out your guy friends too.

A： That's a really good idea, actually, I'll have to call up my girls and get it started. But I only have so many friends. If, at last, I've already met all of my friends' friends, but haven't found one that was good for me, what should I do?

B: Well you can always come up with something crazy, and you never know, it just might work. I saw this story about a girl who said her secret weapon was taking her camera with her everywhere she went. If she saw a guy she liked, she would nonchalantly walk up and ask him to help her take a picture; 99% of guys won't refuse this request. While he was taking her picture, this girl would do really cute or funny poses and try to start up a conversation with the guy afterwards. And you know what? In the end, this approach finally landed her a boyfriend!

A: Aha, that's hilarious! Hmm, I better start thinking...

对 话

A: 我听了你的话，给自己未来的爱人列出了一些标准。但是只有这些标准有什么用啊？我还是单身一人啊！

B: 别着急！你有了标准以后就更容易找到适合你的那个人！可是你得出去找呀——如果你还是像以前一样等着别人来追求你，你所列的那些标准也就失去意义了。

A: 那我应该怎么办呢？难道要我在报纸上登一个征婚广告，把我的灵魂深处展示给全世界吗？我可不想那样做。

B: 不一定要登广告，但是自己中意的人还是要靠自己去找的。首先，你应该扩大自己的交友圈。办法之一是尽可能多地去参加一些社交活动，像舞会啊、晚会啊、外语俱乐部啊等等，这些都是认识陌生人的好地方。

A: 这种办法我试过，但是我在这种场合下总是有些羞怯，很难让别人注意到我。我也不太好意思去特别关注一个人，这样会让对方觉得不舒服。

B: 嗯，还有办法二，你肯定有几个关系很好的女性朋友吧？你们应该凑在一起做些有意思的事，比如爬山啊、唱卡拉 ok 啊，每次聚会你们都带上自己的男性朋友，你有可能从朋友带来的男孩子中发现自己喜欢的。如果你的朋友们也是单身，你带的男孩子可以让她们选择。

A: 这个办法不错，我要找我的朋友们试一试。但朋友总是有限的，如果到最后她们的朋友我已经都认识了，但还是没有一个适合我的，怎么办呢？

B: 你可以做一些疯狂的事情，很难说，这就有用呢。一个女孩子说，她的秘密武器是，她总是随身带着照相机。如果看到比较有感觉的男人，她会若无其事地走上前去，请求对方帮她拍一张照片，99% 的男人都不会拒绝这个请求。在拍照时，这个女孩子会摆出十分可爱的姿态来吸引对方，然后试着和对方聊天儿。你知道吗？最后她用这个方法找到了男朋友！

A: 太有意思了！我也该想一想怎么做了……

Methods for Attracting Members of the Opposite Sex 吸引异性的方法

People have all sorts of methods for finding and attracting members of the opposite sex. There is no foolproof way to get the guy or girl you want, but there is one big step that will at least ensure you have a chance: be proactive. Being proactive means taking the initiative to ask that special someone out to dinner or express your feelings for him or her. Whatever method you use, you'll have a better chance of finding someone you like if you don't just sit around waiting for them to come to you. Take that first step!

人们有很多种方法来寻找和吸引异性。想得到任何你喜欢的男孩或者女孩并没有万无一失的办法，但是有一个很重要的步骤能保证你至少有机会：主动出击。主动出击的意思就是你主动地去请你喜欢的那个人出去吃饭或者向他/她表白你的感受。不管你用什么办法，如果你不是仅仅坐在那儿等人来找你，你都更有可能找到你喜欢的人。迈出第一步吧!

One way of getting someone's attention is by asking for a little favor. Then you two might get to talking, and if the favor is a little bit bigger you can offer to treat the other person to dinner as a way of saying thanks. This is a good way to start getting to know someone, because both of you will be more relaxed than if you were going on a formal date. And if it turns out you like each other, you'll get your chance for those fancy dates later on.

吸引某人注意的办法之一就是请他帮点儿小忙。然后你们可能就会开始交谈，而且如果这个忙比较大，你出于感谢，就得请对方吃饭。这是开始了解一个人的很好的方式，因为你们都会比在正式约会时要放松一些。如果接触以后证明你们是喜欢对方的，你们就可以开始以后的浪漫约会了。

What should you do if you've got a crush on someone but they don't know it? The best thing to do is just to spend a lot of time together. Eat lunch together, go to ball games, study together in the library, and just hang out, either one-on-one or with other friends. This way the person will get a chance to know you, and in the meantime you'll have lots of opportunities to send subtle hints that you're interested in more than friendship. At this point, you're already halfway there. If the other person has feelings for you, they're sure to pick up on your signals.

当你迷恋上某个人，而那个人却不知道，怎么办？最好的方法就是多花时间和他在一起。一起吃午饭，一起看球赛，一起去图书馆看书，或者只是一起闲待着，两个人单独在一起或者和别的人在一起都可以。这样，这个人就有机会了解你，同时，你也有很多机会给他微妙的暗示，你不仅仅是想和他做朋友。这时你已成功了一半。如果那个人对你也有感觉，他就会接受你的信号。

There are tons of ways to get someone's attention if the two of you live in the same apartment building or on the same street. You could come over to ask to if you can borrow an egg when you're cooking, or throw a party for all the neighbors. If there's a nice place to sit in front of your building, you can sit outside with a book in nice weather, and start a conversation when your crush comes by.

如果你们两个人住在一栋公寓楼里或住在同一条街上，你就有很多办法去吸引他/她的注意。你做饭的时候可以去找他借一个鸡蛋，或者举办一个晚会邀请所有的邻居都来参加。如果你的楼前有一小块漂亮的地方，你可以在天气好时坐在那儿看看书，当你喜欢的人经过时，试着和他交谈。

Exercises 练习

Answer these questions.

1. What do you do when you meet someone you like?
2. How can one expand their circle of friends?
3. What's the most creative way you can think of for finding love?

Translate these sentences into English.

1. 如果你只是等着别人来追求你，那你就只能永远地等待下去。
2. 做一些与众不同的事情一定会吸引你喜欢的人的注意。
3. 不仅是寻找爱人，做任何事情都应该主动。
4. 吸引某人注意的办法之一就是请他帮点儿小忙。
5. 他们一见钟情。
6. 给他微妙的暗示，你不仅仅是想和他做朋友。
7. 总有属于你的人，难的是如何找到他。

Complete the following paragraph with these words or phrases.

bump into   create   date   fated   destined   across
each other

When you come ___1___ a girl or guy you like, if you can ___2___ opportunities to see them more often you might be able to make them think that you two are ___3___ to be together, because you always seem to ___4___ each other unexpectedly. After you've run into ___5___ a couple times it's easy to start a conversation and even ask them out on a ___6___. This way your crush will start out believing you two were ___7___ for each other!

 Answers 答案

Translate these sentences into English.

1. If you're just waiting for someone to come find you, you could end up waiting for the right person forever.
2. Doing something original is sure to catch that special someone's eye.
3. You should be proactive in all situations, not just when looking for love.
4. One way of getting someone's attention is by asking for a little favor.
5. They fell in love at first sight.
6. Send subtle hints that you're interested in more than friendship.
7. There's someone for everyone; the hard part is finding them.

Complete the following paragraph with these words or phrases.

1. across   2. create   3. fated   4. bump into
5. each other   6. date   7. destined

词 汇 表

chase
　　　　　追求
show off
　　　　　展示
expand
　　　　　扩大
circle
　　　　　圈子
attract
　　　　　吸引
embarrassed
　　　　　尴尬的
option
　　　　　选择
secret weapon
　　　　　秘密武器
nonchalantly
　　　　　若无其事地
pose
　　　　　姿势
hilarious
　　　　　令人捧腹的
foolproof
　　　　　可靠的
at least
　　　　　至少
ensure
　　　　　保证
initiative
　　　　　主动
turn out
　　　　　证明
get a crush on...
　　　　　迷恋…
subtle
　　　难捉摸的；微妙的
hint
　　　　　暗示
halfway
　　　　　一半
come over
　　　　　拜访
original
　　　　与众不同的

37

10. Long-distance Relationships

异地恋情

Dialogue

A: Hey, what are you up to tonight?

B: I'm going out with this girl...

A: Same one as last week?

B: Yeah.

A: So things are going well then?

B: It's going really well, actually, but the big picture is a little more complicated. I like her a lot, but I'm only going to be in China for a couple more months, and I think a long-distance relationship would be way too hard. I would love to keep seeing her for the rest of my time here, but I don't know if she's interested in a relationship if it's not going to be serious.

A: I think it's wise to think about these issues before you get really involved with her. I agree that a long-distance relationship is a bad idea. A couple years ago I met this guy while I was living in South America. After I left we tried to keep it up long distance, but it's just so hard to stay connected to someone when all you have is the telephone. Maybe if I had had definite plans to go back to Peru it would have worked, but as it was we eventually had to acknowledge that the relationship wasn't going anywhere, and end it.

B: I don't want that to happen with this girl, but it seems silly to give up the time I have with her just because I know that time is limited. On the other hand, I don't know if starting a relationship that has no future is fair to her. I mean, it's different for Chinese girls—it's not as acceptable for them to date casually as it is for American girls.

A: I think you're right, and I think it's especially touchy if the guy is a foreigner. But if you like this girl and you want to keep seeing her in the time you have, then you just have to

38

talk to her about all this. Tell her how you feel, but also make sure she understands that the two of you have no long-term potential. Then she can decide for herself if it's worth it. But I think you have a responsibility to get all this out on the table before it goes much further.

B: True, true. I guess I should probably talk to her tonight, huh?

A: It will only get harder the longer you wait.

B: Yeah, ok. Thanks for helping me think this through!

A: What are friends for? Anyway, let me know how it goes.

B: Will do.

对 话

A: 嗨，今天晚上你做什么？

B: 我要和那个女孩一起出去……

A: 是上个星期的那个女孩吗？

B: 是的。

A: 这么说，你们进展得很顺利啊？

B: 进展得很顺利，但是，实际上，整个情况却有点儿复杂。我很喜欢她，但是我在中国只有几个月的时间了，我觉得异地恋爱会很辛苦。在我留在中国的这段时间里，我很想一直跟她见面，但是我不知道她对这种不一定有结果的恋爱有没有兴趣。

A: 我觉得在你和她真正陷进去之前考虑这件事是明智的。我同意，异地恋爱不是一个好主意。几年以前我在南美生活过一段时间，在那儿，我认识了一个男孩子。我离开以后，我们都尽力保持异地的恋爱关系，但是保持联系太难了，因为所有能用的东西只有电话。如果我有明确的计划回到秘鲁，可能还有用，但是到最后，我们不得不承认我们的关系不能继续了，只好分手了。

B: 我不想和这个女孩发生这样的事情，但是因为知道我的时间是有限的，就放弃和她在一起又好像很蠢。另一方面，我不知道开始一段没有结果的恋爱对她来说是否公平。我的意思是，对中国女孩来说不一样——她们并不像美国女孩那样随便和人约会。

A: 我觉得你说得对，而且如果男方是个外国人就更敏感了。但是如果你喜欢这个女孩，在剩下的时间里，你还想见到她，你就最好和她谈一谈。告诉她你的感受，也让她清楚你们两个人没有长期发展的可能。然后她可以自己决定这样做是否值得。但是我觉得你有责任在你们的关系进一步发展以前把这些放到桌面上说清楚。

B: 对，对，我想今晚就该跟她谈谈，对不对？

A: 你等的时间越长就越辛苦。

B: 是的，很好。谢谢你帮我想清楚这件事情。

A: 朋友是用来干什么的？不管怎么样，有了结果就告诉我。

B: 会的。

Some Tips on How to Make a Long-distance Relationship Succeed
异地恋爱成功的秘诀

Set clear expectations before the separation. This includes the big issues, such as whether you will remain monogamous, and seemingly smaller—but still crucial—issues like how you'll communicate. When it comes to talking on the phone, it's a good idea to make a plan of when and how often you'll talk. That way no one ends up waiting by the phone, or feeling insecure about calling too much. However, it's still important to let your partner know you're thinking of them, so send emails, text messages, small gifts, or make surprise phone calls just to say "I love you."

分开之前确定一个明确的前景。这包括重要的问题，比如你们是否要保持夫妻或男女朋友关系；和看起来很小但实际上很关键的问题，就是你们如何交流。如果你们想通过电话交流，那么最好确定什么时候通电话、多长时间通一次。那样的话，就没有人会白等电话，或是因为打电话太多而感到不安。还有，让你的伴侣知道你在想他也很重要，所以发 email、发短信、送小礼物或者突然给他打个电话只说"我爱你"都是好办法。

Be forthcoming with your thoughts and feelings. There are lots of nonverbal ways of communicating that can let our partner know how we're feeling when we're together, but the same thing doesn't apply to email or phone conversations. Don't pretend everything's fine when in reality you're terribly lonely. Chances are that the other person feels the same way, so pretending you're perfectly happy will make the other person feel like you don't miss them as much as they miss you. On the other hand, if you are doing just fine without the other person, you should be up-front about that too. It could be a sign that you're moving on and that the relationship doesn't have a future.

主动说出你的想法和感受。当我们在一起的时候有很多非言语的交流方式可以让我们的伴侣了解各自的感受，但是这些办法在 email 或电话里却行不通。如果你真的感到特别寂寞的时候，不要假装没事。很有可能，那个人和你的感觉一样，所以如果你装得很快乐会使那个人觉得不像他想你一样想他。另一方面，如果没有那个人，你也生活得很好，你也应该表现出来。这可能意味着你的心已经不在他身上，你们的关系可能没有未来了。

Even though it might seem like a waste to spend the limited time you have to talk to each other on the trivial details of your day, staying in the loop with each other's lives is an important part of staying connected. Modern technology has made it easier—and less expensive—than ever before to keep in touch with a long distance lover, so take advantage of the many different ways you have to communicate. Webcams and text messaging can put you in touch with your partner instantly, but don't overlook the value of writing an old-fashioned love letter or sending a care package.

虽然互相谈一点儿生活中的琐事看起来可能是在浪费双方有限的时间，但是熟悉对方的日常生活也是保持联系的重要组成部分。现代科技使这些保持异地恋爱的方法比以前更容易、也更便宜，所以应该好好利用这些不同的方式去交流。网络摄像头和手机短信可以使你和你的伴侣保持即时联系，但是也别忽视写一封旧式的情书或者寄一个包裹的作用。

It will undoubtedly be questioned or tested in a long-distance relationship, so it's especially important that you go out of your way to make sure your partner trusts you. You can do this with thoughtful gestures and being reliable with phone calls, returning emails, etc. Don't get involved in a long-distance relationship if you've already had questions about the other's faithfulness, because being separated will only compound your insecurities. At the same time, you should also take advantage of your independence. Being in a serious relationship can often make you lose sight of your individuality. Long-distance relationships can be a good thing—you'll be forced to do and learn things on your own, which will only make your relationship stronger when you and your partner are reunited.

异地恋爱毋庸置疑地会受到怀疑和考验，所以极其重要的是你要不惜一切地让你的伴侣信任你。你们可以通过体贴的行为和依靠电话、回 email 等等保持信任。如果你已经对对方的忠诚度有所怀疑的话，就不要卷入异地恋，这只会加剧你的不安全感。同时，你也应该利用你的独立。正式的恋爱关系常常会使你失去自我。异地恋爱可能是件好事，你不得不自己学做事情，当你们团聚的时候，这会使你们的关系更牢固。

Exercises 练习

Answer these questions.

1. Do you think long-distance relationships ususally have a good chance of succeeding?
2. What are some of the ways to help maintain a long-distance relationship?
3. What do you think is most important for maintaining a long-distance relationship?

Translate these sentences into English.

1. 异地恋爱可能会很辛苦。
2. 虽然身处两地，但我们都尽力地保持着恋爱关系。
3. 告诉她你的感受，她可以自己决定是否值得去经历异地恋情。
4. 异地恋要想成功需要付出很多，但也不是不可能。
5. 现代科技使这些保持异地恋爱的方法比以前更容易、也更便宜。
6. 如果你已经对对方的忠诚度有所怀疑的话，就不要卷入异地恋。
7. 正式的恋爱关系常常会使你失去自我。

Complete the following paragraph with these words or phrases.

> thanks to   among   career   entering   military marriages
> serving

___1___ online dating, more people than ever are ___2___ into long-distance relationships. However, in the US, long-distance relationships are still most common ___3___ college students and people ___4___ in the military. Three-quarters of college students say they've been in a long-distance relationship at some point during their college ___5___ , and as many as half of ___6___ are long-distance.

 ## Answers 答案

Translate these sentences into English.

1. A long-distance relationship would be way too hard.
2. We do our best to keep the relationship up even though we're apart.
3. Tell her how you feel and she can decide for herself if a long-distance relationship is worth it.
4. It takes a lot of work to make a long-distance relationship succeed, but it's far from impossible.
5. Modern technology has made it easier—and less expensive—than ever before to keep in touch with a long distance lover.
6. Don't get involved in a long-distance relationship if you've already had questions about the other person's faithfulness.
7. Being in a serious relationship can often make you lose sight of your individuality.

Complete the following paragraph with these words or phrases.

1. Thanks to   2. entering   3. among   4. serving
5. career   6. military marriages

词 汇 表

serious	严肃的；认真的
wise	明智的
involve	卷入
definite	明确的
eventually	最后
acknowledge	承认
silly	愚蠢的
limited	有限的
fair	公平的
casually	随便地
touchy	敏感的
worth	值得
expectation	期望；预期
separation	分开
monogamous	一夫一妻制的
insecure	局促不安的
nonverbal	非言语的
trivial	琐碎的
detail	细节
loop	圈；环
take advantage of	利用
instantly	立即
undoubtedly	毋庸置疑的
faithfulness	忠诚
compound	加剧

11. Metrosexual

都市美男

Dialogue

A: Have you noticed, men these days are becoming more and more interested in how they look? Some of my male friends and co-workers use moisturizers and makeup every day, some even wear jewelry! Every time I come near them I get a whiff of their cologne.

B: I know what you mean! Men in today's society are definitely starting to care more and more about their own image. Some men spend as much time and money on their appearance as most women do—a few even go to beauty salons and get plastic surgery. I've heard that now, one out of every ten people who get plastic surgery is male.

A: It's an interesting phenomenon. Traditionally, women are the ones who are supposed to care most about beauty, but people's values are changing these days, especially in the big cities. A few years earlier, if a man showed he cared about his appearance or clothes, he would be told he was being too feminine, or acting like a girl. But now, plenty of men would willingly describe themselves as "metrosexual" —it doesn't have a negative connotation.

B: I think this has a lot to do with mass media. Many celebrities, especially in the movie industry, are so-called "pretty boys." They are admired and idolized by the public, and many young men want to imitate their clothes and fashions, which is one of the reasons for the "pretty boy" phenomenon in society at large. In reality, whether or not you're a celebrity, a well-groomed appearance can raise your self-confidence and help you make a good impression on other people.

A: True! I think another reason that men are paying more attention to their appearance is that they've realized that women are paying attention to men's appearance! A man who makes an effort to look his best is more likely to win the approval of the opposite gender. Also, many women appreciate a man who doesn't roll his eyes as soon as she mentions anything having to do with fashion.

B: Yeah, I think it's related to the fact that the position of women in society is continuously rising, and they are becoming more and more particular when it comes to choosing a partner. Women have always been more interested in men who are physically handsome in addition to being responsible and economically secure, but now that women can be more selective, men have to work harder to prove themselves the ideal partner. Men are realizing that it pays to be considerate, attentive and well-dressed.

A: So whereas before, women dressed up in order to attract men, nowadays men are also dressing up to attract women. Men and women really are becoming more and more equal in society!

对 话

A: 你有没有发现,现在社会上的男人越来越爱美了?我身边的一些男性朋友和同事,每天都使用护肤品和化妆品,有的还佩戴饰品!每次走近他们,我就能闻到男士香水的味道。

B: 是啊!现代社会的男人的确越来越在意自己的形象了,一些男人在修饰外表上花费的时间和金钱跟大多数女人一样,有的男人甚至进美容院去整容。据说,现在十名整容者中就有一名是男性。

A: 我觉得这个现象很有意思。传统观念认为,女性是最爱美的,但是现在,人们的观念发生了很大的变化,尤其是在大城市。几年前,如果一个男人对自己的衣着和外表太过在意,会被旁人耻笑为"女人气"或者"娘娘腔"。但是现在,很多男人都愿意把自己说成"都市美男",这个词完全没有负面含意了。

B: 我觉得,这和大众传媒的发达有很大的关系。很多明星,尤其是在演艺界,被叫作"花样美男"。他们被大众崇拜和偶像化,很多年轻的男孩子都想模仿他们的穿衣打扮,这是"美男"现象在社会上流行的一个原因。实际上,不管你是不是明星,光鲜靓丽的外表都能提升自己的信心,给人以良好的印象。

A: 对!我觉得男人更注重外表的另一个原因就是他们认识到了女人也很注重男人的外表!一个精心打扮后的男人更容易得到异性的认可。还有,很多女人都很欣赏那些可以和他们聊一聊时尚话题的男性。

B: 嗯,我觉得这和现在女性社会地位的上升也有关,她们在对象的选择上越来越挑剔,女人总是对那些长得很帅又有责任感而且有经济实力的男人更有兴趣。既然女人更挑剔了,男人们就得更努力去证明自己是理想的伴侣。男人们也认识到体贴、细心和精心打扮会有好处。

A: 这么说,以前是女人为了吸引男人而打扮自己。现在男人也为了吸引女人而打扮。男人和女人的社会地位越来越平等了!

Background Reading 背景阅读

Metrosexuals 都市美男们

"Metrosexual" is a term coined by British journalist Mark Simpson in 2002; it denotes an urban man with a strong fashion sense, who puts more effort into looking good than the stereotypical man. Metrosexuals tend to be young urban men with relatively comfortable incomes. They are willing to spend money to take advantage of the shops, hairdressers, gyms and clubs of the modern metropolis. While people used to assume that any man who paid attention to his appearance was gay, "metrosexuals" don't fit into this binary: they are straight man who have a desire to be fashionable and well-groomed in order to attract women or just because it makes them feel good about themselves.

"都会美型男"是英国记者马克·辛普森在 2002 年创造的新词汇,指的是时尚意识强烈、比传统男人更在意外表美丽的都市男性。都市美男往往是收入相当不错的都市年轻男人。他们愿意花钱充分享用现代大都市的商店、美发店、健身房和俱乐部。人们过去以为只要是注重外表的男人就是同性恋,都市美男却并不适合这种假设:他们只是为了吸引女性或仅仅是为了自我感觉良好而追求时尚和外表靓丽的简单男人。

British soccer star David Beckham is, according to journalist Mark Simpson, a classic example of a metrosexual. He is continuously changing his hairstyle, and he's not afraid to take fashion risks, wearing everything from Versace suits, to track suits with gold cuffs, to sarongs, and even on occasion painting his fingernails. Beckham's fashion sense provides a model to stylish young men around the world, including in Asia.

英国足球明星大卫·贝克汉姆被辛普森认为是"都会美型男"的经典代表。他隔三差五就改变自己的发型,而且在追求时尚方面大胆创新,时而身着范思哲西服,时而套上缀有金属亮片的田径服,时而围上裙子,甚至有时还抹指甲油。贝克汉姆的时尚感为全世界,包括亚洲的时髦的年轻男性树立了形象。

One survey of men aged 18 to 60 in seven major Chinese cities estimates that urban Chinese men spend 8.6 minutes a day gazing at themselves in the mirror and shell out 80 yuan a month on beauty products. Beijing and Shanghai were neck-and-neck on whose male residents were most vain. Those in the capital spent the most money on cosmetics—an average of 119 yuan a month—but Shanghai's men looked in the mirror the longest about 17 minutes a day. Chinese consumers are becoming increasingly image conscious as they grow wealthier; this is evidenced by the booming market for beauty products and plastic surgery.

一份针对中国七个大城市里的 18 到 60 岁之间的男性的调查说,中国的城市男性每天要花 8.6 分钟来照镜子,每个月花在美容用品上的钱也达到了 80 元。在男性居民的虚荣程度这方面,北京和上海打了个平手。首都男花在化妆品上的钱最多,平均每人每月用去 119 元;而上海男照镜子的时间最长,平均每天 17 分钟。逐渐富裕的中国消费者越来越注重自己的形象,繁荣的美容用品和整容手术的市场也证明了这一点。

Exercises 练习

Answer these questions.

1. What kind of men fit the term "metrosexual"?
2. Who do you consider a metrosexual idol? Why?
3. Do you think the metrosexual trend is a global phenomenon?

Translate these sentences into English.

1. 现在社会上的男人越来越在意自己的形象了。
2. 很多男人每天使用护肤品和化妆品，有的还佩戴饰品。
3. 光鲜靓丽的外表能提升自己的信心，给人以良好的印象。
4. 很多女人都赞成男人更注重外表。
5. 大多数使用化妆品的男性会通过网络购买化妆品。
6. 很多年轻男性都想模仿电影明星"花样美男"的风格。
7. 都市美男往往是收入相当不错的都市年轻男人。

Complete the following paragraph with these words or phrases.

> technology society standards fashion taste looks
> existed

Men with __1__ & style who know about __2__, art, and culture have always __3__. In past centuries, these kinds of men were confined to the upper crust of __4__ that had the available time and money to pay attention to their appearance. Now, however, __5__ and rising __6__ of living have enabled men from a wider slice of society to fuss over their __7__ almost as much as women.

Answers 答案

Translate these sentences into English.

1. Men in today's society are starting to care more and more about their own image.
2. Lots of men use moisturizers and makeup every day, some even wear jewelry.
3. A well-groomed appearance can raise your self-confidence and help you make a good impression on other people.
4. Many women approve of men paying more attention to their appearance.
5. Most men who use cosmetics purchase them over the internet.
6. Many young men want to imitate the styles of "pretty boy" movie stars.
7. Metrosexuals tend to be young urban men with relatively comfortable incomes.

Complete the following paragraph with these words or phrases.

1. taste 2. fashion 3. existed 4. society
5. technology 6. standards 7. looks

词 汇 表

moisturizer
护肤品
makeup
化妆品
jewelry
珠宝；首饰
whiff
一股（气味）
cologne
男用香水
image
形象
salon
沙龙
plastic surgery
整形手术
negative
否定的；消极的
connotation
涵义；内涵
idolized
偶像化的
admire
崇拜
imitate
模仿
celebrity
名人
groom
修饰；梳妆
approval
认可；批准
attentive
关心人的
gaze
凝视；注视
neck-and-neck
不分上下
vain
爱虚荣的
conscious
有意识的
boom
激增；猛涨

45

12. Tomboys
中性美女

A: Some of my girlfriends have an unusual style. They have short hair, they only wear T-shirts, jeans, and tennis shoes, and they never wear makeup. I think if I didn't know them I wouldn't be able to tell that they were girls!

B: There are a lot of girls like that, but I think they're still really cute. Their style has a nice casual and confident feeling; it looks very natural.

A: Some of them even talk different than other girls; their voices are kind of throaty, low alto quality rather than high-pitched.

B: There are definitely girls who project a more masculine attitude. One good example of this kind of "tomboy" is the 2005 Super Girl contest winner, Li Yuchun. To tell you the truth, the first time I saw her on TV, I couldn't tell she was a girl, but the more I watched the more I liked her style. By the end, I was a dedicated fan.

A: That's true, Li Yuchun has tons of fans even though she doesn't fit the traditional Chinese ideal of female beauty. Tomboys like her defy the idea that women have to be gentle, tender, sweet, and cute in order to be pretty.

B: Tomboys can be graceful and feminine, too, though—it's just a different way of expressing yourself. Some people think girls with a more androgynous style are just sloppy or lazy, but many of them care just as much about their appearance as other girls. Also, just because she's a tomboy doesn't mean a girl isn't well-mannered or polite.

A: I think that this trend toward a more androgynous style for women doesn't just reflect the change of beauty standards and changing fashion trends, it's also an expression of individuality.

B: You could even say that tomboys are an example of the independence and strength of modern women.

A: I think so. This more androgynous form of beauty is really in style these days; fashion designers have started coming out with more androgynous clothes and accessories, and it's becoming a hot trend.

B: But even though this trend is becoming more and more popular, sometimes people make assumptions about other people's personalities based on the type of clothes they wear, but in my experience tomboys aren't any different from girls with a more traditionally feminine style. You can be down to earth, outgoing and attractive to the opposite sex regardless of whether you wouldn't dream of wearing a skirt or you wear a skirt every day.

A: Yeah, in my opinon it's great that girls these days have more freedom to dress however they want and still look cool.

对 话

A: 我的一些女朋友有很特别的风格。她们通常留短发，喜欢穿 T 恤、牛仔裤和帆布鞋，从来不化妆。我觉得如果我不认识她们，我可能看不出来她们是女孩子！

B: 有很多那样的女孩子，不过我觉得她们依旧很可爱，有种随意、帅气的感觉，不做作。

A: 她们说起话来都和别的女孩子不一样，她们的嗓音是有些沙哑的女低音，不是又尖又细的女高音。

B: 她们就是有男人气质的女人，典型的代表人物就是2005年"超级女声"的冠军——李宇春。说实话，当我在电视上第一次看见她的时候，我真的没看出来她是个女生，可是越看越喜欢，到后来，我成了她的忠实粉丝。

A: 是的，虽然李宇春不是典型的中国传统美女，但她有很多粉丝。像她那样的中性美女打破了女孩应该文静、温柔、甜美和可爱才算漂亮的审美观。

B: 中性美女也很优雅、有女人味——这只是展示自己的不同方式。一些人觉得中性风格的女生都很邋遢或什么都不讲究，但是很多中性美女和其他女孩一样很在意自己的外表。还有，一个中性女生并不意味着她的举止不好或没有礼貌。

A: 我觉得女性中性化的趋势不仅反映了人们的审美标准和时尚潮流的变化，更是女性张扬个性的表现。

B: 你甚至可以说中性美女是时代女性独立和自强的代表。

A: 我同意。这种更中性化的风格现在大行其道，很多设计师都开始设计中性的服装和饰品，现在非常流行。

B: 但是虽然这种趋势越来越流行了，有时候人们仍然会根据穿衣风格来判断一个人的性格。但是，根据我的经历，中性女生和传统的女生没什么两样。不管你是从来都不想穿裙子还是每天都穿裙子，你都可以很纯真、外向和吸引异性。

A: 对，我觉得现在的女孩子可以更自由地打扮、想怎么打扮就怎么打扮看起来仍然很酷，这很棒！

Background Reading 背景阅读

Princess Charming 白马公主

Generally speaking, the tomboyish style of dress is more appropriate for women with long and lean figures and athletic dispositions. Tomboys can be very popular; beautiful girls think they're fine, and boys accept them as "one of the guys". Tomboys usually

1. Have an extroverted personality, are humorous, expressive, and not easily scared.
2. Don't use makeup, but use accessories, including: necklaces, earrings, rings, crystals, athletic wristbands, belts, cell phone accessories, etc.
3. Don't wear skirts, always pants, and wear their hair fashionably short.
4. Are straightforward and frank like boys and complex like women.

While fashions come and go quickly, from dresses to pants, from frilly and done up to casual, "tomboys" with their straightforward, casual, and unassuming ways have captured the general public's approval. The beauty standards their styles embody echo society's aesthetic ideals, and because of this they are also considered pretty girls. In order to differentiate them from more traditionally pretty girls, some people have taken to calling this kind of androgynous beauty, tomboyism a fashion term—princess charming.

Pop star Li Yuchun really revolutionized the world of Chinese fashion by showing people how a girl can refuse to follow traditional standards of beauty and at the same time be popular, attractive and endearing. When the 2005 Super Girl contest began, many people didn't know what to make of Li Yuchun's style. But as people got to know her, Li Yuchun's tomboy appearance and personality actually became the reason that many people became her devoted fans! Young girls started imitating her short haircut and confident demeanor, fashion designers started coming up with new tomboy-inspired styles, and boys and girls alike agreed that tomboys are both cute and fun.

通常说来，身材高挑、气质干练的女生比较适合"中性化"的打扮。中性女生广受欢迎，漂亮 MM 觉得她们没有威胁，男生也愿意吸收她们当哥们儿。中性美女通常具有以下特征：

1. 个性开朗、幽默、表情丰富，不怯场。
2. 不施粉黛，但配饰够个性，包括：项链、耳钉、臂环、水晶、运动型腕表、腰链、手机绳等等。
3. 不穿裙子，一年四季适应裤装，前卫短发。
4. 兼具男孩子的豪爽洒脱和女孩子的细腻。

时尚的潮流翻来覆去，从裙装到裤装，从柔美到利落，"中性美女"以其不娇柔、不做作、率性、简洁赢得了众人的喜爱。她们身上所体现的中性美迎合了现在社会的审美需求，因此她们同样被划入美女级别，为了与传统美女区分开来，有人还赋予了"中性美女"一个时尚的代名词——白马公主。

流行歌手李宇春向人们展示了一个女孩可以怎样拒绝遵循传统的审美标准，使中国时尚界发生了革命，她自己也同时走红，受人喜爱。当 2005 年超级女声比赛开始的时候，很多人不知道李宇春的风格是什么。但是随着人们对她的逐渐了解，她的中性外型和性格却使很多人成了她的忠实粉丝！年轻女孩开始模仿她的短发和自信的举止，时尚设计师开始有了新的中性风格的灵感，男孩和女孩同样都认为中性美女又可爱又有趣。

Exercises 练习

Answer these questions.
1. What kind of girl can be called tomboy?
2. What do you think of tomboy?
3. Do you think that tomboy would be popular everywhere?

Translate these sentences into English.
1. "中性美女"们通常留短发,喜欢穿T恤、牛仔裤和帆布鞋,而不穿裙子。
2. 我是她的忠实粉丝。
3. 现在,"中性"成为一种新的流行趋势。
4. 现在的女孩子有想穿什么就穿什么的自由。
5. 传统的审美观也在随着社会的快速变化而变化。
6. 中性打扮是显示独立的一种表现。
7. "中性美女"是时代女性独立和自强的代表。

Complete the following paragraph with these words or phrases.

critics winner defying contest representative style trail

Li Yuchun, the __1__ of the Super Girl __2__ , is popular not only because of her voice, something her __3__ and fans can agree on. She is also popular because of her __4__ , which says "I'm gonna be myself whether you like it or not". By blazing her own __5__ and __6__ cultural norms she has earned the respect and admiration of many, and is a perfect __7__ of this style of androgynous beauty so popular in today's China.

 Answers 答案

Translate these sentences into English.
1. Usually, "tomboys" have their hair cut short, and they prefer to wear T-shirts, jeans, and tennis shoes rather than skirts.
2. I am a dedicated fan of hers.
3. The androgynous style has become a very popular trend nowadays.
4. Girls these days have the freedom to dress however they want.
5. Society is changing rapidly and traditional aesthetic ideals are changing along with it.
6. Dressing androgynously can be an expression of one's individuality.
7. Tomboys are an example of the independence and strength of modern women.

Complete the following paragraph with these words or phrases.
1. winner 2. contest 3. critics 4. style
5. trail 6. defying 7. representative

词 汇 表

casual
　　　　随意的
confident
　　　　自信的
natural
　　　　自然的
throaty
　　　　沙哑的
alto
　　　　女低音
masculine
　　　　有男子气概的
representative
　　　　代表
dedicated
　　　　忠实的
fan
　　　　粉丝;…迷
defy
　　　　打破;违抗
feminine
　　　　女性化的
graceful
　　　　优美的;雅致的
progression
　　　　进步;发展
androgynous
　　　　中性的
figure
　　　　身材
disposition
　　　　气质;性格
charming
　　　　可爱的;迷人的
accessories
　　　　附件;配饰
straightforward
　　　　坦率的
complex
　　　　复杂的
endearing
　　　　受人喜欢的
demeanor

13. Enjoy Being Single

享受单身

Dialogue

A： Hey, I haven't seen you in forever! How are you doing? You still seeing that guy, Danny?

B： No, we broke up a while back. We just weren't compatible, you know?

A： Yeah, I know what you mean. Sometimes it just doesn't work out. Are your parents upset at all?

B： My parents? They just met him once and they liked him alright. But I don't think they felt strongly either way. They just want me to find someone who makes me happy. They don't want to pressure me into something I'm not ready for, you know? So when I told them we had broken up, they just asked if I was doing OK, and if they could do anything to help. I said I'd be fine, they haven't mentioned him since.

A： Oh, that's nice of them. Actually, I'm not with David anymore either. My parents didn't react quite like yours did though they were pretty upset because they liked David a lot they always said he was a nice, dependable young man. Plus, I'd been seeing him for a long time since college and just before we broke up they had started to hint that it was time for me to "settle down". "You're almost 27," they said, "isn't it about time you started planning for the future?" Well, I'm not so sure that I agree. At this point in my life young, and I need freedom, not restrictions.

People are getting married later and later these days and enjoying their
 shouldn't have to worry about marriage when you've barely gotten out
 the job market. Now, if I wanna go out on the weekend, toss a few
d time, I can, and I don't have to feel bad about it.

n! We should plan a Girls Night Out sometime, go out to the bars

50

and dance all night! Or maybe stay in, eat pizza and ice cream and watch a few movies.

B: That really sounds like a lot of fun. I'm so glad I have time now to do things like that. Now that I don't have to plan around what my boyfriend wants to do, I can spend more time with my friends. Sometimes I feel like because of him, I lost touch with some people I really care about.

A: Me too! Well now we can make up for lost time!

B: Great! How about this weekend, say, Friday?

A: Sounds good! Call me with the details!

对 话

A: 嗨，好久不见了！最近怎么样？你还在和那个叫丹尼的人来往吗？

B: 不，我们已经分手一段时间了。我们就是合不来，你明白吗？

A: 是的，我明白你的意思。有时候真的是没办法。你的父母是不是很失望？

B: 我父母？他们见过他一次，他们觉得他还行。但是我觉得他们也并不是特别喜欢他。他们只是希望我找到一个能使我快乐的人。你知道，我没准备好的事情，他们不想给我压力。所以，当我告诉父母我们已经分手了的时候，他们只是问我好不好，他们能给我一些什么帮助。我说我很好，他们就没有再提过他。

A: 哦，你的父母真好！实际上，我和大卫也不在一起了。我父母的表现可不像你父母那样，他们非常失望，因为他们很喜欢大卫，他们总是说，他是一个很好的、可以依靠的年轻人。还有，我们交往很长时间了，从大学就开始了，就在我们分手前，我父母暗示我们是时候应该稳定下来了。他们说："你快27岁了，还不开始为你的将来做打算吗？"我觉得我不能完全同意他们的话。现在我还年轻，我需要自由，而不是限制。

B: 就是！现在人们结婚的年龄越来越晚了，他们要更多地享受年轻的日子。当你刚刚走出校园开始工作的时候，你不应该为了结婚的事情担心。现在，如果周末的时候我想出去，我可以喝两三杯酒，享受一下，我并不觉得糟糕。

A: 听起来很有意思！有时间，我们应该计划一个"女孩之夜"。去酒吧，整夜跳舞！或者待在家里，吃比萨饼、冰激凌，看几部电影。

B: 听起来真的很有意思。我现在能有时间做这样的事情，我真高兴。现在我不用考虑我的男朋友想做什么，我可以有更多的时间和朋友在一起。有时候，我觉得因为他，我跟很多朋友失去了联系，这些朋友都是我很在意的人。

A: 我也是！现在我们可以把失去的时间补回来！

B: 太好了！这个周末怎么样，星期五？

A: 好！想好了给我打电话吧！

Background Reading 背景阅读

Enjoy Being Single 享受单身

Statistics show that in America, the number of married people and people in committed relationships is declining with respect to the number of single people. Being single is no longer an in-between. According to a recent survey of single Americans, of those not in committed relationships, nearly three fourths stated that they were not looking for a partner. This data indicates that singles these days are enjoying being single. Among American singles, men are more than twice as likely as women to be actively seeking a partner. Both women and men are statistically more likely to date for longer periods of time than they used to and marry later than ever before.	有统计表明，在美国，和单身人士的数量相比，已婚和有固定交往对象的人数正在下降。单身不再是中间层了。根据一项最近对美国单身人士的调查，在所有没有交往对象的人中，四分之三的人表示他们并没有在寻找他们的另一半。这项数据表明，当今的单身人士很享受单身。在美国的单身年轻人中，积极寻找对象的男性是寻找对象的女性的两倍以上。男性和女性都希望交往的时间比以前再长一点儿，然后再结婚。
A survey of 1,000 single New Zealanders shows that two thirds of all participants had made an active choice to be single. As for why they were single, nearly 44% of participants reported that they preferred being single, and found it more enjoyable than being in a relationship.	对1 000个单身的新西兰人的调查显示，三分之二的参与者都是主动选择单身的。至于他们为什么单身，将近44%的参与者说他们更喜欢单身，他们发现比起谈恋爱来，单身生活更令人愉快。
In China, the latest surveys show that the number of single women with degrees and career jobs is on the rise. The growth in the total number of single people is attributed to the increasing number of people getting a college education, which often delays marriage plans. Many women may also postpone hunting for a spouse while they develop their careers.	在中国，一项最新调查显示，有学历、有工作的单身女性的数量正在上升。受过大学教育的人越来越多是单身人口数量增长的主要原因，因为上大学通常会使结婚计划推迟。此外，很多女性由于忙于发展事业，找对象的事也被延迟了。
Being single doesn't have to mean being lonely. In fact, not having a significant other can be a blessing in disguise. Singledom gives you more time to appreciate your friends and family. Singles also have more time to themselves and more personal space than their attached counterparts. If you're single, take this time to learn more about yourself and what you want out of life. This can be a really rewarding time!	单身真的不一定就意味着孤独。实际上，没有对象可能会因祸得福。单身状态给你更多的时间可以和朋友还有家人在一起。单身的人也比有对象的人有更多的私人时间和个人空间。如果你现在单身，用这些时间多了解自己和想一想在你的生活中你想要什么。这可能是一段很有意义的时间！
Single people often feel pressured by their friends and family members to "find that special someone" and "settle down." But despite these pressures, people are choosing to wait longer and longer before marriage. Times are changing and being single is an increasingly legitimate lifestyle. People have begun to realize that taking time before marriage to explore and learn about oneself and others is directly beneficial to them later in life.	单身的人常常感到有压力，这些压力通常来自朋友或家人，他们总是催他快点儿找到爱人并且稳定下来。但是就算是有这些压力，人们选择在婚前等待的时间还是越来越长了。时代在变，对一个人来说，单身也越来越切合实际。人们开始认识到婚前用更多的时间去经历、去了解自己和别人，这对他们以后的生活有直接的好处。

Exercises 练习

Answer these questions.

1. What is your attitude towards being single?
2. What are the pros and cons of being single?
3. What has caused the recent increase in the number of single people?

Translate these sentences into English.

1. 你知道吗？我们就是合不来。
2. 他是一个很好的、可以依靠的年轻人。
3. 当今的单身人士很享受单身。
4. 很多女性由于忙于发展事业，找对象的事也被延迟了。
5. 单身真的不一定就意味着孤独。
6. 单身人士常常要面对来自家庭和朋友的让他们"安定下来"的压力。
7. 时代在变，对一个人来说，单身也越来越切合实际。

Complete the following paragraph with these words or phrases.

> appreciate examples feel sorry reevaluate ask for
> discontent

Why do people sometimes __1__ for singles? Because single people __2__ it. There are few __3__ of truly contented singles. Even under a pretense of satisfaction, there often lies a note of __4__ and desire to be in a relationship. Singles, both women and men, should __5__ their attitude and choose to __6__ the advantages of single life.

 Answers 答案

Translate these sentences into English.

1. We just weren't compatible, you know?
2. He was a nice, dependable young man.
3. Singles these days are enjoying being single.
4. Many women may also postpone hunting for a spouse while they develop their careers.
5. Being single doesn't have to mean being lonely.
6. Single people often face pressure from their family and friends to "settle down".
7. Times are changing and being single is an increasingly legitimate lifestyle.

Complete the following paragraph with these words or phrases.

1. feel sorry 2. ask for 3. examples 4. discontent
5. reevaluate 6. appreciate

词 汇 表

compatible
　　　　适合的；相容的
work out
　　　　产生好结果
upset
　　　　　　失望
alright
　　　　　　还可以
mention
　　　　　　提到
hint
　　　　　　暗示
restriction
　　　　　　限制
toss a few back
　　　　喝两三杯酒
lost touch with
　　　　跟…失去联系
committed
　　　　　已确定的
decline
　　　　　　下降
with respect to
　　　　和…比较
state
　　　　　　表明
actively
　　　主动地；积极地
attributed to
　　　　　归结于…
postpone
　　　　　　推迟
significant
　　　　　有意义的
blessing in disguise
　　　　　因祸得福
appreciate
　　　　　　感激
despite
　　　　不管；不看
increasingly
　　　　　越来越…
legitimate
　　　　切合实际的
directly
　　　　　　直接地

14. Slow Food

慢 餐

Dialogue

A： I'm really busy with work these days, most of the time I just eat fast food. It feels like I don't even have taste buds anymore.

B： Aww, you shouldn't eat that much fast food. It's terrible for you.

A： I wish it weren't this way too, but the pace of city life these days is too fast, anything you do needs to be really efficient, if you're even a little bit slower than other people, it could give the impression that you've failed somehow.

B： OK, but when you've got some free time I'll take you out to a special restaurant, and then you just might change your mind.

A： Really? What's so special about this restaurant?

B： It's a "slow food" restaurant—you know, "slow food" as opposed to "fast food". The foods there are all cooked delicately. You also need to take your time while you eat so you can really savor it, and the atmosphere of the place is really peaceful, so when you go out to eat there with friends you can talk and eat at the same time, even spend a few hours there. There's a snail painted on the entrance to the restaurant, expressing the management's hopes that people will enjoy their food at a snail's pace. It's a really a good place to go for the relaxing atmosphere.

A： Sounds really interesting! Who first came up with this idea of "slow food"?

B： In the 80s, a few Italians established a "Slow Food Society" as a way of boycotting fast food. The group started the "slow food" movement to protest fast food, and now the movement has over 10, 000 followers worldwide. This restaurant, Beijing's only "slow food" restaurant, has drawn many fashionistas and white collar professionals to visit.

A： Listening to you describe it makes me realize that the "slow food movement" is actually a kind of return to the more natural beginnings of life. The pace of our lives has gone from slow to fast, and now some people are advocating going from fast to slow. Pretty soon there will be people talking about modern life as "the good old days"!

B: Right, "slow food" doesn't just mean that you eat slowly; it's also advocating food with personality, cuisine prepared according to local tradition. When we enjoy "slow food", we're also respecting those who prepare food and cuisine.

A: Healthy, tasty, and culturally rich! What else are we waiting for, let's go there and eat now!

B: OK!

对 话

A: 这段时间我工作特别忙，常常吃快餐，我感觉我的味觉已经麻木了。

B: 哎呀，你不要吃那么多快餐，那都是垃圾食品，对身体一点儿好处都没有。

A: 我也不想这样。可是现在的城市生活节奏太快了，做什么都讲求高效率，如果你比别人慢一点儿，那可能就意味着失败。

B: 这样吧！你有空的时候，我请你去一家很特别的饭馆吃一顿，然后你的想法可能就会有点儿改变。

A: 真的吗？那家饭馆那么特别吗？

B: 是的。这是一家慢餐馆，之所以叫"慢餐"，就是为了区别于"快餐"。那儿的食物都烹制得极为精致，吃的时候也需要慢慢品尝，而且饭馆的环境也很幽雅，你可以和朋友边吃饭边聊天儿，吃上几个小时都没关系。饭馆的门口还画着一只蜗牛，希望人们用蜗牛的速度去享受美食。那真是一个放松精神的好去处。

A: 听起来很有意思啊！"慢餐"是谁想出来的好主意？

B: 上个世纪80年代，一些意大利人为了抵制快餐，成立了"慢餐协会"组织，并发起了"慢餐运动"。目前，"慢餐运动"在全世界已经有了数万名追随者。在北京，这是唯一的一家慢餐馆，吸引了很多时尚人士和白领光顾。

A: 听你这么说，我倒觉得，"慢餐运动"实际上是倡导回归自然和原始的生活状态。我们的生活节奏从慢到快，现在又有人提倡从快到慢。很快就会有人说现代生活是"过去的好日子"了！

B: 是的，"慢餐"的意思不仅仅是慢慢吃，也提倡保护带有地方色彩的烹饪方式。我们享受"慢餐"，也是对食物和烹制食物的人的一种尊重。

A: 又健康、又美味、又有文化内涵，还等什么，我们现在就去吧！

B: 好啊！

Background Reading 背景阅读

Join the Slow Food Movement 参与慢餐运动

The international Slow Food Movement was founded in 1986 by Italian leftist journalist Carlo Petrini, in a determined effort to wage intellectual war on the homogenization of food around the world. Spurred by the opening of Italy's first McDonald's in Rome, Carlo started the organization determined to save regional foods and small producers from extinction and to revive people's sensual appreciation of food. The Slow Food Movement helps local farmers, regional cuisine traditions, and restaurateurs, and at the same time feeds our hunger for authentic tastes, healthy eating, and a more leisurely, saner style of life. Its members are spreading the message that the pleasure of cooking and savoring delicious food is worth the time and effort.

"国际慢餐运动"是由意大利左翼记者卡罗·培崔尼在 1986 年建立的组织,旨在发起一场知识性战役,坚决反对全球食物同质化。这场运动的导火索是麦当劳要在罗马开设第一家分店,这刺激了卡罗建立这个组织,坚决要保护带有地方色彩的食品和挽救濒临灭绝的小作坊,并复苏人们对食物的感官享受。"慢餐运动"提倡采用当地的农产品、推崇传统的烹饪方式和餐馆,以满足我们对美食、健康饮食的渴求,实现一种更悠闲、健康的生活方式。这个运动的成员所宣扬的观点有:烹饪和享受美食的乐趣是值得花费时间和精力的。

People often regard eating as something you do as quickly as you can, because you have to, so you can go on to something that's more important. But the Slow Food movement views it in a different way. They believe that food is an important part of one's life and should be a wonderful sensual experience that you take the time to appreciate fully. The Slow Food movement will encourage people to recognize how important their environment is; to encourage people to buy foods that are nutritious, attractive, and most of all, delicious, as opposed to foods that only satisfy the pocketbooks of the corporations that are selling them.

人们常常把吃饭看作一种要尽快完成的事情,因为你得这样做,为了可以接着去做更重要的事。但是慢餐运动成员对此有不同的见解。他们认为食物是一个人生活中很重要的组成部分,是一次我们应该花时间去充分体验的完美的感观经历。慢餐运动能鼓励人们认识到自己所处环境的重要性,鼓励人们购买富有营养的、更诱人的,最重要的,是更美味的食物,而不是那些买来唯一的作用是满足了生产商腰包的食物。

How can an average working family join the Slow Food movement? One easy way is to distinguish your meals. You may be too busy to cook an elaborate meal on the weekdays, but during the weekends you can choose to make time for slow food. You can also cook a lot of your meals in preparation for the weekdays, and that will save you preparation time on busy evenings. But again, try to make meals a family experience: cook together, sit together at the table with the family, and do something fun with your meals whenever you have time.

一个普通的工薪家庭怎样才能参与慢餐运动呢? 一种容易的方法就是给食物分类。工作日的时候,你可能忙得没有时间去做一顿精致的饭菜,但是周末真的是你可以抽空准备慢餐的时候。你还可以为工作日准备很多菜,这样到忙碌的晚上时,你就节省了准备时间。不过更重要的是,尽量和家人一起准备:在你有时间的时候,和家人一起做饭,一家人围坐在桌前,一边吃饭一边做一点儿有意思的事。

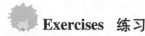 **Exercises** 练习

Answer these questions.

1. What do you think of the International Slow Food Movement?
2. Do you support the goals of the Slow Food Movement? Why?
3. Do you think there is room for Slow Food in a fast-paced urban lifestyle?

Translate these sentences into English.

1. 我感觉我的味觉已经麻木了。
2. 吃太多的快餐对身体非常不好。
3. 现在的城市生活节奏太快了，做什么都讲求高效率。
4. 那家饭馆的环境很幽雅，食物也烹制得极为精致。
5. 他们想挽救濒临灭绝的地方性风味食品和小作坊。
6. 烹饪和享受美食的乐趣是值得花费时间和精力的。
7. 慢餐运动成员认为食物是一个人生活中很重要的组成部分。

Complete the following paragraph with these words or phrases.

workshops explored celebrating far-reaching aspect
individual component

Slow Food Festivals are ___1___, not only acknowledging and encouraging ___2___ artisans, but also ___3___ the role of food throughout every ___4___ of culture. ___5___ where tastes are ___6___ in their cultural context are an important ___7___ of the International Slow Food Movement.

 Answers 答案

Translate these sentences into English.

1. I feel like I don't even have taste buds anymore.
2. Eating too much fast food is terrible for your health.
3. The pace of city life these days is too fast, so everything you do needs to be really efficient.
4. The atmosphere of the restaurant is really peaceful; the foods there are also cooked delicately.
5. They wanted to save regional foods and small producers from extinction.
6. The pleasure of cooking and savoring delicious food is worth the time and effort.
7. The Slow Food movement views food is an important part of life.

Complete the following paragraph with these words or phrases.

1. far-reaching 2. individual 3. celebrating 4. aspect
5. Workshops 6. explored 7. component

词 汇 表

fast food	快餐
taste buds	味蕾
junk food	垃圾食品
pace	节奏
efficient	有效率的
distinguish	区分
delicately	精心地
savor	品尝
atmosphere	气氛
upscale	高雅的
snail	蜗牛
establish	建立
boycott	抵制
protest	反对
draw	吸引
advocate	提倡
cuisine	烹饪法
movement	运动
wage	发起
intellectual	知识的
homogenization	同质化
spur	刺激
extinction	灭绝
revive	使复苏
elaborate	细致的

15. Internet Exchange

网络易物

A: That's a cool mp3 player, is it new?

B: No, I got it on the internet from an exchange; someone traded me their mp3 player for my old cell phone.

A: Really? I've only heard of people buying and selling things on the internet. I didn't know you could exchange things too!

B: Sure, internet exchange has just started up, but it's been developing quickly. Now there are a ton of websites and forums designed specifically for exchanging items.

A: Swapping stuff for stuff, it's such a simple idea! The most advanced form of modern technology has returned us to the most primitive form of exchange.

B: That's an interesting way to look at it. It's cool because as long as you find a willing partner you can swap anything. This is different from spending money to purchase an item, because what matters isn't how much your item is worth, it's how much the other person needs it. Because of this, some, even most exchanges are with items of unequal value.

A: It's really very efficient—you can exchange items you don't need for those you do, and both people benefit without wasting anything. I should get in on this too!

B: Well, those are some of the great things about internet exchange, but there are some flaws in the system too. For example, you can't always be sure about the quality of the items you get through exchange.

A: Have you had many problems?

B: I've actually only exchanged something once, and it was really easy. But some people will go through a whole chain of exchanges before they get the desired item. They'll exchange item A for item B—whether or not they want B—and then exchange item B to get C,

58

then maybe exchange C again to get D. They might go through many exchanges to get the item they want, or they might keep exchanging items indefinitely, just because they enjoy the game of trying to make a match and get something better.

A: Really? So this kind of person doesn't think it's a hassle, instead they think it's fun.

B: No, it's not a hassle at all; the internet makes this kind of thing so easy. You just register and then you can log on as often as you want and check what people have posted. And you'd never imagine what some people end up with. I saw an article that said one person started with a paper clip, and after fourteen exchanges ended up with a house!

A: That's incredible! Now you've made me think about all the things I have that I might be able to exchange. I'm going to go register at an exchange website right now!

对 话

A: 你的 mp3 很酷，是新的吗？

B: 不是，这是我在网上换来的，有人用他的 mp3 换了我的旧手机。

A: 是吗？我以前只听过有人在网上买卖东西，不知道在网上还可以换东西！

B: 是啊，网络易物的确是刚刚兴起，但是发展很快。现在有很多易物网站和论坛，专门为物品交换提供平台。

A: 以物换物，这个想法太简单了！先进高科技又使我们回到了原始的物物交换状态。

B: 你的想法很有意思。这种方式很酷，因为只要你找到一个愿意交换的朋友，你们就可以换任何东西。这和花钱买东西不一样，因为你的东西值多少钱并不重要，重要的是那个人有多需要它。因此，有一些，甚至大部分的物物交换都是不等价的。

A: 这很有效啊——你可以把自己不需要的东西换给别人，这对双方都有利，而且又不浪费。我也应该试试。

B: 你说的是网络易物好的方面，但是它也有不好的一面。比如说，你不能确定换来的东西有质量保证。

A: 你遇到过什么问题吗？

B: 我其实只换过一次，很容易。但是有的人在换到他们想要的东西之前，会经过一连串的交换。他们常常是先用 A 物品和别人交换 B 物品，不管他想不想要 B 物品，然后再用 B 物品去跟别人交换 C 物品，然后他可能再用 C 物品去换 D 物品，他可能会经过很多次交易，换来自己想要的东西；也可能他会一直换下去，就是因为他喜欢这个交换游戏，而且想换到更好的东西。

A: 是吗？这样的人真是不怕麻烦！反而觉得很有意思！

B: 其实一点儿也不麻烦，网络使这样的事情变得特别容易，你只要在网上注册以后，常常登陆，并及时关注别人发布的信息就行了。你一定想不到有人换到了什么。我看过一则新闻，说的是一个人用一个曲别针经过十四次交换换来了一栋房子。

A: 太不可思议了！你让我想到了我所有能交换的东西，我要马上去易物网上注册！

A Red Paper Clip to a House 从红色曲别针到房子

Kyle MacDonald, a Canadian, started with a red paper clip, spent 14 months and negotiated 14 exchanges, and ended up finally with a house. What were those fourteen lucky trades? One red paper clip→a fish-shaped pen→a door knob→a camping stove→a generator→a keg of beer→a snowmobile→a trip to British Columbia→a moving truck→a recording contract→a year of rent in Phoenix, Arizona→an afternoon with musician Alice Cooper→a role in a movie→finally, a house. His trading skill landed him appearances on American, Canadian, and Japanese television. And now? MacDonald has moved into the house with his girlfriend. The publicity surrounding his story has put the small town of Kipling on the map since he moved in. He doesn't plan to live there forever, he says, but for now he wants to settle down and start writing a book.

加拿大人凯尔·麦克唐纳花费 14 个月，经历 14 次交换，用一个红色曲别针换到了一栋房子。他的 14 次幸运交换流程：一枚红色别针→一支鱼形圆珠笔→一个门把手→一台野营微波炉→一台发电机→一桶啤酒→一辆雪橇摩托车→一次去加拿大不列颠哥伦比亚省的免费度假→一辆两用货车→一份录音棚的合同书→美国亚利桑那州凤凰城一所双层公寓一年的使用权→与歌星艾丽斯·库珀喝下午茶的机会→一部电影中的一个角色→一套房子。他的交换技巧使他频频亮相于美国、加拿大和日本的电视台。现在呢？麦克唐纳已经和他的女朋友搬进了那个房子。自从他搬家，他的故事的广告效应使这个叫基普岭的小镇出现在了地图上。他说，他并不想永远住在那儿，但是现在他想安定下来写本书。

Necessity Determines Value 需求决定价值

Web exchange can be about more than trading goods and services over the internet—it can also be fun. Web exchange is based on the idea that necessity determines value, just like the saying, "one man's trash is another man's treasure". You can trade something that's been sitting around unused in the house for many years for something that is a "treasure" to you, even though its current owner sees it as little better than "trash." The two main groups of people who participate in internet exchange are white collar professionals and students, aged 16 to 35. Most prefer to do the actual exchange in person so they can inspect the other person's item before they give their own away. Many exchangers are not looking for anything specific, so under exchange requirements they write, "trade for anything," "whatever's fine," "I'll trade for anything as long as I like it," "trade for interesting and fun things," and so on.

网络易物不只是在网上交换物品和服务，这个过程还很有意思。网络易物遵循"需求决定价值"的理念，就像一句俗话说的"一个人的垃圾是另一个人的财富"。你可以用一件早已闲置在家多年的物品，换得一件心仪已久的"宝贝"，尽管它现在的主人认为它差不多就是垃圾。参与网络易物的两大主要群体是白领和学生，年龄集中在 16 到 35 岁之间。他们大多选择当面验货、当面交易。不少换客都没有明确的换物目标，在换品要求上写着"换什么都行"、"随便"、"只要喜欢就换"、"换有趣的、好玩的"等等。

Benefits of Swapping Stuff 物物交换的优势

1. Maximize the value of an item. Rather than having a fixed inherent value, any item's worth varies in the hands of different people. That's where we get the sayings, "one man's trash is another man's treasure," and "beauty is in the eye of the beholder." Turning your trash into treasure only depends on finding the right person to trade with, and thanks to the internet this is easier than ever before. 2. Protect the environment. People all over the world are becoming aware of the importance of protecting the environment. When we take unused items and exchange them instead of throwing them away, we are contributing to this cause. 3. Find new friends online. If you often exchange a certain kind of product, for example audio and video equipment, then you are likely to meet people who share your interests, and you can form sincere friendships through the internet exchange community.

1. 让物品的价值最大化。虽然任何一件物品都有其固有的价值，但在不同人手里其价值也是不一样的。所以才有这样的说法"一个人的垃圾是另一个人的财富"和"情人眼里出西施"。只要找到合适的人交换就可以把你的垃圾变成宝贝，而网络使这变得比以前容易多了。2. 保护环境。全世界的人都意识到了保护环境的重要性。当我们把多余物品拿出来交换，而不是把它们送到垃圾站，我们就在为环保事业做贡献。3. 在网上认识新朋友。如果您经常交换某类物品，比如音像制品，那么您肯定会认识有共同兴趣的朋友，你们能通过交换关系建立起非常真诚的友情。

Exercises 练习

Answer these questions.

1. What kinds of people are more likely to participate in online exchange?
2. What are the benefits of online exchange?
3. Why might online exchange be risky?

Translate these sentences into English.

1. 我用我的旧手机跟别人换了一个 mp3。
2. 网络易物刚刚兴起，但是发展很快。
3. 网络易物不只是在互联网上交换物品和服务，这个过程还很有意思。
4. 网络易物遵循"需求决定价值"的理念。
5. 网络易物可以让物品的价值最大化。
6. 情人眼里出西施。
7. 一个人要丢弃的垃圾可能是另一个人的宝贝。

Complete the following paragraph with these words or phrases.

a series of staring scoffed instead of spotted until ambitious

One day, Kyle MacDonald was sitting at his computer __1__ blankly into space. He looked down at his desk, __2__ a lone red paperclip, and had an "aha" moment. MacDonald came up with the __3__ idea of trading that little red paperclip for a house. His friends and family __4__ at the idea, but he explained that __5__ trying to trade a paperclip for a house directly, he was going to do __6__ "up-trades" for bigger and better objects __7__ he got the house.

 Answers 答案

Translate these sentences into English.

1. I traded my old cell phone for someone else's mp3 player.
2. Internet exchange has just started up, but it's been developing very quickly.
3. Web exchange can be about more than trading goods and services over the internet—it can also be fun.
4. Web exchange is based on the idea that necessity determines value.
5. Swapping stuff with someone else can maximize the value of an item.
6. Beauty is in the eye of the beholder.
7. One man's trash is another man's treasure.

Complete the following paragraph with these words or phrases.

1. staring 2. spotted 3. ambitious 4. scoffed
5. instead of 6. a series of 7. until

词 汇 表

exchange	交换
item	项目；条款
forum	论坛；讨论会
designate	指明；表明
swap	交换；交流
primitive	原始的；远古的
purchase	购买
unequal	不公平的
quality	质量
desire	愿望；心愿
indefinitely	无限期地
hassle	麻烦
register	注册
log on	登陆
check	检查
gain	收获
paper clip	回形针
settle down	定居
treasure	财富；珍宝
inspect	检查
commodity	商品
online	线上；在线
maximize	使…最大化
trash	废物；劣货
beholder	观看者

16. College Tuition

大学学费

A: I heard that college tuition is really high in America, so for average Americans it's extremely expensive—is that true?

B: Yeah. There are two kinds of universities in America, public and private. The tuition for the average public university is around $10,000, and tuition at the average private university is $35,000 a year. Tuition for graduate students may be even more expensive.

A: Wow! To me, those prices are just sky-high!

B: Although tuition at American universities is very high, schools will provide assistance according to each student's circumstances. For instance, a student whose parents are very rich probably won't receive any financial aid. On the other hand, a student whose family is very poor will usually receive a combination of grants and loans. Universities try to make it financially possible for every accepted student to attend, but if most of the financial aid is in the form of loans, the student might choose to a university where the tuition is cheaper, because they don't want to be thousands of dollars in debt when they graduate. But students can pretty much always find somewhere to go, even if it's not their first choice.

A: That's great that even people who don't have much money can still go to college.

B: I thought that in China college tuition isn't that high, so why are so many people still unable to go to college? I heard that even some students who had already been accepted to university had to give up the opportunity because they didn't have the money.

A: To middle-income families who live in cities, college tuition isn't that expensive, but to a rural family, especially those in remote and underdeveloped areas, it's actually an incredibly large expense.

B: So if a low-income student wants to attend college, what can he or she do in that kind of situation?

A: Before, his or her parents would borrow money from friends and relatives to pay the child's tuition. Nowadays, the government is paying more and more attention to education, so students can apply for loans from the school and pay them back after graduation.

B: Many students in America also take out loans to pay their tuition. But besides loans, there are all kinds of scholarships funded by the federal government, state governments, and individuals.

A: Many students also get a job to help pay for college, right? I think that's the best way to do it. You can pay your debts and get experience for later jobs at the same time!

B: Yeah, even if you can't pay your entire tuition that way, it's a great way to learn to be self-reliant.

对 话

A: 我听说美国大学的学费特别贵，对一般的美国人来说也非常贵，是吗？

B: 是的。美国的大学分为公立大学和私立大学，一般的公立大学的学费是 10 000 美元左右，私立大学的学费差不多是 35 000 美元。研究生的学费可能要更贵一些。

A: 哇！对我来说，简直是天文数字！

B: 虽然美国大学的学费贵，但是学校会根据每个学生的具体情况为他们提供帮助。比如说如果一个学生的父母很有钱，那么他可能就得不到经济援助。另一方面，如果一个学生的家里没有钱，他通常会得到助学金和贷款。大学会尽量使被录取的学生能够上得起学。但是如果大部分的经济援助都是以贷款的形式提供给学生的，那么学生可能会选择去一个学费便宜一点儿的大学，因为他们不想一毕业就背上数千美元的债。虽然那可能不是他们的首选，但是他们也有地方可去。

A: 真不错！这样就不会有人因为没钱而不能上大学了。

B: 我觉得在中国，大学的学费不是那么贵啊，为什么还有很多人上不起大学呢？我听说，甚至有的学生已经考上了大学，可是因为没有钱，却放弃了上大学的机会。

A: 对于居住在城市的中等收入的家庭来说，大学的学费不算特别贵，但是对农村家庭，尤其是生活在比较偏远和落后地方的人们来说，大学的学费却是一笔不小的开支。

B: 那么如果一个贫困学生，他很想上学该怎么办呢？

A: 以前，他/她的父母会向亲戚和朋友借钱来付孩子的学费，现在，政府越来越重视教育了，所以学生可以向学校申请助学贷款，毕业以后自己偿还。

B: 在美国，很多学生也贷款付学费。但是除了贷款以外，我们还有各种形式的奖学金和助学金，这些资金来源于联邦政府或州政府或个人的捐助。

A: 很多学生也打工自己赚学费，对不对？我觉得这种办法是最好的。又能赚钱，又能为以后的工作积累经验。

B: 对，虽然这不够支付全部学费，但也是学会自力更生的好办法。

Background Reading 背景阅读

Grants, Loans and Scholarships 助学金、贷款和奖学金

Going to college in the United States can be very expensive. Between tuition, books, and room and board, one year at a private university often costs nearly $ 40,000! Public universities are less expensive, with total cost averaging $ 10,000 - 12,000 per year. However, if you do not live in-state, tuition at a public university might be almost as much as at a private university. In order to help students who might not otherwise be able to afford a college education, most universities offer financial aid. This can take the form of grants, loans, and/or "work-study," where the university gives the student a job to help them pay for tuition. Still, the vast majority of college students in the US must take out loans to pay for college, but student loans enjoy a very low interest rate, and the interest usually doesn't start accruing until the student graduates.

在美国上大学非常贵。一个私立大学一年的总费用包括学费、书费、住宿费和伙食费通常会高达 40 000 美元! 公立大学稍微便宜一点儿,总费用一般在每年 10 000 到 12 000 美元之间。但是,如果,你不是大学所在州的公民,那么即使大学是公立的,你的学费也和私立大学差不多一样贵。为了帮助那些有可能付不起学费的学生,大多数的大学都会提供经济援助。这种经济援助可能以助学金、贷款或者"工作—学习"(就是学校给学生提供工作,然后相应的免除他们的学费)的方式提供给学生。除此之外,相当多的美国学生得用贷款来支付学费,但是学生的贷款可以享受低利息,而且在学生毕业之前,贷款是不计利息的。

Funds for scholarships come from the state and federal governments as well as private individuals. To qualify for need-based assistance, families must fill out a questionnaire called the FAFSA. Because the American government, like the Chinese government, is realizing the increasing importance of education in a global society, many politicians are pushing for the government to provide more financial assistance to low-income students. Scholarships provided by private donors may have different criteria depending on the donor's preference.

奖学金的专款来源于州政府和联邦政府,也来自个人。想要得到以需要为基础的帮助,申请家庭必须要填一张叫做 FAFSA 的问卷。因为美国政府,和中国政府一样,正在认识到在全球社会中教育的重要性,很多政治家敦促政府向低收入的学生提供更多的经济援助。由个人捐助者提供的奖学金可能有不一样的标准,那取决于捐助者个人的喜好。

Many students in America receive scholarships from private donors rather than the government or the university. For example, the Morehead-Cain scholarship, provided to outstanding students at the University of North Carolina at Chapel Hill, is awarded to approximately fifty students every year. This scholarship covers tuition, fees, books, room, board, and so on. It also provides for students to study abroad and do internships that would otherwise be unpaid.

在美国,很多大学生从个人捐助者处得到奖学金而不是从政府或大学得到奖学金。比如说,为北卡罗来纳大学的优秀学生提供的 Morehead-Cain 奖学金,每年差不多授予 50 个学生。这个奖学金包括学费、书费、住宿费、伙食费等等。它也向学生提供海外留学和实习的费用,不然,这些钱是由学生自己来付的。

Exercises 练习

Answer these questions.

1. What are some ways that American students pay their college tuition?
2. Why can't some Chinese students afford college, even though tuition is so much cheaper than in the US?

Translate these sentences into English.

1. 美国大学的学费非常贵，甚至对一般的美国人来说都很贵。
2. 美国的大学会根据每个学生的具体情况为他们提供帮助。
3. 中国大学里贫困的学生多半来自农村。
4. 有的父母会向亲戚和朋友借钱来付孩子的学费。
5. 现在，学生可以向学校申请助学贷款，毕业以后自己偿还。
6. 在美国，奖学金的专款来源于州政府和联邦政府，也来自个人。
7. 在美国，很多大学生从个人捐助者而不是政府或大学得到奖学金。

Complete the following paragraph with these words or phrases.

contribute scholarships offer graduation options defray

For those who do not receive either merit or need-based __1__ , there are still many __2__ to help with expenses. Most universities __3__ a work-study program, in which students work at jobs on campus and can __4__ to their tuition. Even if they're not participating in a work-study program, many students decide to work during college to help __5__ the costs. There are also student loans, which can be paid back after __6__ .

 Answers 答案

Translate these sentences into English.

1. College tuition is really high in America, so even for average Americans it's extremely expensive.
2. American universities will provide assistance according to each student's circumstances.
3. Most of the impoverished students in Chinese universities come from villages.
4. Some parents would borrow money from friends and relatives to pay the child's tuition.
5. Nowadays, students can apply for loans from the school and pay them back after graduation.
6. In the US, funds for scholarships come from the state and federal governments as well as private individuals.
7. Many students in America receive scholarships from private donors rather than the government or the university.

Complete the following paragraph with these words or phrases.

1. scholarships 2. options 3. offer 4. contribute
5. defray 6. graduation

词 汇 表

tuition
            学费
average
            一般水平的
public
            公立的；公共的
private
            私立的；私有的
around
            大约；在…周围
graduate student
            研究生
financial
            财政的；金融的
aid
            援助；帮助
grant
            助学金
loan
            贷款
remote
            偏远的；遥远的
underdeveloped
            落后的
impoverish
            使…贫穷
fund
            资金；基金；专款
federal
            联邦的
debt
            债务；欠款
board
            伙食费
interest
            利息
as well as
            也
questionnaire
            问题表；问卷
politician
            政治家
donor
            捐献者；馈赠者
criteria
            标准
award
            授予；颁发
approximately
            近似的

17. Student Evaluation

学生测评教师

Dialogue

A: There's a teacher at our school whose lectures are really boring, so students are always skipping her class. I don't really enjoy it either, but at least I always go to class.

B: Has anyone ever told the professor why no one's ever at lecture? In the US, students at most universities write evaluations of the class and the teacher at the end of each semester.

A: Really? Students can criticize the teacher and the course?

B: Absolutely, in the US, student feedback is encouraged. Students are given evaluation forms where you can write down the things that were unsatisfying about the course or the teacher. This can also be helpful to students who are thinking of taking the class in the future.

A: Can students really say whatever they want?

B: Yes, the evaluations are always anonymous, and the teacher isn't even in the room when the students are filling them out.

A: What kind of things are on the evaluation?

B: Well, let's see... common questions would be things like, were the readings relevant, were the lectures well-presented and was their content interesting and useful, was the professor well-prepared for class and available for extra help outside of class, that sort of thing. So students definitely have plenty of opportunity to let the professor know if there's something that could be better.

A: Wow, that's great. Do professors pay attention to what the students say?

B: Of course not all professors are the same, but I'm sure no professor wants their class to be boring, so most of them probably listen to the criticism.

A: Have you written negative evaluations?

B: Yeah, definitely. Not many, because I've really enjoyed most of my classes, but there have been a couple that I didn't like. Most of my bad evaluations have actually been for teaching assistants, not professors. I think giving TAs honest evaluations is really important because most of them are going to be professors later on, so being a teaching assistant is their opportunity to practice and get better.

A: You're right; I think criticism—as long as it's constructive—can be really useful. Students should respect their professors, of course, but professors should also be trying to improve themselves too.

B: I agree. That's why I always write detailed evaluations—regardless of whether they're good or bad.

对 话

A: 我们学校的一个老师，上起课来很无聊，有很多学生逃课，我虽然每次都去上她的课，但是也不太喜欢。

B: 有没有人告诉过她，为什么有人会逃课？在美国，大多数大学的学生在每个学期结束的时候都会给课程和老师做评估。

A: 是吗？学生可以评价老师和课程吗？

B: 当然，在美国，学生的反馈会受到鼓励。学生会收到评估表，在上面填写对课程和老师不满意的地方。这样做对于那些下学期想要选修这门课程的学生也有帮助。

A: 学生们真的能想说什么就说什么吗？

B: 是的，评估一般都是匿名的，学生们做评估的时候，老师甚至不会在教室里。

A: 那评估表上通常都有什么？

B: 嗯，让我想想，一般的问题是这样的，阅读材料贴切吗，课讲得好不好，上课内容有没有意思、有没有用，老师备课备得好不好，课外是否愿意帮助学生，就是这些。所以学生们当然有很多机会让教授知道还有没有可以改进的地方。

A: 哇，真是太好了。老师们会在意学生们说的话吗？

B: 当然不是所有的老师都一样，但是我确定没有一个老师希望自己的课无聊，所以他们大多会接受批评。

A: 你在评估上写过什么不满的话吗？

B: 当然写过。不太多，因为大部分的课我都很喜欢，但是也有几门不太喜欢的。我写的不好的话都是针对助教的，而不是教授。我觉得给助教们最真实的评估很重要，因为他们以后大多会成为教授，所以当助教是他们实践和提高自己的机会。

A: 对，我觉得批评——只要是建设性的——真的很有用。学生当然应该尊敬老师，但是老师们也需要提高自己。

B: 我同意。所以我总是很认真地写评估——不管好的还是不好的。

Background Reading　背景阅读

How Would You Rate the Course?　你怎么评价这门课?

In the US, formal evaluations of teachers by students are not considered disrespectful at all. Indeed, the opposite is in fact true: if a student takes the time to fill out an evaluation in detail, it shows that they care about the class and respect the professor, even if some or all of their comments are negative. They will never take the class again, but they still care about the experience of the students who will come after them.

在美国，学生对老师做的正式评估完全不会被认为是对老师的不尊重。事实正相反：如果一个学生花时间认真写评估，尽管他们的评论部分或全部是否定的，但这表明他很在意这门课、尊敬这位老师。他们不会再选这门课了，但是他们仍然在意将要选这门课的学生们的经历。

People tend to think of teaching as just imparting knowledge. But teaching is about getting the students to truly understand what is being taught, and no one is a better judge of whether they are learning something than the students themselves. At most American universities, students get evaluation forms in the final 15 minutes of the last day of a course and are asked to fill them out anonymously.

人们往往觉得教学只是传授知识。但是，教学是为了让学生真正理解他们学到的东西，没有人比学生们自己更能判断他们是否学到了东西。在美国的大部分大学里，学生们在某一门课的最后一堂课的最后 15 分钟会拿到评估表，并匿名填写。

At Stanford University, the course guide has been computerized. Students are able to use a terminal to find out all the courses taught on a certain day or the names of the courses taught by a certain professor or what requirements a given course fulfills. At the end of each course description is a student evaluation section, which has questions like, "What are the best things about the class? How would you rate the course? What would you say to a student taking this course?" In addition, individual faculty members are encouraged to devise their own questionnaires for their students. These are used to help faculty members to improve their teaching and to help universities evaluate professors for tenure. Sometimes, however, the range of comments you get on the evaluation forms is so extreme that you wonder if all the students were taking the same course!

在斯坦福大学，课程指导已经计算机化了。学生们可以用一台电脑的终端机来找到某一天的所有的课程或者某一位教授所教的所有课程或者一门特定的课程有哪些具体要求。每一门课程介绍的最后就是学生评估的部分，包括这样的问题，"这门课最好的方面是什么? 你会怎么评价这门课? 你会对要选这门课的学生说什么?"除此之外，校方也鼓励个别的教师或工作人员为他们的学生设计自己的调查问卷。这些评估可以帮助教师提高教学水平和帮助大学测评教授以签订长期合同。有时，你从评估表上得来的评论差别极大，所以你不由得怀疑这些学生选的是不是同一门课。

Exercises 练习

Answer these questions.

1. Do you support student evaluation of professors? Why or why not?
2. What kinds of questions are on a typical evaluation?
3. How do you think professors should regard students' evaluations?

Translate these sentences into English.

1. 在美国，学生可以把对课程和老师不满意的地方写在评估表上。
2. 评估总是匿名的，学生做评估的时候，老师甚至不会在教室里。
3. 没有一个老师希望自己的课无聊，所以他们大多会接受批评。
4. 我觉得批评——只要是建设性的——真的很有用。
5. 学生当然应该尊敬老师，但是老师们也需要提高自己。
6. 没有人比学生们自己更能判断他们是否学到了东西。

Complete the following paragraph with these words or phrases.

later on in addition to grade undergraduate run practice office hours

Teaching Assistants are graduate students who, __1__ attending their own classes and doing their own research, have a job helping professors teach __2__ courses. They do things like help the professor __3__ papers and exams, hold __4__ for students who have questions, and __5__ discussion sections. Most of them are going to be professors __6__, so being a teaching assistant is their opportunity to __7__ and get better.

 Answers 答案

Translate these sentences into English.

1. In the US, students can write down the things that were unsatisfying about the course or the teacher on the evaluation forms.
2. The evaluations are always anonymous, and the teacher isn't even in the room when the students are filling them out.
3. No professor wants their class to be boring, so most of them probably listen to the criticism.
4. I think criticism—as long as it's constructive—can be really useful.
5. Students should respect their professors, of course, but professors should also be trying to improve themselves too.
6. No one is a better judge of whether they are learning something than the students themselves.

Complete the following paragraph with these words or phrases.

1. in addition to 2. undergraduate 3. grade 4. office hours
5. run 6. later on 7. practice

词 汇 表

boring
　　　　　无聊的
skip class
　　　　　逃课
unsatisfying
　　　　不令人满意的
helpful
　　　　　有益的
criticize
　　　　　批评
feedback
　　　　　反馈
semester
　　　　　学期
anonymous
　　　　　匿名的
fill
　　　充满；装满
relevant
　　　　　材料
content
　　　　　内容
pay attention to
　　　　　注意
teaching assistant
　　　　　助教
later on
　　　　　以后
as long as
　　　　　只要
constructive
　　　　建设性的
respect
　　　　　尊敬
comment
　　　　　评论
negative
　　　否定的；消极的
impart
　　　　　传授
faculty
　　　　全体教师
administrator
　　　　行政人员
tenure
　　　　任职期限
judge
　　　　　判断
terminal
　　　　电脑终端

18. Household Education

家庭教育

Dialogue

A: I heard that in China parents can beat their children, is this true?

B: It's true—some people think hitting children is a kind of useful method of education. There is an old Chinese saying about it, "If you don't beat your child, he won't be successful." When I was a kid, my mother often beat me.

A: Really? That's terrible! In America, beating a child is a federal crime. If a social worker discovers that it is happening, the government can charge the parents with the crime and take their children away.

B: Chinese and American traditions are not the same! Americans care about freedom and equality; Chinese believe that children should unconditionally obey their parents.

A: Why did your mother hit you?

B: The main reason was grades. To tell you the truth, my grades were always pretty good, but if one test grade dropped, she would hit me because she thought during that time I hadn't studied well enough.

A: Oh my God! I just can't imagine it.

B: My mom hit me, but she also really loved me. She was always making delicious food for me, and never made me do chores. She just made me devote all of my energy to studying, so that I could test into a good college. My mom did not have the chance to go to college because of the Cultural Revolution, so she placed all of her hopes on me, she wanted me to achieve the dream that she never had a chance to achieve herself.

A: Yeah, Chinese parents believe that grades are more important than anything else.

B: So how did your parents teach you? Did they let you have a lot of freedom? Could you do whatever you liked?

A: When I did something wrong, my parents would talk to me about it. If I kept on doing

70

what I was doing, they would take away privileges, or make me do chores. But they never beat me for getting bad grades.

B: Actually, I think that parents love their children just the same, whether they're Chinese or Westerners. The only difference is that the methods of education are different. But that's related to every country's culture and traditions.

A: Well then can I ask you, when you have children will you hit them?

B: Of course not! When my mom hit me, it really hurt. I don't want the same thing to happen to my child. If he is disobedient, I'll just reason with him.

对 话

A: 我听说，在中国，父母可以打孩子，这是真的吗？

B: 是的，有的人觉得打孩子是一种很有用的教育方法。中国还有一句俗话，叫"不打不成材"。我小的时候，我妈妈就常常打我。哈哈！

A: 真的吗？这简直不可思议！在美国，打孩子是犯法的。如果社会工作者发现了这件事，政府可以判父母有罪，然后把孩子带走。

B: 中国和美国的传统不一样啊！美国人注重自由、平等；中国人则认为孩子必须无条件地服从父母。

A: 你妈妈为什么打你？

B: 主要是因为我的学习成绩。说实话，我的学习成绩一直不错，但是如果某一次考试我的成绩下降了，她就认为我这段时间没好好学习，然后就打我。

A: 天啊！我无法想像。

B: 我妈妈虽然打我，但是她也特别爱我，她总是给我做好吃的饭菜，从来也不让我做家务活，就让我一心一意地学习，为了能考上一所好大学。我妈妈因为文化大革命而失去了上大学的机会，所以她把一切希望都寄托在我身上，希望我能实现她的梦想。

A: 对，中国的父母觉得孩子的成绩是所有事情中最重要的。

B: 你的父母是怎么教育你的呢？他们是不是给你很大的自由，你想做什么就做什么？

A: 当我做错事情的时候，我父母就会和我谈一谈。如果我还是这样做，他们就会限制我做一些事情，或者让我做家务。但是他们从来没有因为我成绩不好而打过我。

B: 其实我觉得，无论中国还是西方的父母，他们都是一样的爱孩子，只是教育方式不同。但是这跟各个国家的文化和传统也有关系。

A: 那我问你一个问题，以后你会打你的孩子吗？

B: 当然不会！我妈妈打我的时候，我真的很疼，我不要这样的事情再发生在我的孩子身上。如果他不听话，我会跟他讲道理。

Different Methods of Education 不同的教育方式

Because of the differences in traditions, culture, and society, Chinese and Western concepts of "household education" are very different. Most western parents believe that from the very day of their birth, children are individual people. Nobody can dominate their behavior and make choices for them. Most Chinese parents, however, require their children listen to them and be obedient. Western parents believe if the child is able, they usually make her do the task on her own. This is a way of respecting her individuality. Chinese parents, on the other hand, will often do whatever they can for their children. Western parents don't plan out every detail of their child's future. They work hard to raise their children so that they can adapt to all sorts of environments and can lead independent lives. Chinese parents want their children to become successful, so they care most about their children's studies. In order to ensure their children get good grades, they don't let children do anything but study, and developing the child's psychological health and their ability to lead an independent life and participate in civil society is less of a priority.

由于历史传统、社会文化背景的不同，中西方的家庭教育观念存在着巨大的差异。西方家长普遍认为孩子从出生那天起就是一个独立的个体，任何人都没有权力去支配他的行为，也不能替他做选择。而中国家长则大都要求孩子顺从、听话。西方家长一般都相信如果孩子能做到的，就让他自己做，这是对孩子独立性的尊重。而中国家长常常是能替孩子做多少就做多少。西方人并不煞费苦心地设计孩子的未来，而是努力把孩子培养成为能够适应各种环境，具备独立生存能力的人。中国的许多家长望子成龙，所以家长最关心的是孩子的学习。为使孩子学习成绩好，学习之外的事情家长都不让孩子干，而对孩子的独立生活能力、心理健康程度、公民意识等则关心很少。

Do Not Beat Your Children 不要打孩子

Many Chinese parents beat their children because they think it will make them learn well and behave better. In truth, it is a violent, harmful, and ineffective way of treating children. It does much more harm than good to children's psychological health and physical well-being. The incidence of child abuse, however, is still very high. Many children suffer permanent physical, mental, and emotional damage from these beatings. Children who are beaten can develop deep-seated resentment toward their parents and some try to run away to escape the abuse. Others might live in a state of perpetual fear and tremble at the very sight of their parents. How could this kind of situation possibly be beneficial to children?

很多中国父母打他们的孩子，因为他们觉得这样做可以让孩子学好并表现得更好。事实上，这是一种暴力的、有害的和没有用的教育方法。这对孩子的心理和身体健康都有更多的坏处。然而，对儿童滥用暴力的比率仍然很高。很多孩子在身体、精神和情感上都受到了永久的伤害。被打的孩子可能会对父母有根深蒂固的憎恨，一些孩子为了躲避被打骂可能会离家出走。其他一些孩子可能一看见父母就会感到没完没了的恐惧和紧张。这种情况怎么可能对孩子有好处呢？

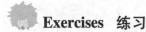

Exercises 练习

Answer these questions.

1. Would you ever beat your children?
2. Do you think physical punishment is always wrong?
3. What are some differences between how Chinese and American parents raise their children?

Translate these sentences into English.

1. 我小的时候，我妈妈常常打我。
2. 中国人认为孩子必须无条件地服从父母。
3. 我妈妈把一切希望都寄托在我身上，希望我能实现她的梦想。
4. 当我做错事情的时候，我父母就会和我谈一谈。
5. 我父母从来没有因为我成绩不好而打过我。
6. 无论中国还是西方的父母，他们都是一样的爱孩子。
7. 中西方家庭教育观念存在着巨大的差异。

Complete the following paragraph with these words or phrases.

in truth   afterwards   negotiation   regret   respect   guilt

Parents who beat their children may be torn __1__ by pangs of __2__ and remorse. Many parents even say, "Trust me, this hurts me more than it hurts you." However, the __3__ parents feel does not justify the beating. __4__, children are people too, and they should be treated with __5__. Parents should be understanding and guide them with reason, and __6__.

Answers 答案

Translate these sentences into English.

1. When I was a kid, my mother often beat me.
2. Chinese believe that children should unconditionally obey their parents.
3. My mother placed all of her hopes on me, she wanted me to achieve her dreams.
4. When I did something wrong, my parents would talk to me about it.
5. My parents never beat me for getting bad grades.
6. Parents love their children just the same, whether they're Chinese or Westerners.
7. Chinese and Western concepts of "household education" are very different.

Complete the following paragraph with these words or phrases.

1. afterwards   2. regret   3. guilt   4. In truth
5. respect   6. negotiation

词汇表

saying	格言；谚语
crime	罪；罪行；犯罪
charge	控告；指控
chore	家务
concept	概念；观念
dominate	支配
behavior	行为；举止
obedient	顺从的
raise	培养
adapt	适应
violent	暴力的
harmful	有害的
ineffective	无效的
psychological	精神的
physical	身体的
well-being	健康
incidence	发生率
abuse	滥用；辱骂
permanent	永久的
mental	精神的
deep-seated	根深蒂固的
resentment	不满；怨恨
escape	逃跑
perpetual	没完没了的

19. EQ Is More Important than IQ

情商比智商更重要

Dialogue

A: I saw on the news yesterday that a college student in Beijing killed himself by jumping off a building. Just since the beginning of this year, Beijing has already seen 15 college students commit suicide. To me this is a really worrisome trend.

B: Wow, that's terrible. But in China, many people envy college students, they're the pride of their parents and they have such a bright future. Why would someone like that want to kill himself?

A: I think there are many reasons why college students or recent graduates might be unhappy or feel like they're under a lot of pressure. They might feel desperate because they're failing in their studies, or they're having a hard time finding a job. They might have broken up with their boyfriend or girlfriend, or they could be facing financial pressures, or there might have been a death or other crisis in their family.

B: But these are all external factors. I think the internal factors play at least as big a role. I wonder if there's something particular to these college students that makes them more emotionally fragile.

A: Well, nowadays most college students in China are only children. If their parents have always helped them solve their problems, they don't have experience overcoming obstacles and they can't deal with things on their own very well. Once they encounter a problem that's a little hard to solve, they lose all confidence, and a few feel so desperate that they impulsively decide to commit suicide.

B: Have you heard about this idea called "EQ"? It's like IQ, but instead of measuring how smart you are, it's a way of thinking about how good a person is at dealing with the emotional aspects of life. It seems to me that the current educational model puts too much emphasis on IQ and not enough on EQ, and maybe that's part of the reason things turn out so tragically sometimes.

A: Hmm, that's interesting: so instead of just depending on education, IQ, family background, and luck, maybe success depends on a person's EQ as well.

B: Oh, definitely. In fact, it's becoming more and more common for companies to give a questionnaire to job applicants that tries to determine the person's EQ, in addition to looking at their school and employment history.

A: Then it really is important for our educational system to help students become more emotionally mature and self-reliant, because in addition to preventing really tragic outcomes like suicide, a good EQ is important for everyone's success.

B: I agree!

对 话

A: 昨天的新闻里说，北京又有一个大学生跳楼自杀了。从今年年初到现在，北京已经有 15 名大学生自杀身亡了。这种状况真令人担忧啊！

B: 真糟糕！在中国，大学生是很多人羡慕的对象，他们是父母的骄傲，拥有光明的前途。为什么有人要自杀呢？

A: 我觉得大学生或刚毕业的人会感觉不高兴或压力大有很多原因，比如说学习失败、就业难、感情失意、经济压力、家庭变故等都可能使他们感到绝望。

B: 但这些都是外在原因，我觉得内在原因的作用更大。我很想知道是什么特别的事情让这些大学生的心理更脆弱。

A: 现在的大学生大部分都是独生子女，如果家长一直替他们解决问题，他们自己就没有克服困难的经历，因而处理问题的能力就差。只要有一点儿解决不了的困难，他们就失去信心，感到绝望，冲动之下，就轻易的选择自杀。

B: 你听说过"情商"吗？和智商一样，但情商并不是用来衡量你有多聪明，而是一种考察一个人在情感方面处理问题的方式。我们现在的教育模式好像过于重视开发智商而忽视对情商的培养，这可能是事情变得不幸的部分原因。

A: 嗯，很有意思：所以一个人的成功不仅仅取决于他的受教育程度、智商、家庭背景和运气，还取决于他的情商。

B: 当然！事实上，除了要看他们的学习和工作经历以外，很多公司还让申请人填写问卷以确定他们的情商，这种现象已经越来越普遍了。

A: 所以，帮助学生在情感上变得更加成熟和自立对我们的教育体制很重要，除了可以防止像自杀这样的悲剧重演，还对每个人的成功都有好处。

B: 我同意！

Background Reading 背景阅读

EQ—A Greater Predictor of Success 情商——未来成功的预示

In the past many people believed that IQ was the best measure of human potential. In the last 10 years, however, researchers have found that this isn't necessarily the case—that in fact, your emotional intelligence quotient (EQ) might be a greater predictor of success.

以前，人们相信智商是衡量人的潜力的最好的标准。但是，在过去的10年里，研究人员发现事实不一定是这样——实际上，你的情商可能对你未来成功与否有着更准确的预示作用。

American psychologists hold that there are several components to having high "emotional intelligence." First is self-awareness, because you can only be in control of your life and your relationships if you know yourself. Second is being able to properly manage your emotions, so you can control your feelings rather than letting them control you. Third is being self-motivated, and being able to get through tough times and start over. The fourth is being receptive to other people's emotions, which is crucial for effective communication and healthy relationships. The fifth is being able to manage your relationships, which includes leadership and professional management skills.

美国心理学家认为，高情商包括以下几个方面的内容：一是自我意识。因为只有认识自己，才能成为自己的生活和与人关系的主宰。二是能妥善管理自己的情感，这样你可以控制你的情绪，而不是让情绪控制你。三是自我激励，能使自己走出生命中的低潮，重新出发。四是认知他人的情感。这是与他人顺利沟通、建立良好关系的基础；五是人际关系的管理，包括领导能力和专业的管理技巧。

There are many examples of people who have become very successful in business despite they fact that they never went to college. They have what are called "street smarts." One also finds people in all segments of society who seem very put together and have good "people skills"—these people have a high level of EQ One well-known American research institute investigated 188 companies, assessing the EQ and IQ of every company's upper-level executives. The study then analyzed the results of the EQ and IQ assessment together with each person's workplace performance. The results showed that among those in leadership positions, the influence of EQ was 9 times as important as IQ Those with a low IQ but a higher EQ could also succeed.

有些人在没有上过大学的情况下，却在做生意方面非常成功。他们拥有"城市环境中巧妙生活的能力"。我们也能发现在社会各个领域中有一些人总是很善于和人相处、和人交往——这些人就有很高的情商。美国一家很有名的研究机构调查了188个公司，测试了每个公司的高级主管的智商和情商，并将每位主管的测试结果和该主管在工作上的表现联系在一起进行分析。结果发现，对领导者来说，情商的影响力是智商的9倍。智商略逊的人如果拥有更高的情商指数，也一样能成功。

Exercises 练习

Answer these questions.

1. What are some aspects of EQ?
2. How could being an only child affect your EQ as a young adult?
3. Which factor do you think is most important in determining success?

Translate these sentences into English.

1. 这些学生的心理太脆弱。
2. 现在的中国大学生大部分都是独生子女。
3. 我们现在的教育模式好像过于重视开发智商而忽视对情商的培养。
4. 情商对一个人的成功或失败起到决定性作用。
5. 情商包括一个人应该对自己的优点和缺点都有清醒的认识。
6. 以前，人们相信智商是衡量人的潜力的最好的标准。
7. 智商略逊的人如果拥有更高的情商指数，也一样能成功。

Complete the following paragraph with these words or phrases.

determined ability understanding ranging from improve
street smarts appropriately

EQ is a person's __1__ to understand his or her own emotions and the emotions of others, and to act __2__ based on this __3__ . A lot of one's success in society is __4__ by non-IQ factors, __5__ social class to educational opportunity, and even luck. EQ is another very important factor, and fortunately it is something a person can work to __6__ , no matter how old they are. There are also some kinds of intelligence, like " __7__ ", which are not measured by traditional IQ tests.

 # Answers 答案

Translate these sentences into English.

1. These students are too emotionally fragile.
2. Nowadays most college students in China are only children.
3. It seems that the current educational model puts too much emphasis on IQ and not enough on EQ.
4. EQ is a crucial factor in determining a person's success or failure.
5. EQ includes being aware of one's own talents and flaws.
6. In the past many people believed that IQ was the best measure of human potential.
7. Those with a low IQ but a higher EQ could also succeed.

Complete the following paragraph with these words or phrases.

1. ability 2. appropriately 3. understanding 4. determined
5. ranging from 6. improve 7. street smarts

词 汇 表

jumping off
　　　　从…跳下去
commit suicide
　　　　　自杀
envy
　　　羡慕；嫉妒
pride
　　　　　骄傲
external factor
　　　　外在因素
internal factor
　　　　内在因素
fragile
　　　　　脆弱的
only children
　　　　独生子女
obstacles
　　　障碍（物）
impulsively
　　　　冲动地
current
　　　　　目前的
model
　　　　　模式
tragically
　　　　不幸地
tragic
　　　　　悲剧
outcome
　　　结果；后果
measure
　　　量；测量
predictor
　　　　预言者
psychologist
　　　　心理学家
component
　　　　组成部分
investigate
　　　　　调查
upper-level
　　　　高层的
executive
　　　　执行官
assessment
　　　评价；评估

20. Different Styles of Education

不同的教育方式

Dialogue

A: I've heard that Chinese high school students are incredibly busy and tired. Every day in addition to going to class and doing their homework, they still have to attend extra classes. Even over the summer it's the same way—they never do anything just for fun!

B: That's how most Chinese high school students are. The only thing that matters is their scores—to their parents, to their teachers, for getting into college—so they spend all their time studying.

A: Well scores are important in America, too, but it's not the only thing that matters. For instance, when you apply to college they look at your grades and your standardized test scores, but the college is also interested in what else you've done. In fact, colleges prefer students who have lots of extracurricular activities too, like sports or theater or student government. And there's also an application essay, which is by nature much more subjective.

B: That's so different from China—here the only factor determining whether you get into college is your score on the college entrance exam.

A: Yeah, I don't think deciding solely on the basis of one test is very rational, because you could be talented at so many things that just aren't on the test. But there are certainly other ways in which I think the Chinese educational system is better. Like basic math and science education, for example—Americans are terrible at math!

B: Haha, I've heard that too.

A: Exactly. American education gives students more freedom and puts more importance on creativity, but one result is that not as many students choose to work really hard at subjects like math. I mean, freedom is important, but not if a good foundation in certain core subjects comes as the price.

B: Then maybe there are times when testing and scores are really important—maybe students would learn more if they had to take harder tests, and if their scores really mattered.

A: Some people in the US think that that's exactly how we should fix the problems with education: have more and harder tests. But harder tests won't make students learn more if they're not being well taught; you have to look at all aspects of the problem.

B: That definitely makes sense. But the Chinese educational system just goes too far in that direction, at the expense of all the things that aren't on the exam.

A: Well, I think the point is that both systems have their strengths and weaknesses, so both countries have something to learn from the other.

对 话

A: 我听说中国的中学生学习特别忙、特别累，他们每天除了上学和做作业以外，还要参加各种辅导班，甚至在暑假期间也是这样，他们从来没有时间玩儿。

B: 那是现在大多数中国高中生的状况。对于他们的父母、老师以及升学来说，唯一重要的就是分数，所以他们所有的时间都用来学习了。

A: 在美国，分数也很重要，但并不是升学的唯一标准。举个例子，当你申请大学时，他们不仅要看你的成绩和标准化测试的分数，还要看你在学习之外做了些什么。实际上，大学更喜欢有很多课外活动经历的学生，像体育、戏剧表演或是学生会。而且他们申请大学时还得写一篇文章，这能很自然地体现他们的主观想法。

B: 这和中国太不一样了。在这儿，决定你能否进入大学的唯一因素就是升学考试的分数。

A: 是的，我觉得只根据一次考试来决定升学不太科学。因为你可能在很多方面有才能，但就在考试这个方面做得不好。但是我觉得当然也有一些方面，中国的教育制度更好。比如数学和自然科学教育，美国人的数学真的很糟糕！

B: 哈哈，我也听说过。

A: 没错。美式教育给了学生更多的自由，而且更重视创造性，但是一个后果就是很少有学生选择努力学习像数学这样的科目。我的意思是，自由当然重要，但是不能以核心基础学科作为代价。

B: 那么可能当考试和分数变得非常重要，并对升学有很大影响的时候，学生们就会为应付较难的考试而努力学习了吧。

A: 一些美国人认为这正是解决教育问题的方法：更多、更难的考试。但是如果学生们不能接受更好的教育的话更难的考试也不会让他们学到更多；你不得不考虑到问题的各个方面。

B: 很有道理。但是中国的教育制度在这方面做得太过了，牺牲了除考试之外的所有东西。

A: 嗯，我觉得关键是两种制度都有优缺点，两个国家也需要互相学习。

Different Education Systems in China and America 中美不同的教育体系

The Chinese style of education has its roots in a strict examination system developed over two millenia ago. The competition in the Chinese system now is just as intense as it was those thousands of years ago. All high school students take the same examination and their score is the number one determining factor in where they are admitted. In America, however, not nearly as much emphasis is put on the SAT, and more is put on grades and after-school activities. Colleges want well-rounded students who have demonstrated initiative and leadership ability. Another important factor is the application essay, through which students may demonstrate intelligence and creativity while describing some of their life experiences.

中国的教育方式根源于一种严格的考试制度，这种制度产生于两千多年前。中国教育体制中的竞争和几千年以前一样紧张。所有的高中生要参加一样的考试，他们的分数是他们被承认的决定性因素。然而，在美国，人们不是那么重视高考，而比较重视成绩和学生们参加的课外活动。大学想要那些显露出主动性并且有领导才能的全面发展的学生。另一个重要的因素就是申请作文，因为通过描写他们生活中的一些经历，学生们可以证明自己的智力和创造性。

While in China the National College Entrance Examination serves as a standardized test and a college application, the same is not true in the US. Applying to colleges is an entirely separate process from taking the SAT. Applications are different for each individual school and students can select which colleges they would like to apply to. This illustrates a key aspect of the college application process in America: applying to college is not about trying to get into the "best" college, but trying to find a college that is the "best fit" for you as an individual.

在中国，全国高考既是一次考试，也是进入大学的申请书，在美国却不是这样。申请上大学除了参加高考以外，还有几个独立的步骤。每个学校的申请程序都不一样，学生们必须选择他们想去的大学。这说明在美国申请上大学的一个关键的方面：申请上大学并不是一定要去"最好的"大学，而是尽力找到一个对你个人来说"最合适的"大学。

Almost all American colleges require an essay from their applicants, but the questions ask can vary widely. A common question is, "Write about a risk you have taken or tough choice you have made and how it has impacted your development." Colleges that require essays on these types of questions are trying to find out more about how the applicant has experienced personal growth and become a better person because of it. The University of Chicago, however, has asked question like, "How do you feel about Wednesday?" These more off-the-wall questions are opportunities for applicants to demonstrate creativity.

几乎所有的美国大学都要求申请人写一篇文章，但是这个文章的要求范围很广。一个很常见的问题是，"写你曾经经历过的一次冒险或者很难做的一次决定以及这件事情对你的发展有什么影响。"大学之所以要求学生的文章涉及这类问题，是想知道申请人是怎么因为这些事情而经历成长和成为更好的人的。芝加哥大学问了一个这样的问题"你对星期三有什么感觉？"这些更不寻常的问题恰恰给了申请人展示创造性的机会。

The never-ending debate between China and America, and even within the American education system, is how to evaluate performance. On the one hand, it is fairly easy to evaluate a student's knowledge of set material through graded examinations. On the other hand, such examinations may not give insight into whether the student has a good understanding of the material. Understanding and critical analysis, some of the foundations of traditional Western education, are difficult and perhaps impossible to evaluate objectively.

存在于中国和美国之间的、甚至在美国教育体系内的从未结束过的争论就是怎么来测评一个人的表现。一方面，通过分级考试很容易就可以测评出一个学生对某些材料的知识；另一方面，这样的考试恐怕不能让我们清楚这个学生是否对这些材料理解得很好。对知识的理解和批判式的分析等等一些传统西方教育的基础，很难或者也许不可能很客观地进行评价。

Exercises 练习

Answer these questions.

1. What do American colleges look for in their applicants?
2. Why do college applications in the US ask students to write an essay?
3. What is one advantage of tough standardized testing?

Translate these sentences into English.

1. 在中国，决定你能否进入大学的唯一因素就是升学考试的分数。
2. 你可能在很多方面有才能，但就在考试这个方面做得不好。
3. 当然也有一些方面，中国的教育制度更好，比如数学和自然科学教育。
4. 因为有更多教育上的自由，很少有学生选择努力学习像数学这样的科目。
5. 在中国，全国高考既是一次考试，也是进入大学的申请书。
6. 在美国，申请上大学并不是一定要去"最好的"大学，而是尽力找到一个对你个人来说"最合适的"大学。

Complete the following paragraph with these words or phrases.

standardized scores admission reasons requiring weight

Even though the SAT is not the only criterion for college __1__ in the US, some people think that it should get even less __2__ than it does now. Critics of the SAT say that __3__ tests are inherently unfair, citing consistently lower __4__ for non-white students, for example. For this and other __5__, some colleges have stopped __6__ that applicants submit SAT scores.

 Answers 答案

Translate these sentences into English.

1. In China the only factor determining whether you get into college is your score on the college entrance exam.
2. You could be talented at so many things that just aren't on the test.
3. There are certainly other ways in which the Chinese educational system is better, like basic math and science instruction.
4. With more educational freedom, fewer students may choose to work really hard at subjects like math.
5. In China the National College Entrance Examination serves as a standardized test and a college application in one.
6. In the US, applying to college is not about trying to get into the "best" college, but trying to find a college that is the "best fit" for you as an individual.

Complete the following paragraph with these words or phrases.

1. admission 2. weight 3. standardized 4. scores
5. reasons 6. requiring

词 汇 表

extra
　　　　额外的
matter
　　　要紧；有关系
score
　　　　　分数
standardized
　　　　标准化的
extracurricular
　　　　　课外的
theater
　　戏剧表演；剧场
essay
　　　　　文章
subjective
　　　　主观的
solely
　　　　　仅仅
rational
　　合理的；有理性的
talent
　　天才；才能；才干
creativity
　　　　创造性
foundation
　　　　　基础
core
　　　　核心的
root
　　　　　根源
competition
　　　　竞争
intense
　　　　紧张的
admit
　　　　承认
demonstrate
　　　　证明
leadership
　　　　领导能力
application
　　申请书；求职信
illustrate
　　　用例子说明
tough
　　难做的；棘手的
fairly
　　　　相当的
insight
　　见识；深刻的了解

21. Lightning Marriage
闪 婚

Dialogue

A: I went to a friend's wedding yesterday. I was so happy for them—the bride and the groom looked like a match made in heaven. But I almost couldn't believe it was happening because they only met 3 months ago, and now they're married!

B: I think this kind of situation is becoming more widespread. I've heard there's even a new word for it: "lightning marriage." You know, like getting married as fast as a bolt of lightning. As far as these lightning marriages go, a relationship of three months is considered comparatively long, I heard about some people who only knew each other for seven hours before they got married!

A: This is really an era that requires speed and stresses efficiency! Even relationships and marriage aren't exceptions. Do you think these "lightning marriages" can be happy and fulfilling?

B: I think "lightning marriages" are really interesting. If it was love at first sight for two people and they got married immediately, it would definitely be exciting, and after marriage their lives would be full of a sense of mystery and newness. Besides this, "lighting marriages" also have a great advantage: they can save the cost, including saving time and money.

A: I certainly believe that falling in love is something that can happen in the blink of an eye, but married life requires long-lasting, steady love. So I think "lightning marriages" seem like a big gamble. They're turning love into a game.

B: On the other hand, there are a lot of people who have been in very long term relationships, but in the end, because they waited so long, their relationship loses the passion it had in the beginning and they break up, which is really painful for them both.

82

I think "lightning marriages" are still better than that kind of situation!

A: But if the two people in a "lightning marriage" haven't known each other very long, and don't completely understand each other, don't you think after they get married they'll have a hard time avoiding conflicts?

B: I think a married couple's happiness isn't measured by how long they were together before they got married, so a "lightning marriage" doesn't have to lead to instability. Any marriage can succeed or fail.

A: I still think it's too risky; I think these "lightning marriages" will end up in "lightning divorces," and that's much worse for the two people than if they hadn't married at all.

B: It's true, "lightning marriages" aren't right for everyone; only those who have courage and the right attitude can take the risk!

对 话

A: 昨天我去参加了一个朋友的婚礼，新郎和新娘看上去很般配，我很为他们高兴，但让我感到不可思议的是，他们刚刚认识3个月就结婚了。

B: 现在这种情况已经并不少见了，而且还有了一个相应的新词"闪婚"，意思就是"像闪电一样很快很快的结婚"。3个月的恋爱期在闪婚中算是比较长的了，听说还有认识7个小时就结婚的人呢！

A: 这真是一个追求速度、讲究效率的时代啊！连恋爱、结婚也不例外。你觉得"闪婚"会幸福吗？

B: 我觉得"闪婚"挺好玩儿的！如果两个人一见钟情就结婚，肯定很刺激，而且婚后生活也会充满神秘感和新鲜感。此外，"闪婚"还有一个很大的好处，就是能节约恋爱成本，包括金钱成本和时间成本。

A: 我相信爱上一个人可能是一瞬间的事情，但是婚姻生活需要的是长久的、稳定的爱情，所以我觉得"闪婚"就好像是在赌博，把爱情当成游戏。

B: 可是也有很多人经历了马拉松式的恋爱，最后就因为恋爱时间太长、缺少恋爱初期的激情而分手了，而且双方还都很痛苦，我觉得这种情况还不如"闪婚"呢！

A: 可是"闪婚"的双方恋爱时间短，互相了解不充分，在婚后的生活中难免会出现矛盾。你说呢？

B: 我觉得婚姻幸福不幸福，不是用恋爱的时间长短来衡量的，所以闪婚并不意味婚姻不稳固，任何婚姻都可能成功或失败。

A: 可我还是觉得这样做太冒险了，我担心"闪婚"之后很快就会离婚，那真的是比没有结婚还痛苦。

B: 的确"闪婚"并不适合每个人，有勇气、而且心态好的人才能尝试！

Background Reading 背景阅读

Lightning Marriage—A Kind of Individual Act 闪婚——一种个人行为

The instance "lightning marriages" in cities is fairly high, and is most common among white collar young people. This is because of a few of this class's characteristics. Metropolitan professionals are very economically independent, and because of this they make their own decisions about things: if they want to buy something, they only consider personal preference. Marriage has become like this; they don't need to take into account other factors. They only care about their own feelings: marriage has already become a kind of individual act. At the same time, the white collar class has become more open-minded, with modern ideas, and this is one reason for this "lightning marriage" phenomenon.

闪婚在城市出现较多，并主要集中在年轻的白领阶层，这是由这个阶层的一些特质决定的。都市白领们经济独立，使他们可以决定自己的事情，买什么东西全凭个人喜好。婚姻也是如此，不用过多考虑其它的因素。他们只在乎自己的感受，婚姻已经变成一种个人的行为。同时，白领阶层的思想开放、观念现代，也是他们出现"闪婚"现象的原因之一。

"Lightning marriages" meet a certain group's requirements; they suit a certain group's nature. "Lightning marriage" is their preference and method of choice, and you could also say it is their creation. The arrangement of marriage wasn't originally meant to be permanent; for instance, in Western Europe and North America, more and more people are deciding not to marry, and is one kind of lifestyle people choose. This reveals that marriage laws are not perfect; otherwise people would not try to change them. But it is still difficult to determine whether or not the arrangement of marriage will cease to exist.

"闪婚"满足了一部分人的需求，符合这部分人的天性。"闪婚"是他们对婚姻的选择和做法，也可以说是他们的创造。婚姻这种形式本来就不是永恒的，比如在西欧和北美，越来越多的人选择不结婚，这是人们选择的一种生活方式。这也说明了婚姻制度本身是存在缺陷的，不然人们不会想到要去改变它。但婚姻这种形式是否会消亡，又是很难断定的。

The concept of marriage has evolved over the years. The traditional concept of marriage was more about responsibility, whereas the modern concept of marriage is more about emotions than responsibility. This indicates that marriage is more a matter of how to make one happier and increase quality of life. This concept of marriage is better suited to individualism. If a "lightning marriage" can make both parties happier, then getting married quick and divorced quick isn't necessarily a bad thing. Overemphasizing responsibility in marriage is also not necessarily a good thing. Many people in relationships in Western Europe and North America choose not to marry: according to statistics, 50% choose to cohabit. 1/4 of all people in America and France choose not to marry, but that doesn't mean they don't lead happy lives.

"婚姻"这个概念有一个演变的过程，传统的婚姻观多定义为责任，而现代的婚姻观则更多地定义为感情而非责任。这说明婚姻更关注的是如何使生活更快乐，生活的质量更加提高。这种婚恋观也就更符合人性。如果"闪婚"能使双方更快乐，那快结快离也不一定不是好事啊。将婚姻过多定义为责任也不见得是好事，西欧、北美有很多情侣并不选择进入婚姻，根据资料显示西欧有50%的人选择同居，而美国和法国也有1/4的人选择不结婚，但并不能因此就说他们过得不幸福。

Exercises 练习

Answer these questions.

1. What do you think about "lightning marriage"?
2. What do you think are the good and bad aspects of "lightning marriages"?
3. Would you have a "lightning marriage"? Why or why not?

Translate these sentences into English.

1. 他们是很般配的一对。
2. 闪婚几乎都出现在城市，并主要集中在年轻的白领阶层。
3. 闪婚的流行反映了一种文化，速度就是一切。
4. 网恋、一夜情、快速约会和闪婚在大城市变得普遍起来。
5. 传统的婚姻观多定义为责任。
6. 现代的婚姻观更多地定义为感情而非责任。
7. 很多人选择不结婚，但并不能因此就说他们过得不幸福。

Complete the following paragraph with these words or phrases.

| as long as   views   lifestyles   tolerant   acceptance   opposed |

According to a China Youth Daily report, Chinese people are becoming more open in their __1__ on marriage, and more __2__ of new and different __3__. However, there are varying levels of __4__ for specific kinds of life choices. For example, while 62.7% of those surveyed said it was ok to stay unmarried __5__, you're happy, 51.5% were __6__ to "lightning marriage"

 Answers 答案

Translate these sentences into English.

1. They are a well-matched couple.
2. Nearly all "lightning marriages" occur in cities, and they are most common among young white collar professionals.
3. The popularity of "lightning marriages" reflects a culture where speed is everything.
4. Online dating, one-night stands, speed dating and lightning marriage have been common in big cities.
5. The traditional concept of marriage was more about responsibility.
6. The modern concept of marriage is more about emotions than responsibility.
7. Many people choose not to marry, but that doesn't mean they don't lead happy lives.

Complete the following paragraph with these words or phrases.

1. views 2. tolerant 3. lifestyles 4. acceptance
5. as long as 6. opposed

词汇表

imagine	想像
widespread	普遍的
lightning	闪电
comparatively	比较地
era	时代；年代
exception	例外
fulfilling	满足
love at first sight	一见钟情
exciting	令人兴奋的
mystery	神秘
blink	眨眼
steady	稳固
gamble	赌博
passion	激情
avoid	避免
conflict	矛盾
imply	含有…的意思
divorce	离婚
class	阶层
metropolitan	都市
permanent	永久的
cease	终止；结束
concept	概念
evolve	演化
cohabit	同居

22. Moonlight Group

月光族

Dialogue

A: I hope I can get my paycheck a few days early, I'm broke again.

B: You really are a true "moonlight girl".

A: What do you mean by "moonlight girl"?

B: In modern society there are some young people who spend however much money they make; they live paycheck to paycheck, hand to mouth: these people are called "the moonlight group", and you are a "moonlight girl".

A: Haha, that's really interesting! That name is really fitting! I really am a "moonlight girl." Pretty clothes, fashionable shoes, and top of the line cosmetics are my favorite things. More than two thirds of my monthly salary goes towards buying these things. I like to go out to eat with friends, and go out drinking and dancing. In these ways, I spend money untill I'm broke.

B: Like you, the majority of this "moonlight group" live in large cities, are open minded, follow fashion closely and care a lot about their consumption. "Being good to one's self" is the first thing they consider when they're buying things.

A: Well yeah, the whole point of earning money is so you can enjoy life better!

B: Not gonna lie, I'm the same as you. Before, I was part of the "moonlight group" too. I think I was the kind of person who strived to attain a certain quality of life; I hoped I could enjoy life to the fullest, so when I spent money I usually didn't think too hard about it. As long as I thought it was worth it, I just spent it. But later, I realized that this kind of habit of consumption is not beneficial for a person's development in the long run, and I gradually got rid of it.

A: What exactly was not beneficial?

B: For example, if you don't have any savings at all, how will you support yourself when you're old? If something unexpected happens, how will you deal with it?

A: What you say makes sense, how do you get rid of these bad spending habits?

B: I got rid of my credit cards, and got my mom to guard my debit card. Of course once in a blue moon I get the urge to buy things, but since I don't have money or cards, there's no way, so I just look and that's all.

A: That method sounds like it could work...

B: After that I also studied up on financial management, put some effort into allotting my salary: for example, making a budget.

A: Well how's your financial situation now?

B: Now I already have put away a bit of savings, haha.

A: That's really cool! Looks like I should take a page from your book, quit being a "moonlight girl".

对 话

A: 我希望能早几天发工资，我的钱又花光了。

B: 你可真是名副其实的"月光小姐"啊！

A: "月光小姐"是什么意思呢？

B: 现在社会上有一些年轻人，他们挣多少钱就花多少钱，每个月都把自己的收入全部花光，这样的人叫"月光族"，你就是一个"月光小姐"！

A: 哈哈，太有意思了！这个名字真合适！我就是一个"月光小姐"！漂亮的衣服、时尚的鞋子、一线品牌的化妆品，都是我的最爱，我每月工资的三分之二以上都花在这上面了。平时，我还喜欢和朋友一起去吃饭、喝酒和跳舞，我的钱就这样花光了。

B: 和你一样，"月光族"大多生活在大城市，他们思想开放，喜欢追求时尚，对于自我消费非常重视，以"善待自己"为消费的出发点。

A: 那当然，挣钱的目的就是为了更好的享受生活嘛！

B: 不瞒你说，我以前也和你一样是个"月光族"，我觉得我是一个追求生活品质的人，我希望能够最大限度地享受生活中的乐趣，所以我花钱的时候基本上不会考虑太多，只要我自己觉得值，就付钱。但是后来，我认识到这样的消费习惯对一个人的长期发展很不利，就慢慢改掉了。

A: 有哪些不利呢？

B: 比如说，如果你一点儿积蓄都没有，你将来怎么养老？如果生活中有了突发事件，你怎么应付？

A: 你说的有道理，你是怎么改掉这乱花钱的坏毛病的呢？

B: 我戒掉了信用卡，工资卡也交给妈妈保管。虽然偶尔还有冲动购物的欲望，但无奈手上没钱又没卡，所以看看就算了。

A: 这个办法比较可行。

B: 然后我还学习了一些理财知识，尽量合理地分配我的收入。比如说，做个人预算。

A: 那你现在的财务状况怎么样呢？

B: 我现在已经有一笔积蓄了，呵呵。

A: 真不错！看来我也应该向你学习，摘掉"月光小姐"这顶帽子。

Background Reading 背景阅读

A Prevalent Consumption Way 一种流行的消费方式

China's economy is developing very quickly, and has brought with it a culture of consumption more prevalent with each passing day. At the same time, it has brought into being an educated group of young people who enjoy capitalist consumption way. They're used to spending money as soon as they get it every month, and so are called "the moonlight group". This word came into being during the 90s, to make fun of those born into wealth, who have received a high education, and who appreciate fast food culture.

中国经济的高速发展，带来了消费文化的日益盛行，同时也催生了一批具有高学历，充分享受资本主义消费模式的年轻人，他们习惯于当月工资当月花，因而被称为"月光族"。"月光族"一词出现于上世纪90年代后期，是用来讽刺那些出身富裕、接受高等教育、充分享受快餐文化的年轻人。

China's "moonlight group" are by and large only children born after China began to implement the One Child Policy in 1973. They grew up in an environment with four grandparents, a mother, a father, and one child. They hold pocket change from 6 people in their hands, and don't have to worry about food or clothing: everything's lovingly prepared for them; they're really "little emperors" and "little princesses". They fall into a culture of consumerism very easily, as soon as they enter society they become members of the "moonlight group".

中国的"月光族"基本上是1973年开始实施独生子女政策后出生的独生子女。他们在爷爷、奶奶、外公、外婆、父母和一个小孩的环境中成长，手里攥着六个人给的零花钱，衣食无忧，备受宠爱，是名副其实的"小皇帝"、"小公主"，他们很容易接受消费文化，一旦他们开始步入社会，很快就会成为"月光族"。

It is said that among Chinese young people who have just graduated college and entered the real world, 30% belong to "the moonlight group". Their parents helped them financially with their studies and they are gaining employment. Their wings of independence appear to be strong but in actuality they are still quite weak. Economically speaking, most of them can't be totally financially independent, and are still heavily dependent on their parents. After marriage, they not only have to take care of 4 elderly people, but also have to take care of children. It looks like the future for the "moonlight group" isn't that bright.

据说，在大学毕业后开始社会生活的中国年轻人中，"月光族"的比率占30%。他们在父母的资助下完成学业，走向工作岗位。看起来似乎已经拥有了坚强的翅膀，但事实上他们的翅膀依然非常稚嫩。在经济上，他们很多人都无法完全自立，对父母仍有较强的依赖性。结婚之后，他们不仅要赡养4位老人，还要照顾小孩。看起来，"月光族"的明天不甚明朗。

Xinhua News Agency surveyed 6,500 urban young people, and found that most of the "moonlight groups" work in IT, finance, publishing, media, the arts, and other professions. Their expenditures are mainly in clothes, makeup, eating out, tobacco, alcohol, and travel, among others.

新华社对6 500名城市青年进行的问卷调查的结果显示，"月光族"主要集中在IT、金融、出版、媒体、艺术等领域。其主要的消费支出是：服装、化妆品、外出聚餐、烟酒、旅行等。

Exercises 练习

Answer these questions.

1. What kind of people can be called "moonlight group"?
2. What kind of jobs do "moonlight group" usually do?

Translate these sentences into English.

1. "月光"是对那些在月底之前把自己的工资和收入全部花光的人的调侃。
2. "月光族"大多生活在大城市，他们思想开放，喜欢追求时尚。
3. 挣钱的目的就是为了更好的享受生活。
4. 我花钱的时候基本上不会考虑太多，只要我自己觉得值，就付钱。
5. 这样的消费习惯对一个人的长期发展很不利。
6. 中国的"月光族"基本上都是独生子女。
7. 看起来，"月光族"的明天不甚明朗。

Complete the following paragraph with these words or phrases.

> cell phone   management   hand-to-mouth   finances   lifestyle
> paycheck-to-paycheck

Money __1__ may not be that difficult, but mismanaging money is far easier. However, this mismanagement may cost us very dearly later on, and so it important to do some planning when it comes to your __2__. Instead of living __3__ and __4__, most people would do better to live a less flashy __5__, with a less expensive __6__ and certainly a less expensive car.

Answers 答案

Translate these sentences into English.

1. "Moonlight" is the moniker for people who always spend all their salaries or earnings before the end of the month.
2. The majority of the "moonlight group" live in large cities, are open minded, follow fashion closely.
3. The whole point of earning money is so you can enjoy life better.
4. When I spent money I usually didn't think too much. As long as I thought it was worth it, I just spent it.
5. This kind of habit of consumption is not beneficial for a person's development in the long run.
6. China's "moonlight group" are by and large the only children.
7. It looks like the future for the "moonlight group" isn't that bright.

Complete the following paragraph with these words or phrases.

1. management   2. finances   3. paycheck-to-paycheck
4. hand-to-mouth   5. lifestyle   6. cell phone

词 汇 表

paycheck	工资
hand to mouth	勉强糊口
consumption	消费
strive	奋斗；力求
attain	获得；达到
in the long run	最后
got rid of	摆脱；去掉
guard	保管
once in blue moon	难得有一次
urge	激励
allot	分配
budget	预算
prevalent	流行的
capitalist	资本主义的
wealth	财富
born into	出身于…
implement	执行
One Child Policy	独生子女政策
consumerism	消费主义
financially	财政上地
wing	翅膀；羽翼
independent	独立的
expenditure	支出

23. Astrology

占星术

Dialogue

A: Do you understand astrology?

B: Not really, because astrology is too complicated, but I really believe in it. Every time I first meet someone, I always use it to determine their personality and what kind of things they like, see if we have the potential to become good friends.

A: Astrology really is very complicated. I have a friend who is an expert on astrological signs, but ironically she isn't very lucky in love.

B: Is that so? I'd really like to know why.

A: My friend is a Scorpio girl, and first love was an Aquarius guy.

B: Scorpio girls and Aquarius guys, they aren't really compatible.

A: You're right, but when she first met this guy, she didn't know a thing about astrology. After they broke up, she stumbled across something on the internet that explained their signs weren't good together. Since then, she slowly came to believe in astrology, and that she should find a boyfriend of a compatible sign.

B: Has she found one?

A: Afterwards she had another boyfriend. The first time they went out, she asked him about his birthday and blood type so she could go back and check out his sign; see if they could be compatible. If they were, she would continue to see him, and if not, then she wouldn't.

B: That's terrible! Guys definitely don't like to be asked those sorts of questions.

A: Right. That guy thought she was too superstitious, and didn't want to see her anymore. My friend didn't think it was so bad. She said, if he didn't respect astrology it was like he didn't respect her, so she didn't feel it was necessary to keep seeing him. Afterwards she continued to search for the type most compatible with her, a Pisces guy.

B: I think her standards for guys are too exact, and too narrow-minded.

90

A： Afterwards she really went online to find a Pisces guy, and when they first started to go out they both like each other very much. My friend thought she had found true love, but later in the course of events discovered many other ways they weren't good for each other. Now she doesn't know how to go about it.

B： I think your friend should give up this idea that you can figure everything out with astrology, and use a more natural method for making friends. This is the only way you can find a person who is really good for you.

A： I agree. Her problem proves that when judging people, astrology should only be a reference, and not the primary resource. Your own feelings are still the most important thing.

对 话

A： 你了解占星术吗?

B： 我不太了解，因为占星术实在是太复杂了，可是我很相信它。每当我新认识一个人的时候，我都会用占星术来估测一下他的性格和喜好，看看我有没有可能和他成为好朋友。

A： 占星术的确很复杂，我有一个朋友，她简直是星座专家了，但是她的爱情却并不顺利。

B： 是吗? 我很想知道为什么?

A： 我的朋友是个天蝎座女孩，她的初恋情人是水瓶座男孩。

B： 天蝎座女孩和水瓶座男孩其实并不般配。

A： 你说对了。可是她刚认识那个男孩子的时候，对星座一无所知。他们分手以后，她无意中在网上发现，他们的星座不相配。从那以后，她开始慢慢相信星座，觉得应该找个星座相配的男朋友。

B： 她找到了吗?

A： 后来她又遇到了一个男孩。第一次出去约会时，她就问对方的生日和血型，想回去查查星座，看他们配不配，如果相配就交往下去，不相配就不要交往。

B： 真糟糕! 男孩子肯定不喜欢被这样问的。

A： 是的，那个男孩子觉得她对星座过于迷信，不想跟她交往。我的朋友也不觉得可惜，她说，不尊重星座就是不尊重她本人，所以也没有交往的必要。然后她就继续寻找跟她最配的双鱼座男生。

B： 我觉得她找男朋友的标准太绝对了，也太单一了。

A： 后来，她果然在网上找到了一个双鱼座的男生，刚开始的时候，他们都很喜欢对方，我的朋友以为自己找到了真爱，可是后来在进一步的接触中又发现了很多不合适的地方，她现在都不知道该怎么办好了。

B： 我觉得你的朋友应该放弃用星座来衡量一切的想法，用自然的方式去结交朋友，这样才能找到真正适合自己的人。

A： 我也这样想。通过她的例子，我觉得衡量人的时候，星座只能作参考，不能起决定作用，还是自己的感觉最重要。

What Is Your Sign? 你的星座是什么？

If you are interested in (or intrigued by) astrology, the first thing you need to know is your sun sign (also known as the zodiac sign). Sign—as in "What's my sign?"—is a word the average reader of horoscope columns in newspapers thinks of as a "label" for a stereotype applied to him simply because he was born in a certain one-month time period.

如果你对占星术感兴趣，那么你需要知道的第一件事就是你的太阳星座（也就是黄道带星座）。"我是什么星座的？"，这里所提及的"星座"就是报纸上占星算命栏目的普通读者心目中的一种"标签"，用以表示他属于某种类型的人。这种对人的典型类型的划分，是由他所出生的特定月份决定的。

Each of the twelve signs of the zodiac is a 30-degree arc in a 360-degree imaginary belt around the Earth (360/12 =30).

黄道带是围绕地球360度的假想带，分为12宫，其中每个宫是一个30度的弧线（每个宫都按星座命名）。

Along with the increasing study of astrology in the past few years, everyone has become more aware of it, and has stopped asking, "What's your sign", and started asking "What's your sun and moon sign, and rising sign?" Actually, there aren't many people who can distinguish sun, moon, and rising signs. We often use the month and day of birth to determine an individual's sign: for example, people born between September 23 and October 23 are Libras. This is the sun sign, which the sun located at when you were born. The sun sign just tell you general personality and spirit. But it is the moon sign which the moon located at when you were born that influences the inner you and emotions. The rising sign, determined by the time of birth, is the sign that was rising in the east when you were born; it determines one's outer image, speech and the beginning of one's career.

随着近年占星学的流行，大家对占星学的认识多了，开始由问"你的星座是什么"转而问"你的太阳、月亮星座和上升星座是什么"了！实际上，真正能分辨太阳、月亮和上升星座的人并不多。我们通常根据出生的月、日来确定自己的星座（sign），如：9月23日至10月23日期间出生的人是天平座（Libra）。这是指的太阳星座（sun sign），即出生时，太阳所处的星座。太阳星座所表示的是一个人的大致性格和精神等。但影响我们内心世界和感情的是月亮星座（moon sign），即我们出生时，月亮所处的星座。上升星座（rising sign）是指出生时，东方升起的星座，它主宰一个人的外在形象、言行举止及事业的开端。

Sun Sign 太阳星座

Aries (3/21 −4/19)　　　　　　　　白羊座（3 月 21 −4 月 19）
Taurus (4/20 −5/20)　　　　　　　金牛座（4 月 20 −5 月 20）
Gemini (5/21 −6/21)　　　　　　　双子座（5 月 21 −6 月 21）
Cancer (6/22 −7/22)　　　　　　　巨蟹座（6 月 22 −7 月 22）
Leo (7/23 −8/22)　　　　　　　　狮子座（7 月 23 −8 月 22）
Virgo (8/23 −9/22)　　　　　　　处女座（8 月 23 −9 月 22）
Libra (9/23 −10/23)　　　　　　　天平座（9 月 23 −10 月 23）
Scorpio (1/24 −11/21)　　　　　　天蝎座（10 月 24 −11 月 21）
Sagittarius (11/22 −12/21)　　　　射手座（11 月 22 −12 月 21）
Capricorn (12/22 −1/19)　　　　　摩羯座（12 月 22 −1 月 19）
Aquarius (1/20 −2/18)　　　　　　水瓶座（1 月 20 −2 月 18）
Pisces (2/19 −3/20)　　　　　　　双鱼座（2 月 19 −3 月 20）

Exercises 练习

Answer these questions.

1. Do you believe in astrology?
2. Would you consider using astrology to determine suitability when picking your future spouse?

Translate these sentences into English.

1. 天蝎座女孩和水瓶座男孩不一般配。
2. 她相信星座，觉得应该找个星座相配的男朋友。
3. 她对星座过于迷信。
4. 她找男朋友的标准太绝对了，也太单一了。
5. 星座是占星家们用来定义天空某个部分的一种形式。
6. 很多人都知道自己的太阳星座，这是由你的生日决定的。
7. 一旦你知道了自己的太阳星座，你就可以看到你每天、每周、每月和每年的星座运程了。

Complete the following paragraph with these words or phrases.

> technically referred as influenced astrologers specific
> stars based

Astrology is the study of how events on earth are __1__ by the sun, moon, __2__ and planets. __3__, "horoscope" is the term __4__ use for a chart showing the relative positions of the stars and planets at a __5__ time. It is like a snapshot of a particular place in time and space. But the horoscope familiar to most people is the forecast astrologers make __6__ on the chart. These daily, monthly or yearly predictions are often __7__ a "horoscope", and are published in newspapers and on the Web.

 Answers 答案

Translate these sentences into English.

1. Scorpio girls and Aquarius guys, they aren't really compatible.
2. She believes in astrology, so she wants to find a boyfriend of a compatible sign.
3. She was too superstitious about astrology.
4. Her standards for guys are too exact, and too narrow-minded.
5. "Sign" is a term used by astrologers to denote a sector of the sky.
6. Most people know their sun sign, which is based on your birthday.
7. Once you know your sun sign, you can start reading your horoscopes daily, weekly, monthly or yearly.

Complete the following paragraph with these words or phrases.

1. influenced 2. stars 3. Technically 4. astrologers
5. specific 6. based 7. referred as

astrology
　　　　占星术
complicated
　　　　复杂的
potential
　　　　可能性
determine
　　　确定；测定
expert
　　　　专家
ironically
　　　　讽刺地
first love
　　　　初恋
stumble across
　　　　偶然发现
superstitious
　　　　迷信的
exact
　　　　绝对的
narrow-minded
　　　思想狭隘的
figure out
　　　想出；领会
reference
　　　　参考
primary
　　主要的；初级的
resource
　　　寄托；资源
intrigue
　　引起…极大的兴趣
sign
　　　　星座
horoscope
　　　占星算命
column
　　　　栏目
stereotype
　　　固有的看法
imaginary
　　　　假想的
aware
　　　意识到的
influence
　　　　影响
inner
　　　里面的
emotion
　　　　感情

93

24. Singles' Day

光棍节

Dialogue

A： Do you know what holiday falls on November 11th?

B： I've heard that a lot of young people call this day "Singles' Day"! But how did it come from?

A： It is said it originated from the early 1990s, when college students first put forward the idea of choosing the day of November 11 (1111) as a day for single people. It became popular and turned into a cultural event on campus even society.

B： Then, How do they celebrate Singles' Day?

A： There are tons of ways to celebrate it! At some universities, student organizations have singles parties, to give single guys and girls an opportunity to meet and stop being single; some people go out singing and drinking, let off steam about being single; and some people go on blind dates looking for suitable partners; some people get together with other single friends to just have a good time. Singles' Day has also become a holiday even people who aren't single, on this day lots of people with partners pretend they are single again, together tasting their old single life.

B： That's really cool! Looks like this holiday is a lot of fun for a lot of people.

A： It is, in China, the number of single people has increased. Before, being "single" had a connotation of being lonely, lonesome, and unloved, but now it is no longer the substitute name for sadness, it means more independence, more freedom and unrestrained way of life.

B： So what you're saying is, before they were "passively" single, and now they're "actively" single?

A： Some people are that way, but definitely not all of them. There are still lots of people these days who are sad about being single, and want to escape it somehow, but more and more young people think that marriage isn't something one has to do, they aren't looking for partners, and they don't want to get married. They consider themselves very young at heart, and still have a lot of other things to do.

B： It looks like the economy has developed, society is changing, and people's values are also changing!

A： In the past many older young people just married for the sake of marriage. But nowadays young people's ideas about marriage and values have changed. They value intellectual exchange more, and require a common language of communication.

B： Perhaps this trend of singlehood will have a definite negative impact on society! If the number of single people increases, the existence of society and humanity may both be threatened. In some western countries, this trend has already become apparent.

A： Yep! So, some experts say, this kind of lifestyle deserves respect, but shouldn't be advocated!

对 话

A： 你知道 11 月 11 日是什么节日吗？

B： 我听说过，很多年轻人管这一天叫"光棍节"！但是这个节日是怎么来的呢？

A： 据说它起源于 90 年代初期的大学校园，一些单身的大学生们首先提出了这个想法，就是把 11 月 11 日作为单身人的节日。之后，这个节日越来越流行，成了校园文化乃至社会文化中的一件大事。

B： 那么，他们怎么庆祝"光棍节"呢？

A： 庆祝的花样可多了！在一些大学，学生组织会举办单身晚会，为众多单身男女创造机会，结束单身；有的人会去 K 歌或喝酒，发泄自己身为一名"光棍"的郁闷；也有人去参加"陌生约会"，寻找适合自己的另一半；也有一些都是单身的好朋友会借这个机会聚会玩乐。还有，光棍节也成为越来越多非单身者的狂欢节日，许多人在这一天与爱人扮回单身状态，来回味自己久违的单身生活。

B： 真有意思！看来这个节日给很多人都带来了快乐！

A： 是的，在中国，现在单身的人越来越多了。以前，单身就意味着孤独、寂寞和没有人爱；可是现在，单身不再是伤感的代名词，它代表着一种更独立、更自由和没有约束的生活方式。

B： 这么说，他们以前是"被动单身"，而现在是"主动单身"了？。

A： 有些人是这样，但并不是所有的。现在还有很多人因为单身而痛苦，想摆脱单身；但是越来越多的年轻人不认为结婚是必须的，他们不是找不着对象，而是不想婚恋，他们认为自己的心理年龄还很小，还有很多事情要做。

B： 看来经济发展了，社会在变，人们的观念也在变啊！

A： 过去不少大龄青年是"为结婚而结婚"，但现代青年的婚姻观、价值观都发生了改变。他们更看重思想的交流，要求有共同语言。

B： 可是单身的趋势也必然会给社会带来一定的负面影响啊！如果单身的人越来越多，社会和人类的存在都会受到威胁。在一些西方国家，这种趋势已经越来越明显了。

A： 是的！所以，有的专家提出，这种生活状态值得尊重，但不应该提倡！

Celebrating Singles' Day 庆祝单身

"Singles' Day" falls on every November 11th, and as the name indicates, this relatively new holiday is one exclusively for people who are still living the single life. It got its name for this reason, and because the date is comprised of four "ones." China is the only country in the world that has set aside a special day for singles to celebrate their lives.

每年的 11 月 11 日是"光棍节",就像这个节日的名字所表达的,这个新的节日专为那些仍旧单身的人设立。它因这个原因而得名,也因为这一天有 4 个 1。中国是唯一为单身的人们设立节日的国家。

"Singles' Day" was first celebrated at various universities in Nanjing, capital city of Jiangsu Province during the 1990s. It got the name "Singles' Day" because the date is comprised of four "ones". These college students have since graduated, and carried their university tradition into society. Singles' Day is now a special day for all fashionable youths. The main way to celebrate "Singles' Day" is to have dinner with your single friends, but it's important that each person pay their own way to show their independence. People also hold "blind date" parties in an attempt to bid goodbye to their single lives.

90 年代,"光棍节"最早是在江苏省南京市的各个大学中流传的。光棍节的名字来源于那一天有 4 个 1。这些大学生毕业后把这个大学的传统带到了社会上,于是现在光棍节就成为单身青年们的节日了。这个节日主要的庆祝方式是和单身朋友一起共进晚餐。重要的是,每个人都要各付各的,以显示各自的独立性。人们也会举行"陌生约会"派对,以争取告别单身生活。

These days, many young people are choosing to get married on "Singles' Day," which falls on November 11. Some young people see the four "ones" in the date as a good omen that can be interpreted as "united as having one heart and one soul, and living together all their lifetime." Some other young people plan to get married on the day after Singles Day, because they want to celebrate their last special day of being single.

最近有很多年轻人选择在 11 月 11 日——光棍节这天结婚。一些年轻人把 4 个 1 看作好兆头,将它解释为"一心一意一起过一生"。另一些年轻人选择在光棍节的下一天结婚,因为他们想庆祝单身时期最后的特别日子。

It is no longer a taboo to be single in China, especially in big metropolises. Many people do not think bachelordom is the substitute name for loneliness, solitude and boredom. On the contrary, singleness sometimes means more independence, more freedom and unrestrained planning of life. As the joke goes "single is simple; double is trouble". Being single means you are master of yourself. You can hang out with friends all the time, not worrying that they are going to be picky and demanding as your other half. Social environment has become more tolerant and being single is facing less pressure of public opinion.

在中国,单身已经不再是人们忌讳的现象了,尤其是在大都市。人们不再认为单身就是孤独、寂寞和厌烦的代名词了。相反,单身有时候意味着更独立、更自由和没有束缚的生活。就像一个笑话说的"单身就是简单;成双就是麻烦"。单身意味着你是自己的主人。你可以和朋友在一起玩乐,不用担心他们像你的另一半那样太过挑剔或要求你。社会环境变得更宽松了,单身面对的来自社会舆论的压力也小了。

Exercises 练习

Answer these questions.
1. What's the origin of "Singles' Day"?
2. How do young people celebrate "Singles' Day"?
3. What will you do on "Singles' Day"?

Translate these sentences into English.
1. "光棍节" 是专为那些仍旧单身的人设立的。
2. "光棍节" 起源于 90 年代的中国大学校园。
3. 人们会举行 "陌生约会" 派对，以争取告别单身生活。
4. 酒吧和 KTV 会举办一系列活动来庆祝 "光棍节"。
5. 以前，单身就意味着孤独和寂寞。
6. 在中国，单身已经不再是人们忌讳的现象了。
7. 单身面对的来自社会舆论的压力比以前小了。

Complete the following paragraph with these words or phrases.

special someone   blind date   heart   in addition to
say goodbye to   marry

Many singles also choose to __1__ their single lives on this day.
Many attend " __2__ " parties and many people choose to __3__ on
this day. __4__ meaning "single" the four "ones" of the date can
also mean "only one" as in "the only one for me." Some people will
use this date and this meaning to tell their __5__ that they are the only
"one" in their __6__ .

 Answers 答案

Translate these sentences into English.
1. "Singles' Day" is exclusively for people who are still living the single life.
2. "Singles' Day" originated during the 90s in Chinese universities.
3. People will hold "blind date" parties in an attempt to bid goodbye to their single lives.
4. Bars and KTV clubs are promoting a series of activities to celebrate "Singles' Day".
5. Before, being "single" had a connotation of being lonely and lonesome.
6. It is no longer a taboo to be single in China.
7. Being single is facing less pressure of public opinion than before.

Complete the following paragraph with these words or phrases.
1. say goodbye to   2. blind date   3. marry   4. In addition to
5. special someone   6. heart

词 汇 表

originate
　　起源
celebrate
　　庆祝
let off steam
　　发泄郁闷
blind date
　　陌生约会
pretend
　　假扮；装
connotation
　　含义
substitute
　　代替品
passively
　　被动地
actively
　　主动地
escape
　　逃走
sake
　　缘故
negative
　否定的；负面的
impact
　　影响
threaten
　　威胁
advocate
　　提倡
exclusively
　　仅仅
comprise
　　包括
attempt
　企图；争取
bid
　致意；道别
taboo
　　禁忌
metropolis
　　大都市
solitude
　　孤独
boredom
　厌烦；无聊
picky
　　挑剔的
tolerant
　宽松的；可容忍的

25. Starting a Family

结婚生子

Dialogue

A: Guess what? My brother and his wife are having a baby!

B: Wow, congratulations! I didn't even know your brother was married!

A: Yeah, they had been dating for about two years when my brother proposed a year ago. They got married last summer.

B: They must be so excited!

A: Definitely. I am too, but it's so sudden! He's only 26... maybe it's because I still think of him as being 15 or something, but it's really weird to me that he's suddenly all grown up. And 26 seems so young to start a family.

B: In China 26 isn't young at all for starting a family, especially in the countryside. But even in the cities people often get married when they're in their mid-20's and have a child soon after.

A: In the US lots of people get married in their late 20's or early 30's too, but for me 26 still seems really young—there's just so much I want to do before I start having kids.

B: Well it depends a lot on your career. I mean, if you get a stable job right out of college, then you can start having kids pretty soon. But if your career path is a little more non-traditional, or if it's something that takes longer before you have a good regular income, then it's better to wait until you have a little bit more of that stability.

A: Yeah, my brother is in medical school right now, so his future had a pretty clear path already. If he becomes a doctor as soon as he graduates he'll have no trouble providing for a family and a child. But for me it's also that there are so many places in the world where I want to live, and you can't just move to a different country every few years if you have a kid.

B： It's true, having kids means sacrificing other things, because if you become a parent your most important responsibility is to do your utmost to give your child the best possible environment to grow up in.

A： That's why I think I'm going to wait until I'm in my early-or mid-30's, so I can have time to do some of those things first, and by that time my life and my career will be more stable. What about you?

B： I don't know, I guess for me the main things are finding the right person to start a family with, and a job that's good enough to support a family. Once I have that there's not much else holding me back.

A： Sounds good, just don't forget to invite me to the wedding!

对 话

A： 你猜怎么着？我哥哥和他太太快有孩子了！

B： 太棒了！祝贺你们！我甚至不知道他们已经结婚了。

A： 是的，他们已经交往两年了，一年以前，我哥哥向他女朋友求婚了，去年夏天，他们结婚了。

B： 他们一定特别兴奋！

A： 当然了，我也很兴奋，但是这件事太突然了！我哥哥才 26 岁，我觉得他还是 15 岁左右，真是不可思议，他一下子就长大了。但是，26 岁就建立家庭也有点儿太早了。

B： 在中国，26 岁结婚一点儿也不早，尤其是在农村。就算是在城市里，人们一般在二十五六岁时也就结婚了，然后很快就生孩子。

A： 在美国，人们一般要到快 30 或 30 出头的时候才结婚，在我看来，26 岁实在是太早了，在生孩子之前，我还有那么多事情要做呢。

B： 生不生孩子和你的工作有很大关系。我的意思是，如果你一毕业就有了很稳定的工作，你就可以很快要孩子。但是如果你的职业道路不是那么中规中矩的，或者你得过很长时间才能有份稳定的收入，那你最好等稳定了以后再生孩子。

A： 对，我哥哥现在在医学院读书，他的前途一片光明，如果他毕业以后就当医生，那么供养家庭和孩子都没问题。但是我呢，我还想去世界上很多地方看看，所以每过几年就搬一次家的生活可不适合生孩子。

B： 对，生孩子就意味着牺牲其他一些事情，因为一旦你成了父母，就得尽父母应尽的责任，尽量给他最好的成长环境。

A： 是的，所以我想等到我 30 岁多一点儿的时候再生孩子，这样我可以把我想做的事情先做完，而且那时候我的生活和工作也应该比较稳定了。你呢？

B： 我不知道，我觉得，对我来说，最重要的事情是找到一个合适的人建立家庭，找到一份合适的工作来供养家庭。如果我有了这些，就没有什么困难了。

A： 听起来不错啊！结婚的时候别忘了邀请我参加婚礼！

Background Reading 背景阅读

Get Married！ 结婚吧！

According to the Chinese tradition, marriage is important to perpetuate the family line. In some cities like Beijing and Shanghai, arranged marriage managed by the parents, relatives, or friends is no longer widely accepted because it is regarded as old-fashioned, whereas liberal marriage (so-called love marriage) is more practical because it allows a person the freedom to choose their future spouse without the assistance of a go-between or matchmaker. However, some studies have shown that arranged marriages last far longer than "love marriages" in which the two people choose for themselves.

根据中国的传统，婚姻对延续家庭很重要。在像北京和上海一样的城市，被父母、亲戚和朋友安排的相亲已经不再被大多数人接受了，因为这被认为已经过时了。而自由婚姻（所谓的爱情婚姻）现在更实际，因为它给了一个人选择未来伴侣的自由，这种婚姻并不用中间人和媒人的帮助。然而，一些调查显示，相亲的婚姻比自己选择的以爱情为基础的婚姻持续的时间更长。

Today, a lot of young Chinese have very pragmatic ideas about marriage. Once a person is of a certain age, it is time to get married, plain and simple. Even if the person has not found the love of their life, he or she might find someone they can get along with and make a match. In general there is more pressure on young women to get married right away. Most parents want to see their kids married, as marriage equals happiness in the minds of many Chinese. Not getting married simply is not an acceptable option.

当前，大部分中国年轻人对婚姻抱有非常实际的想法。一旦某个人到了一定的年龄，他就应该结婚，这是很清楚、很简单的。即使这个人没找到生命中的真爱，他或她仍然可能会找到一个可以相处的人，变成一对。一般来说，要求年轻女人马上结婚的压力更大。大部分的父母想看到他们的孩子结婚，因为结婚在中国人心中是一件喜事。不结婚并不是一个容易被接受的选择。

Parents are often much more concerned about their child not finding a marriage partner in time than about what their child may want. Still, nowadays the young man and woman usually make the final decision about marriage between the two of them, though they still seek the advice and approval of their parents and their go-between. Some people feel that romantic love is not the most important ingredient in a successful marriage, but a steady job, a good income, and having an apartment are the major factors determining whether or not someone is a suitable candidate.

对没找到结婚对象的人来说，他们的父母比他们本人还着急。虽然现在的青年男女还是会向父母和中间人来寻求建议和认可，但是最后的决定通常还是由他们自己来做。一些人觉得浪漫的爱情并不是成功婚姻的最重要的组成部分，而稳定的工作、较高的收入、有没有房子则是选择合适伴侣的决定性因素。

The modern system of arranged marriage in China is somewhat similar to blind dating in the West. When a person reaches marriageable age, his or her parents (or relatives and friends) compile a packet of information about them, including a photograph and descriptions of their family background, education, hobbies, accomplishments, and interests. They then inquire among their friends and acquaintances to see if anyone knows a young man or woman who would be a suitable marriage partner. If a possible match is found, information packets will be exchanged, the go-between will arrange a meeting between them, and if all goes well they'll begin dating, with marriage as a possible—but not inevitable—result. It is not uncommon for someone to have 10 or more such introductions before he or she finds the right person to marry.

在中国，现代的相亲有点儿类似于西方的陌生约会。当一个人到了该结婚的年龄，他或她的父母（或者亲戚和朋友）就会把他们的信息整理在一起，包括照片、家庭情况、教育背景、喜好、成就和兴趣等等。然后他们就像周遭的朋友和熟人询问他们认识不认识可以成为合适的结婚对象的年轻男性或女性。如果找到了合适的人，就交换双方的信息，中间人会为他们安排一次见面，如果顺利的话，他们就开始交往，最后的结果可能是结婚，也可能不是。如果一个人在找到合适的人结婚之前相过 10 次或更多次亲，这一点儿也不奇怪。

Exercises 练习

Answer these questions.

1. What do you think is the best age to get married and have a child?
2. What are the advantages and disadvantages of arranged marriage?
3. Could you accept an arranged marriage?

Translate these sentences into English.

1. 我哥哥和他太太快有孩子了。
2. 一年以前，我哥哥向他女朋友求婚了。
3. 去年夏天，他们结婚了。
4. 26 岁就建立家庭有点儿太早了。
5. 在中国城市里，人们一般在二十五六岁时就结婚了，然后很快就生孩子。
6. 在美国，人们一般要到快 30 或 30 出头的时候才结婚。
7. 对我来说，最重要的事情是找到一个合适的人建立家庭，找到一份合适的工作来供养家庭。

Complete the following paragraph with these words or phrases.

based on   in order to   attitudes   practically   traced
soul mate   relationship

The different __1__ toward arranged marriage between young people in China and the US can be __2__ in part to different ideas of why one gets married. In China, people get married __3__ start a family, and the __4__ between husband and wife is seen more __5__ as a partnership. In the US, most people want to find their "__6__", fall deeply in love, and then get married because they want to spend the rest of their life with that person. Americans want to start families, too, but they want that partnership to be __7__ romantic love.

 Answers 答案

Translate these sentences into English.

1. My brother and his wife are having a baby.
2. My brother proposed a year ago.
3. They got married last summer.
4. Twenty-six seems so young to start a family.
5. In Chinese cities people often get married when they're in their mid-20's and have a child soon after.
6. In the US lots of people get married in their late 20's or early 30's.
7. For me the main things are finding the right person to start a family with, and a job that's good enough to support a family.

Complete the following paragraph with these words or phrases.

1. attitudes   2. traced   3. in order to   4. relationship
5. practically   6. soul mate   7. based on

propose
　　　　求婚
get married
　　　　结婚
excited
　　兴奋的；激动的
sudden
　　　　突然
weird
　　不可思议的
grow up
　　　　长大
path
　　道路；小径
sacrifice
　　　　牺牲
to do one's utmost
　　　竭尽全力
invite
　　　　邀请
wedding
　　　　婚礼
perpetuate
　　使…不间断
arrange
　　安排；准备
line
　世世代代；家系
liberal
　　　自由的
assistance
　　帮助；协助
go-between
　　　中间人
matchmaker
　　　　媒人
pragmatic
　　　　务实的
diminish
　　下降；减少
ingredient
　　　组成部分
compile
　　汇编；编辑
inquire
　　　　询问
acquaintance
　　　　熟人

26. Blogging

博 客

Dialogue

A： Hey, I heard you have a blog!

B： Yeah, I started it when I came to China because when I left America there were so many people who said, you have to write to me and tell me all about your year abroad! So this way everyone gets to hear all of the stories—and I only have to tell them once.

A： Sometimes I think I'm the last person on earth who doesn't have a blog!

B： I know; it's so crazy how only a couple years ago no one even knew what a blog was, and now it's such a huge phenomenon all over the world.

A： What kind of stuff do you write about?

B： There isn't any overarching theme, I just post when I have something to say that I think is interesting or funny. So I've posted about what life in Beijing is like, or stories from the times when I've traveled to different places in China, or fun new Chinese words that I've learned, stuff like that.

A： How often do you post?

B： It's totally random. Sometimes I'll post a couple times a week, and then I'll go two months without writing anything. I posted much more often when I first got here, because everything was so new and exciting. Now that I've been in China for almost a year, being here doesn't feel like some crazy adventure, it just feels like my life.

A： I know what you mean. There are still moments when it feels like a crazy adventure, but you no longer have the need to write emails with lengthy descriptions of the glories of Kung Pao Chicken.

B： Totally. My perspective about blogging also changed after my parents came to visit. Before then, I was telling stories to try to give my friends and everyone back home a sense of what I was experiencing. But when my parents got here they were completely surprised by everything, including the things I had written about on my blog and even talked to them about on the phone. It made me realize that some things just can't be shared unless both people have experienced them first-hand.

A： Hmm, that's an interesting point.

B： I mostly stopped posting after that, I guess partly because I had to reevaluate my whole purpose for blogging in the first place, but also just because I was too busy all the time.

A： That seems to be inevitable, doesn't it? Everyone I know who's started a blog posts constantly for a couple months and then it peters out until they stop posting altogether.

B： Guilty as charged!

对 话

A： 嗨, 我听说你有个博客!

B： 是的, 我来中国才开始写博客的, 在我离开美国的时候, 很多人都说, 你一定要写信给我告诉我你在国外的生活。用博客, 每个人都可以知道我的故事, 而我只要写一次就可以了。

A： 有时候, 我觉得我是世界上最后一个没有博客的人!

B： 我知道, 几年以前几乎没有人知道博客是什么, 现在却是如此普遍的一个现象, 全世界到处都是。

A： 你通常都写点儿什么?

B： 没有什么特别的主题, 当我发现有意思或好玩儿的事情我就会写。所以我写了北京的生活是什么样的、在中国不同的地方旅行时的一些故事, 还有我学到的一些中文的新词语, 就是这些内容。

A： 你多长时间写一次?

B： 真的很随意。有时候一周写几次, 也可能两个月什么都不写。我刚来中国的时候常常写, 因为这里的一切都是新鲜的、令我兴奋的。但是现在我在中国已经差不多一年了, 不再感觉像是经历疯狂的冒险, 而只是平淡的生活了。

A： 我明白你的意思。虽然有时候你还会有一些冒险般的感受, 但你已不会为了称赞宫保鸡丁而写一封长长的电子邮件了。

B： 总的来说, 在我父母来过中国以后, 我对博客的看法也有所改变。之前, 我把故事写下来, 想让我的朋友们和家人知道我体验到的东西。但是, 当我的父母真的来到中国时, 他们对所有的事物都很惊奇, 包括那些我曾经在博客里写到过甚至在电话里讲到过的事情。这件事让我意识到有些事除非双方都亲身经历过, 否则根本不可能共同分享。

A： 嗯, 这个观点很有意思。

B： 在那儿之后, 我几乎停止写博客了。我想部分原因是我不得不重新审视一下我写博客的目的, 还有也因为我那时一直都很忙。

A： 那是不可避免的, 不是吗? 我知道有博客的人都是在开始的几个月不断地把文章放在博客上, 然后逐渐减少, 直到完全停止写文章!

B： 真是惭愧!

Background Reading 背景阅读

What Is a Blog? 什么是博客?

The word "blog" is an abbreviation for "web log," and it's an extremely easy way for individuals to publish information. Just like registering for a free email service, writing a message, and sending it, anyone can create, publish and update a web page all their own. Many blogs are like personal online diaries; others provide commentary or news on a particular subject. If an online forum is like a free and open public square, then a blog is a private individual's free and open space of their own. A typical blog combines text, images, and links to other blogs, web pages, and other media related to its topic. The ability for readers to leave comments in an interactive format is an important part of many blogs. "Blog" can also be used as a verb, meaning to maintain or add content to a blog.

"博客"一词是"网络日志"的缩写,是一种十分简易的个人信息发布方式。它让任何人都可以像免费电子邮件的注册、写作和发送一样,完成个人网页的创建、发布和更新。大多数博客很像在线日记;其他的则是关于某一特别主题的新闻或观点。如果把论坛比喻为开放的广场,那么博客就是一个私人的开放房间。一个典型的博客包括正文、图片和与之链接的其它博客和与这一主题相关的网页和媒体等的链接。能让读者在互动版块留下自己的观点对很多博客来说是最重要的。"博客"也可以作为一个动词,意思是对博客进行维护或添加内容。

A Short History of Blogs 博客简史

Blogs as we know them today evolved from online diaries, where people would keep a running account of their personal lives. The term "web log" was coined by Jorn Barger in December 1997, and the short form, "blog," was coined in 1999. Since 2002, blogs have gained increasing importance in breaking news stories and shaping how they're covered. Bloggers have published anthologies of their online writings, and bloggers have also appeared as analysts on radio and television. Merriam-Webster's Dictionary declared "blog" as the 2004 Word of the Year.

今天被我们所熟知的博客是由网络日志发展来的。人们可以持续地在上面记录自己的个人生活。"网络日志"这个词是由约翰·巴杰在 1997 年 12 月创造的,而它的缩略词"博客"是在 1999 年出现的。从 2002 年起,博客在爆料新闻及揭露新闻背景方面变得越来越重要。博客写手们出版了他们的博客文集,还以分析家的身份出现在广播和电视上。韦氏词典称"博客"是 2004 年的年度词语。

Blogs in China 博客在中国

The number of blogs in China hit 34 million in August 2006, 30 times more than that just four years ago when the on-line writing phenomenon began to sweep the country. 75 million Chinese people regularly read blogs, and more than 17 million people in China consider themselves blog writers, offering personal insights and opinions on any topic they choose, according to a report on China's blog market. The report also points out that nearly 70 percent of the blogs, or about 23 million of them, are classified as dormant, as they have remained unchanged for more than a month. The rapid growth of blog sites in China also brought potential business opportunities to the advertising industry. Some blogs written by celebrities attract millions of daily readers. Nearly 40 percent of bloggers said they would accept advertisements on their blogs and over half of blog readers who were interviewed said they would continue to read blogs with advertisements, according to the report. Market observers suggested experts conduct further surveys to probe the commercial value of blogs.

截至 2006 年 8 月,中国的博客用户已经达到 3 400 万,这个数量是 4 年前网络写作刚开始在中国流行时的 30 倍以上。据一份关于中国博客市场的研究报告称:在中国,博客的经常性阅读者达到 7 500 万;有超过 1 700 万人自命为博客写手,他们就任何感兴趣的主题发表个人见解和观点。该报告同时指出,近 70% 的博客(约 2 300 万)因为超过一个月没有更新被归为"休眠博客"。博客门户网站的飞速增长同时给广告产业带来了巨大的商机。一些名人博客每日的点击量超过百万。研究报告称在受访人群中,近 40% 的博客写手愿意在自己的博客中发布广告,超过半数的博客读者表示他们仍将持续阅读带广告的博客。市场预测专家建议相关专业人士进一步调查研究,以开发出博客更多的商业价值。

Exercises 练习

Answer these questions.

1. Do you have a blog? What do you usually write about on your blog?
2. Do you often read other people's blogs? What topics are you interested in?

Translate these sentences into English.

1. 博客对很多人来说是一种生活方式。
2. 一些名人博客每日的点击量超过百万。
3. 博客写手们可以就任何感兴趣的主题发表个人见解和观点。
4. 有的博客写手出版了他们的博客文集。
5. 坚持写博客说起来容易做起来难。
6. 一个好的博客写手应该坚持发表文章，最好有一个明确的更新日程表。
7. 有大量的博客是"休眠博客"，这意味着他们至少有一个月的时间没有更新博客了。

Complete the following paragraph with these words or phrases.

| in public   focus on   stress   battlefield   vent |
| personal interests |

Unlike Western bloggers who often __1__ news and politics, the Chinese bloggers see __2__, complaints and gossip as their priorities. They, under the __3__ of work, study and life in general, have made blogging another platform to __4__ their emotions and express their personal opinions __5__. Blogs have also become the newest __6__ of the war of words and more celebrity blogs have been shut recently.

 Answers 答案

Translate these sentences into English.

1. Blogging is a new lifestyle for many people.
2. Some blogs written by celebrities attract millions of daily readers.
3. Bloggers can offer personal insights and opinions on any topic they choose.
4. Some bloggers have published anthologies of their online writings.
5. Maintaining a fresh blog is easier said than done.
6. A good blogger must be committed to publishing consistently, with a specific blogging schedule.
7. A huge number of blogs are considered dormant, which means they have not been updated in at least one month.

Complete the following paragraph with these words or phrases.

1. focus on 2. personal interests 3. stress 4. vent
5. in public 6. battlefield

词 汇 表

all over	遍及…
stuff	材料；东西
post	贴出；公布
random	随意的
adventure	冒险
lengthy	冗长的
description	描述；叙述
glory	值得夸耀的事
perspective	视角
first-hand	第一手的
reevaluate	重新评定
inevitable	不可避免的
constantly	不断地
peter out	逐渐消失
guilty	有罪的；内疚的
commentary	评论；评价
combine	使结合
link	链接
interactive	互动
format	版块
derived from	派生；引出
anthology	诗文集
insight	洞察力；见识
dormant	休眠的，蛰伏的
probe	探索；查探

`Cyberworld 网络`

27. Telecommuting

远程办公

Dialogue

A: Life in a big city is really troublesome. There are lots of people and heavy traffic; every day I spend more than two hours going to and from work. It would be fine if only I could just work at home.

B: I once worked at home, but later I gave it up and returned to the office.

A: Really? Were you freelance when you worked from home?

B: No, you know I'm an editor, right? An editor's main job is reading drafts and polishing pieces: all you really need to work is a computer. As it happened, telecommuting had just become popular at that time, so the publishing company I worked for decided to jump on the bandwagon. We didn't need to go to work everyday; we could just work from home.

A: That's really great! So then your life got a lot easier all of the sudden, right?

B: Yeah, for the employees, this type of work meant more flexible working hours and reduced the time and money spent on transportation. The company also saved on office space and other costs. At the beginning, we all thought it was a good idea!

A: Seems like a great idea to me!

B: But later, problems gradually began to pop up. First it was technology: telecommuting requires all employees to be technologically proficient with their computers. I don't understand computers very well, so when I first started working from home, I experienced a lot of setbacks because of computer glitches.

A: Yeah, after all, there aren't that many people who are really good with computers.

B: Later on, once all the technological problems had been resolved, new problems came up. It was just that, because I wasn't working within a team anymore, I started to feel more and more let down and lonely. I had lost "face to face" time with my colleagues.

106

Although we used the internet to communicate the same as before, it was still truly different from speaking face to face.

A: You had a feeling of isolation.

B: Yeah, because I didn't have opportunities to interact socially with coworkers. So back then, if neighbors came to borrow things or the postal service came to deliver the newspaper, I would suddenly become really friendly. Then, the person who had come would give me a strange look, like I'd scared them!

A: So it got worse and worse!

B: My coworkers felt the same as I did, so then we all returned to the office.

A: Looks like telecommuting has its benefits and its costs!

对 话

A: 生活在大城市真是麻烦，人多车挤，我每天上下班花在路上的时间就要两个多小时，要是能在家上班就好了。

B: 我曾经有过一段在家工作的经历，但是后来我放弃了，又回到了办公室。

A: 是吗？那时候，你是自由职业者吗？

B: 不，你知道，我是个编辑，编辑的工作主要是阅读稿件、整理作品，只要有电脑就可以工作。正好那时候开始流行远程办公，我们出版社也采用了这种办法，我们就不需要每天去办公室上班了，在家工作就可以了。

A: 真不错！你一下子就轻松了好多吧？

B: 是的，对员工来说，这种工作方式提供了灵活机动的工作时间并节省了花在交通上的时间和费用；对公司来说，节约了办公场地和成本。开始时，我们都觉得这是个好主意！

A: 的确是个好主意！

B: 可是后来，问题就逐渐出现了。首先是技术方面，远程办公要求工作人员精通电脑技术。因为我对电脑技术懂得不太多，所以在远程工作之初，我因为技术故障而受到很多挫折。

A: 是啊，精通电脑技术的人毕竟不多。

B: 后来，技术问题总算解决了，新的问题又来了。那就是，因为我不在一个团队中工作，我越来越感到失落和孤独。我失去了跟同事们"面对面"的时间，虽然我们利用网络同样可以沟通，但那真的和面对面的交谈不一样。

A: 有一种被隔离的感觉。

B: 是的，由于我错过了跟同事的社交机会，那时候，如果邻居来找我借东西或者邮递员来我家送报纸，我会马上变得热情起来，然后对方都用奇怪的眼神看着我，好像被我吓着了！

A: 越来越糟了！

B: 我的同事们也有同感，所以后来我们又都回到办公室了。

A: 看来远程办公有利有弊啊！

Background Reading 背景阅读

Telecommuters 远程办公者

Telecommuters are employees who work from home or from other places besides the office. According to statistics, 16,500,000 American telecommute at least once a month, and 9,300,000 telecommute at least once a week to deal with work-related matters. In the past ten years, the number of people who telecommute has increased along with the development of the internet.

远程办公者是指那些在家办公或者在其它非公司的办公地点工作的雇员。目前据估计在美国有1 650万雇员每月至少有一次、930万雇员每星期至少会有一次机会通过远程办公处理工作上的事情。在过去10年内，随着互联网的发展，远程办公的人数越来越多了。

Telecommuting in America 远程办公在美国

One-quarter of the U. S. work force could be doing their jobs from home if all those able to telecommute chose to do so, and all those people working from home could translate into annual gasoline savings of $3.9 billion, according to the national technology readiness survey. However, many people still elect to work at the office although they have the option of telecommuting, or have jobs conducive to the practice.

根据全美技术条件调查的结果，如果所有具备条件的人都选择远程办公的话，那么美国的劳动大军中将有四分之一会在家工作，而这意味着美国每年将因汽油消耗减少而节省39亿美元的支出。不过，许多人还是选择了去办公室上班，尽管他们拥有远程办公的选择或是做着可以远程办公的工作。

The Benefits 好处

The benefits of telecommuting are obvious: it saves time spent going to and from work, and it also cuts down on transportation costs. It saves gasoline and reduces the pollution that that causes. It can also reduce expensive office costs. Employees who work from home usually have a greater level of enthusiasm for work and a higher level of efficiency. This is largely due to the relaxing atmosphere of the home office. But of course, not everyone is suited for telecommuting. Those who work at home require a stronger sense of self-discipline and a certain ability to overcome problems with office equipment.

远程办公的好处很明显，节省了上下班的时间并减少了交通费用，节约燃油并减轻了由此带来的污染，还可以节省高昂的办公费用。在家办公的员工往往有着更高的工作热情和工作效率，这在很大程度上与家庭办公所提供的宽松工作环境有关。但并不是所有的人都适合远程办公，家庭办公用户需要有更强的自律性和一定的排除办公设备故障的能力。

New Problems 新问题

During the course of its development, telecommuting has encountered a few new problems, for instance: a decline in opportunities for interpersonal interaction, and business secrets possibly being leaked, and finally increased difficulty for management.

远程办公在发展过程中遇到的一些新问题，例如这一模式减少了人际间的交往机会、企业的一些商业秘密有可能外泄、人事管理难度增加等等。

Exercises 练习

Answer these questions.

1. What do you think are the good and bad aspects of telecommuting?
2. Do you think that telecommuting will replace working at office in the future? Why or why not?
3. If your job allowed, would you choose work from home? Why or why not?

Translate these sentences into English.

1. 随着互联网的发展，远程办公的人数越来越多了。
2. 远程办公可以节省上下班时间，还可以节省交通费。
3. 虽然工作允许远程办公，但许多人还是宁愿去办公室上班。
4. 整天待在家里的话，人们就会错过社交的机会。
5. 远程办公要求工作人员精通电脑技术。
6. 网络连接不好时让人感到沮丧。

Complete the following paragraph with these words or phrases.

solving proficient however self-discipline interaction face decline

Working from home seems like the answer to all sorts of problems. __1__ , it also brings with it some new problems that telecommuters must be prepared to __2__ . They must be __3__ in the technology used as well as resourceful about __4__ technological problems. Also, they must have a high level of __5__ . Finally, they must be willing to accept the __6__ in opportunities for __7__ with coworkers: this may be the most difficult part of all.

 Answers 答案

Translate these sentences into English.

1. The number of people who telecommute has increased along with the development of the internet.
2. Telecommuting can reduce time spent going to and from work, and also cut down on transportation costs.
3. Many people would rather work at the office even if their job allowed telecommuting.
4. Being at home all day can cause people to miss social interaction.
5. Telecommuting requires the employees to be technologically proficient with their computers.
6. It can be frustrating when the connection is poor.

Complete the following paragraph with these words or phrases.

1. However 2. face 3. proficient 4. solving
5. self-discipline 6. decline 7. interaction

词 汇 表

troublesome
令人心烦的
freelance
自由职业者
draft
草稿
polish
使完美
jump on the bandwagon
随大流
flexible
灵活的
reduce
减少
pop up
出现
proficient
精通的；熟练的
setback
退步；挫折
glitch
缺点；小差错
came up
出现
let down
失望
isolation
隔离；隔绝
scare
使害怕
annual
每年的
gasoline
汽油
conducive
有助于…的
pollution
污染
enthusiasm
热情；积极性
self-discipline
自律
overcome
战胜；克服
encounter
遇到；遭遇
leak
泄露

28. Google

谷 歌

Dialogue

A: Hey, what's a podcast? I know what a blog is—are they the same thing?

B: I don't know either, but it doesn't really matter. There's a new word almost every day. You just need to google it to find out what it means.

A: Good call! I'll try it out.

B: I use google to search the web almost every day. If I want to go out to eat at a restaurant, I can google it to find out the address and reveiwers' ratings; if I forget the URL of a website, I can just google it; if I hear a new word, I can use google to learn its exact meaning... all in all, if there's anything I don't know or am unclear about, google can help me get it straight.

A: Have you ever googled yourself?

B: Of course. It's interesting to see what kind of personal information ends up on the internet. You should give it a try.

A: Do you use google's other features?

B: Of course! I use google's email, gmail. It has a really big storage capacity and it's really easy to search for emails. There's also a talk feature, so you can chat online. But my favorite is a different google feature; can you guess what it is?

A: It has to be google earth, right? I've used it a couple times too; it's actually pretty fun!

B: Right, I really enjoy exploring and traveling, but you can't possibly make it to every famous landmark in the whole world, so it's fun to look for things on google earth instead. Also, just like you can google your own name, you can use google earth to find your home! I found my neighborhood, even my building.

A: That's so weird! It's like your life depends on google! When did the internet become such an indispensable part of everyone's lives?

B： Yeah, to be exact, it's not just me who can't live without google; everyone has come to depend on it. Google is already much more than just the most popular search engine—it's even become a verb in the English language. Actually, we use it as a verb in Chinese sometimes too.

A： That's true, but I don't know if this is a good thing or a bad thing for the Google Corporation. Some people say that as the name becomes more commonly used, it becomes less of a brand, detracting from its proprietary nature.

B： Who knows? But I think the Google Corporation has a pretty bright future either way.

对 话

A： 嗨，播客是什么意思？我知道博客，他们是一回事吗？

B： 我也不知道，但是没关系，现在差不多每天都出现一些新词语，你 google 一下就知道了。

A： 好办法！我会试一试的。

B： 我差不多每天都会用 google 来搜索。如果我想去一家饭馆吃饭，我可以 google 它的地址以及网友对它的评价；如果我忘了一个网站的网址，我也可以 google 一下；如果我听到一个新词语，我也可以 google 一下它确切的意思……总之，所有我不知道和我不确定的东西，google 都可以告诉我、帮我确定。

A： 你 google 过你自己吗？

B： 当然了。看看自己的个人信息在网上变成了什么样子，这很有意思！你也可以试一下。

A： 你还使用 google 的其它产品吗？

B： 当然了！我用 google 的邮箱，gmail，容量很大，而且找邮件的时候特别方便，还有个 talk 功能，可以在线聊天。但我最喜欢的是 google 的另一个产品，你猜是什么？

A： 一定是 google earth 吧？我也用过一两次，确实很好玩儿！

B： 是的，我特别喜欢旅行和探险，但是你不可能把世界上所有有名的地方都去到，所以用 google earth 看一看，是个好办法！而且，就像你可以 google 到自己的名字一样，用 google earth 还可以找到你的家呢！我就找到了我住的小区，甚至我住的那栋楼都能用 google earth 看到。

A： 太神奇了！好像你的生活离不开 google 了！网络什么时候变成我们生活中不可缺少的一部分了？

B： 是的，准确的说，不是我一个人离不开 google，而是所有人包括他们的生活都离不开 google。google 已经不只是一个搜索引擎的品牌，它已经作为动词进入英语语言了。其实，在中文中，有时候，我们也把它当作一个动词来用了。

A： 的确是这样，但我不知道这对 google 公司来说是好事还是坏事。因为有人说，当一个名字使用得越来越普及，它作为一个品牌的属性就越来越弱。

B： 谁知道呢？但是我相信 google 公司的前途还是一片光明！

Background Reading 背景阅读

Google: A Part of Our Life 谷歌：我们生活的一部分

The word Google is a variant on Googol (meaning 10^{100}), a term coined by the 9-year-old nephew of American mathematician Edward Kasner, who asked him to think of a name for a very large number. One googol represents a one followed by one hundred zeroes. A googol is an extremely large number: there's not enough of anything in the universe to make a googol: not even stars, specks of dust, or atoms.

我们现在常用的"Google"一词是数学用词 Googol（表示 10 的 100 次方）的变异，这个词是由美国数学家爱德华·卡斯纳9岁的外甥米尔顿·西罗塔杜撰出来的，当时爱德华请他想一个词来表示一个极大的数目。1 个 Googol 所代表的数字为 1 后面加上 100 个零。Googol 是一个非常大的数字，宇宙中没有什么物质的数量可以达到 1 个 Googol——无论是星星、尘埃还是原子。

Within a few short years Google has become the top search engine in the world and has earned the most esteemed privilege in contemporary pop culture it has become a verb（"I googled you and found out you were lying to me about your PhD. And you had a prison record!"）. Google has spawned products, concepts, and imitations galore. It is safe to say that Google is not just an Internet search engine, but has become something of a phenomenon.

在短短的几年里，Google 成了世界上最有名的搜索引擎，而且还在当代流行文化中获得了最值得尊敬的殊荣——它变成了一个动词。（我 google 了你的背景，发现你骗我说你有博士学位，另外，你还有过蹲监狱的记录！）Google 也带来了大量的附属产品、概念和丰富的仿制品。可以很确定的说，Google 不仅是一个网络搜索引擎，它已经变成了一种现象。

No one is anonymous anymore. Try a search on your best friend's name in Google, and chances are he/he will be somewhere on the internet, especially if they're under 30. From websites to chat rooms, most Internet users leave a trail easy to pick up.

没有人可以再隐姓匿名下去了。用 Google 搜一下你最好朋友的名字，很有可能你就在网上发现他，尤其是 30 岁以下的人。从网站到聊天室，大部分的互联网用户都留下了很容易让别人找到的痕迹。

Everybody can get information if they learn how to look for it. Irritated that you can only remember half the lyrics of a song? Need a recipe for Kung Pao Chicken? In pre-Internet days, finding the answer would have involved looking through reference books, scanning a newspaper or even making a trip to the library—all with no guarantee of finding the information. Now Google, the Internet search engine, can deliver even the most obscure bits of information to your computer screen within a matter of seconds. Spend a little time on the help pages at google. com to hone your search skills and the vast information warehouse that is the web will soon be at your fingertips.

如果人们愿意学习怎么去找，那么每个人都可以得到信息。为只记得某一首歌一半的歌词而感到不爽？需要做宫保鸡丁的菜谱？在没有互联网的日子里，找到这些答案可能需要花费巨大的精力查阅参考书、浏览报纸或甚至去一趟图书馆——而且还不一定找得到。现在，Google，这个互联网搜索引擎，可以在几秒钟内，把甚至最晦涩的信息送到你的计算机上。花点儿时间研究"google. com"的帮助页面来磨练你的搜索技能，互联网巨大的信息库很快就近在咫尺了。

Exercises 练习

Answer these questions.
1. What search engine do you usually use?
2. How useful do you think the Internet is as a source of information?
3. How do you think Google compares to other search engines?

Translate these sentences into English.
1. 通过搜索引擎，人们可以方便快捷的查询任何信息资料。
2. Google 已经不只是一个流行的搜索引擎了，它已经作为动词进入英语语言了。
3. Google 有很多附属产品，但大多数人还是把它当作搜索引擎来用。
4. Gmail 容量很大，而且找邮件的时候特别方便。
5. Google 不仅是一个网络搜索引擎，它已经变成了一种现象。
6. 有时候，你想在网上准确找到你想要的东西需要花很长时间。
7. 网络让人们的生活变得更容易但同时也让人们的生活更复杂了。

Complete the following paragraph with these words or phrases.

| fear | challenge | convenience | icons | offerings | ubiquitous |

Google has recently begun to __1__ other internet __2__ such as Microsoft, MSN, and Youtube with similar __3__. Some people say that google is becoming too __4__, too all-knowing, and __5__ that Google is turning into "big brother." Others argue that the added __6__ simplifies people's lives and does more good than bad.

 Answers 答案

Translate these sentences into English.
1. With internet search engines, people can quickly and conveniently investigate all kinds of information and material.
2. Google is already much more than just the most popular search engine—it's even become a verb in the English language.
3. Google has a wide variety of features, but most people use it as a search engine.
4. Gmail has a really big storage capacity and it's really easy to search for emails.
5. Google is not just an Internet search engine, but has become something of a phenomenon.
6. Sometimes it can actually take a long time to find exactly what you want online.
7. The internet has made life simpler and more complicated at the same time.

Complete the following paragraph with these words or phrases.
1. challenge 2. icons 3. offerings 4. ubiquitous
5. fear 6. convenience

词 汇 表

rating	评价
ends up	结果变成
feature	部分；特征
storage	贮藏；保管
capacity	容量；能力
explore	探险
landmark	地标
weird	不可思议的
detract from	减损
proprietary	私有的
coin	创造
mathematician	数学家
esteem	尊重；认为
privilege	特殊的荣幸；特权
contemporary	当代的
spawn	大量生产
anonymous	匿名的
chat room	聊天室
trail	痕迹
lyrics	歌词
recipe	菜谱
scan	浏览
guarantee	保证
obscure	晦涩的
warehouse	仓库

29. Infomania

资讯癖

Dialogue

A: I haven't gotten any emails today? That's so weird! I haven't even got spam.

B: It makes you uncomfortable, hmm? I've been there before. Once, I didn't get a single text message from anyone all day. I was continuously looking at my cell phone; I even suspected it might be broken. In the end, I didn't relax until I sent a few text messages to a friend and received a reply.

A: Looks like we've become so accustomed to these "disturbances" that if we aren't disturbed for a whole day, we can't bear it.

B: Actually, this is a kind of disease, called "information anxiety disorder," or "infomania."

A: No way—can it really be possible that sending and receiving emails and text messages too often is a disease?

B: Well it's not like cancer or anything, but because information and communication technologies have become so highly developed, and so many ways of communicating have accumulated, we have developed a strong need to be "in touch." Because of this, if we enter into a situation where we're cut off from information, we won't be able to sit still and might become anxious and jittery.

A: But in recent years people's work and life has become inextricably tied to the internet, cell phones, etc. Are you telling me that everyone has this sickness?

B: Generally speaking, extroverts are more prone to it. Because they like to interact with people, they may get addicted to being in constant contact with others through online chatting or text messaging. This can bring them a sense of security and confidence.

A: But couldn't some introverted people become "infomaniacs" too? I mean, because less outgoing people aren't as comfortable expressing themselves, so in real life they might get nervous interacting with people face to face, but sending and receiving emails and text messages isn't the same. They don't have to immediately reply, so they have enough time to think about it and then answer.

B: That's a really good point. But the drawbacks are that we increasingly depend on the internet, and I think people's actual ability to interact face to face will decrease. Maybe at some point in the future, when people meet face to face they won't say anything; they'll just use their cell phones or computers to communicate.

A: Ooooo, scary! Looks like high technology is really a double-edged sword! After all, not even the best technology can compensate for our personal shortcomings.

对　话

A: 我今天居然没有收到一个邮件？真奇怪！连垃圾邮件都没有。

B: 觉得不舒服，是吧？我也遇到过这种情况，有一次，我一天都没收到任何人的短信，我就总是去看手机，甚至怀疑是我的手机坏了，后来给朋友发了几条短信，收到了回复，才放心。

A: 看来我们已经习惯被别人"打扰"了，一天没人打扰，自己先受不了了。

B: 其实，这是一种病，被称为"信息焦虑综合症"，也叫"资讯癖"。

A: 不可能，难道频繁收发邮件和短信也是病吗？

B: 这并不是癌症或其它的病，但是由于现在的通讯技术太发达了，资讯太丰富了，所以我们对信息的需求也很大，因此，一旦我们进入信息隔绝的状态，就会坐立不安，甚至会产生烦躁。

A: 可是近些年，人们的工作和生活都离不开网络和手机啊，难道每个人都有这种病吗？

B: 一般来说，外向的人更容易这样，他们喜欢与人交往，他们可能会沉溺于跟别人在网上聊天儿或收发手机短信，这会给他们带来安全感和自信。

A: 可是难道内向的人不会也有资讯癖吗？这类人不善于表达，在现实中跟别人进行面对面的交流时可能会有问题；但是收发邮件和短信就不一样了，他们不需要立刻回应，有足够的时间思考，然后再做出回应。

B: 说得对！这种病的害处就是我们会越来越依赖网络，我担心人们的实际交往能力会下降。可能将来有一天，面对面的两个人不是用嘴说话，而是用手机或者电脑才能交流。

A: 好可怕啊！看来高科技真是一把双刃剑啊！但是，甚至最发达的科学技术也不能弥补我们人类的弱点。

Background Reading 背景阅读

Addictive Communications 让人上瘾的交际手段

Discover magazine reports: "A recent study for the company found that British workers' IQ test scores drop temporarily by an average of 10 points when juggling phones, e-mails, and other electronic messages—more of an IQ drop than occurs after smoking marijuana or losing a night's sleep." "This is a very real and widespread phenomenon," said Glenn Wilson of the Institute of Psychiatry at the University of London, who conducted the tests on some 1,100 volunteers. "Just how long it takes to recover is unclear." The study found that modern-day communications have become addictive: Sixty-two percent of adults check work messages after office hours and on vacation. Half of those surveyed reply to an e-mail immediately or within 60 minutes. About 20 percent were "happy" to interrupt a business or social meeting to respond to a telephone or e-mail message. Yet 89 percent of those surveyed found it rude for colleagues to do so.

《发现》杂志报道: "一项最近的调查发现,经常为收发电邮和手机短信分神的人,智商会暂时下降多达 10 分,比抽大麻和一夜没睡觉的人的智商下降得还要多。" "这是一个真实而普遍的现象," 英国伦敦大学精神病学研究所的格伦·威尔逊说。他组织了对 1 100 名志愿者的测试。"用多长时间才能恢复还不清楚。" 这项研究发现,现代的交际手段让人上瘾: 62% 的成人表示即使在家里或放假时都要不时查阅工作短信或邮件;五成人表示会立即回复邮件或在 60 分钟内回复;20% 的人 "很愿意" 打断工作或者会议,即时回复电话或电子邮件;还有 89% 的人认为,如果同事这样做是很不礼貌的。

Symptoms of Infomania 资讯癖症状

If you have five or more of the symptoms listed below, be careful! You might contract "infomania"! 1. Every day you check your email over and over, and even if you only have spam you'll wait a little while and check again. 2. The first thing you do when you turn on your computer is log on to QQ and MSN, sign in to lots of chat rooms, skim all of your messages and send short replies. 3. You can't control the urge to forward text messages; if the receiver doesn't reply you become very unhappy. 4. If you don't receive messages you will feel you were forgotten and become dejected. 5. If no one sends you messages, you will take the initiative and send them to others. 6. You like to forward all kinds of email, with content ranging from jokes to personality tests, and you like to send text messages to groups of people. 7. Even when you're on vacation, you still check your email and text messages as often as before.

如果你有 5 个以上下面谈到的症状,小心哦,你可能患上 "资讯癖" 了! 1. 每天一定要一次又一次地打开邮箱,即便是只看到垃圾邮件也要过一会儿就再看一下。2. 一开电脑就要把 QQ 和 MSN 等即时通讯工具都打开,加入很多聊天群,有任何信息都要浏览一下,回复几句。3. 控制不住想要转发短信,如果对方不回就会很不高兴。4. 收不到信息会觉得自己被遗忘了,很沮丧。5. 如果没人给你发信息,你就会主动发信息给别人。6. 喜欢转发各种邮件,内容从笑话到性格测试,极其喜欢群发短信。7. 即便是放假,也要像平常一样不时地查收邮件和短信。

Exercises 练习

Answer these questions.

1. Do you have infomania?
2. What are the harmful effects of infomania?
3. How can you overcome infomania?

Translate these sentences into English.

1. 大多数人每天的工作都从查收电子邮件开始。
2. 许多人对检查电子邮件和收发手机短信简直上瘾了。
3. 过度收发短信和电子邮件会降低生产效率。
4. 因为痴迷于电子产品而造成的智力衰退相当于一夜失眠。
5. 我每天挂在网上。
6. 我无法想像，如果没有像 MSN 这样的即时通讯工具，生活会是什么样。
7. 我很讨厌收到垃圾邮件。

Complete the following paragraph with these words or phrases.

> addicted suffer warned productivity switch
> claimed found

Workers distracted by email and phone calls __1__ a fall in IQ more than twice that __2__ in marijuana smokers, new research has __3__. The study for computing firm Hewlett Packard __4__ of a rise in "infomania", with people becoming __5__ to email and text messages. The firm said new technology can help __6__, but users must learn to __7__ computers and phones off.

 Answers 答案

Translate these sentences into English.

1. Most people begin their workday by checking their email.
2. Many people are literally addicted to checking email and text messages.
3. Overuse of text messages and e-mails can lower productivity.
4. The IQ drop caused by electronic obsession is equivalent to the drop in IQ after a sleepless night.
5. I use the internet every day.
6. I can't imagine what life would be like without instant messaging systems like MSN.
7. I really hate receiving spam.

Complete the following paragraph with these words or phrases.

1. suffer 2. found 3. claimed 4. warned
5. addicted 6. productivity 7. switch

词 汇 表

spam	垃圾邮件
continuously	不断地
suspect	怀疑
disturbance	打扰
bear	忍受
accumulate	积累；积聚
cut off from	与…隔绝
jittery	焦虑；紧张
prone to	易于…的
express	表达
drawback	弊端；障碍
double-edged sword	双刃剑
shortcoming	缺点；短处
electronic	电子的
marijuana	大麻
institute	研究所
psychiatry	精神病学
conduct	领导；指挥
addictive	上瘾的
interrupt	打断
symptom	症状
over and over	一遍又一遍
forward	转发
dejected	垂头丧气的
switch off	避而不听

30. Apartment Hunting Online

网上找房

Dialogue

A: Ugh, I'm so stressed out! I've spent all week looking for a place to live this coming semester.

B: But don't you go to school in Boston? How do you find an apartment there while you're here at home?

A: There's this website that has tons of ads for apartments or rooms for rent—people post ads if they're moving, or subletting, or just looking for a roommate. So I've been looking at the different ads and making lots of phone calls and sending lots of emails.

B: That's so much easier than it used to be, though. Just a few years ago if someone was trying to rent their apartment they could only put an ad in the newspaper, which made it practically impossible to look for an apartment if you weren't already in that city.

A: That's true, it could be much worse.

B: So are you going to Boston to check a few places out before you choose?

A: Yeah, I'm going to drive out next week and stay with my aunt for a day or two while I look at apartments. I'm trying to cram as many appointments as possible into a short amount of time, because if I don't find a place I don't know what I'm going to do.

B: Well that's good that you're going to go check them out in person. You can't really tell if you'll like a place until you see it.

A: I did it once before, though. Three years ago I got a job in Washington, D. C. for the summer, but it was too far away to make a whole trip just to look at apartments, so I just had to do the whole thing online. Some people sent me pictures of the places they were renting, but in the end I had to just take a chance.

118

B： Man, that's crazy! Did it work out?

A： Actually I was really lucky. The apartment I ended up renting was really nice, even though it was kind of small. It was in a great location too.

B： Wow, you did get lucky!

A： Yeah, but I'm glad I don't have to do it that way again. This whole process is stressful enough as it is.

B： I'm sure you'll find something, and if it's not perfect it's just for one semester, right?

A： Right. But I could stay next year too if I really like the place.

B： Sounds like a plan. Good luck!

对 话

A： 啊，我烦死了！我已经用了一整个星期来为下个学期找一个住处。

B： 但你不是在波士顿上学吗？你在家里，怎么能在那儿找房子呢？

A： 这个网站上有很多出租公寓和房间的广告——如果人们搬家、转租，或者找同屋，他们就会登广告。所以我一直在看这些不同的广告，打了很多电话，发了很多邮件。

B： 这比过去容易多了。几年以前，如果有人想出租他们的公寓，只能在报纸上登广告，所以如果你不在那个城市里，想找房子几乎是不可能的。

A： 是的，麻烦得多。

B： 所以在你确定之前，你会去波士顿调查几处地方吗？

A： 是的，下个星期我就会开车去我姑妈家，在那儿待两天，顺便找房子。我争取在最短的时间里尽可能多看几处房子，因为如果我找不到地方，我就不知道我应该去哪儿了。

B： 嗯，你能亲自去看看，这样很好。只有亲眼看见了，你才能知道自己到底喜欢不喜欢那个地方。

A： 我以前也这样做过一次。三年前的夏天，我得到了一个在华盛顿的工作，但是如果只是为了看房子而去一趟华盛顿太远了，所以我就在网上完成了一切。一些人给我发了他们要出租的房子的照片，最后我不得不冒险碰碰运气。

B： 你疯了！有用吗？

A： 其实我很幸运。我最后租的房子虽然有点儿小，但是很不错，而且位置非常好。

B： 哇，你真幸运！

A： 是的，我很高兴我不用再那样做了。这整个过程太麻烦了。

B： 我确定你会找到的，如果不太好的话，也只住一个学期，对吗？

A： 对。但是如果我喜欢，明年我也会住在那儿。

B： 很好的计划。祝你好运！

Craigslist. org

Of all the websites providing classifieds—for housing or anything else—by far the most popular is craigslist. org. Founded in 1995 as a social network for the San Francisco bay area, Craigslist now has webpages for more than 450 cities in 50 countries around the world. The website gets more than 5 billion page views each month, making it in the top 50 sites worldwide, and in the top 10 US websites. The ads on Craigslist are for much more than housing, though: Craigslist is also one of the biggest websites in the world for job listings, with ads from both employers and people seeking employment. The other main sections of the site include "for sale" ads, community announcements, services, personal ads and discussion forums. Craigslist founder Craig Newmark says that the most important reason Craigslist is successful is that it creates a kind of community online where people can have a voice.

在所有为住房或其它东西提供分类广告的网站中，到目前为止，craigslist. org 是最流行的。它是一个于1995年创立于旧金山的海湾地区的社会网络，可是现在 Craigslist 的网页涵盖了50多个国家的450多个城市。这个网站每个月就新增50亿个网页，这使它成为世界上前50名、美国前10名的网站。Craigslist 上面的广告不只是住房广告：它也是世界上最大的工作信息网站，来自雇主和想找工作的个人的广告都有。这个网站的另一个主要的部分包括"卖东西"的广告、社区通知、服务、个人广告和论坛。Craigslist 的创办者克雷格·纽马克说，Craigslist 成功的最重要的原因就是它创造了网上社区，在那儿人们可以畅所欲言。

How to Hunt an Apartment Online? 怎样在网上找房子？

Doing your apartment hunting online? Nothing can compare to actually seeing an apartment, but if you're trying to find a place long-distance, there are some things you can do to be more prepared. First, it's important to think about what you want ahead of time. Do you want to live with roommates? What locations are convenient to your school or job? After you've scanned the ads and found some that look promising, you should get in touch with the person renting each apartment and ask lots of questions. How much do the utilities cost? Are there internet and TV connections installed already? Does the building have an elevator? Is there parking or a safe place to store your bike? Finally, ask if they can email you some digital pictures, or if you have a friend who lives in that city, ask them to go over and take a look in person.

想在网上找房子吗？没有什么可以和实地去看房子相比，但是如果你决定尝试一下，你可以做一些事情，这会使你更有准备。首先，事先考虑好你要什么样的房子很重要。你想和别人一起住吗？什么地方对你上学或工作更方便？当你浏览了广告找到了一些算是符合要求的，你就应该联系出租人，问很多问题。水、电、煤气等公用设备多少钱？网络和电视都已经安装好了吗？楼里有电梯吗？有车位吗？放自行车的地方安全不安全？最后，问他们可不可以发给你一些数码照片，或者，如果你有朋友住在那个城市，让他亲自去看看。

Live with Roommates 合租

Most people in their twenties choose to live with one or more roommates, usually because they can't afford to live alone, and because living with roommates is more fun. Finding the right roommates is at least as important than finding the right apartment, and it's still possible even if you're doing your apartment hunting online. In addition to asking questions to help you find out about your potential roomate's personality, you should ask specific questions to let you know what kind of roommate they'll be. Are they clean or messy? Do they like to play music and watch TV, or do they prefer quiet? Do they go to bed early or late? Do they have any pets? Do they cook often? These things can help you find out if you will get along with your new roommates.

很多人20多岁的时候都选择和一个或几个同屋一起住，这通常是因为他们负担不起一个人住的费用，还因为和同屋一起住更有意思。找到合适的同屋至少像找到合适的房子一样重要，在网上找同屋也是可能的。除了问一些问题以弄清楚可能成为你同屋的这个人的性格，你还应该问一些具体的问题以确定他会成为什么样的同屋。他们干净还是邋遢？他们喜欢听音乐、看电视，还是喜欢安静？他们习惯早睡还是晚睡？他们有宠物吗？他们常常做饭吗？这些可以帮助你确定自己是否能跟他们合得来。

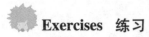 **Exercises** 练习

Answer these questions.

1. How does the internet make it easier to find an apartment from out of town?
2. What are some important questions to ask when you're looking for an apartment?
3. What are some important questions to ask potential roommates?

Translate these sentences into English.

1. 我烦死了！
2. 过去，想要在另一个城市里找房子几乎是不可能的。
3. 我要争取在最短的时间里尽可能多看几处房子。
4. 最后我不得不冒一次险。
5. 找到一个位置方便的房子很重要。
6. 和同屋一起住可以更便宜，还更有意思。
7. 找到合适的同屋至少像找到合适的房子一样重要。

Complete the following paragraph with these words or phrases.

| provide critical ads revenue futile earn |

Some people are ___1__ of sites like Craigslist because they are making life difficult for local newspapers that used to ___2__ most of their profit from paid classified ___3__. However, it seems ___4__ to criticize sites like Craigslist, because they ___5__ a service people need. Local newspapers will just have to find a new source of ___6__.

 Answers 答案

Translate these sentences into English.

1. I'm so stressed out!
2. It used to be practically impossible to look for an apartment in another city.
3. I'm trying to cram as many appointments as possible into a short amount of time.
4. In the end I just had to take a chance.
5. It's important to find an apartment in a convenient location.
6. Living with roommates can be cheaper, and more fun.
7. Finding the right roommates is at least as important than finding the right apartment.

Complete the following paragraph with these words or phrases.

1. critical 2. earn 3. ads 4. futile 5. provide 6. revenue

词 汇 表

apartment
公寓；房子
rent
出租；租
post
发布
move
搬家
sublet
转租
cram
短时间内拼命做…
in person
亲自
take a chance
碰运气
location
地点
classified
分类的
housing
住房
bay
海湾
worldwide
世界范围的
in print
在印刷物上
forum
论坛
convenient
方便的
scan
细看；搜索；浏览
install
安装
elevator
电梯
go over
查看；仔细检查
find out
找出；查明
messy
邋遢的；凌乱的
pet
宠物
get along with
相处

121

31. The White Collar Workers' Health Crisis

白领们的健康危机

Dialogue

A: You look tired today—you have really dark circles under your eyes. Did you not sleep well last night?

B: Yeah, I've been working till two in the morning the past three days, going home to nap a little, and coming back to work again, so I'm really tired.

A: Is your work really that busy?

B: Yeah, it's extremely busy. Our group just got a project that was very important for the company, so we've been spending the last few days looking for the best proposal.

A: It doesn't matter how busy you are, you should take care of yourself!

B: I want to rest too, but I just don't have time! I'm often so busy I don't even have time to eat, and most mornings I want to sleep a little more so I don't have time to eat breakfast. I just have fast food a lot for lunch to save time: everyone has a hamburger while we're in a meeting. But because we're working overtime, dinner is usually a little bit better, and we usually have a lot of meat dishes.

A: Oh my God! I think your diet is way too unhealthy! It's the exact opposite of what nutritionists advocate. Breakfast is the most important meal of the day, but you don't actually eat breakfast; lunch plays a large role too, because at most companies the time spent at work is longer after lunch during the afternoon than from morning till noon, so you should eat a nutritious lunch. For dinner you should eat a somewhat smaller meal, because people exercise very little in the evenings and don't need as much energy.

B: I would love to lead a healthy lifestyle, but right now I have to throw myself into work or I'll never get a promotion!

A: What about exercise? I assume you don't have time for that anymore either.

B：Oh! I know exercise is very important for your health, so I got a year-long membership to a gym near my house, but I'm really embarrassed to say, half a year has already passed and I've only gone twice.

A：Do you ever have time to relax?

B：Not very often, but every time we successfully complete a project, we all go out together to a bar and celebrate. We drink, chat, dance, and have fun until really late or very early the next morning. Then we go home and sleep the whole next day. That sure is relaxing!

A：Going out to the bar and drinking is a way to relax, but it's not good for your health at all. The air at most bars is really smoky and it doesn't circulate enough, so it's easy to come down with a respiratory infection. Also, bars are usually really noisy, which is terrible for your ears. Oh, workaholics like you make me so worried for your health!

对 话

A：今天你看起来很累，黑眼圈很严重，昨晚睡得不好吗？

B：是啊，我连续三天晚上都在公司加班到凌晨两点，回家小睡一下，就又来上班了，所以很累。

A：你的工作真有那么忙吗？

B：是的，特别忙。我们组刚接了一个对公司来说很重要的项目，这几天都在寻找最佳解决方案。

A：无论你怎么忙，你都应该注意身体！

B：我也想休息好，但是根本没时间啊！我现在常常忙得连吃饭的时间都没有，早上常常为了多睡一会儿就不吃早饭；午饭的时候常常吃快餐，为了节省时间，大家一边吃汉堡一边开会；因为晚上要加班，所以晚饭吃得稍微好一点儿，常常吃很多肉菜。

A：天啊！我觉得你的饮食方式太不健康了！和营养学家提倡的恰好相反。早餐是一日三餐中最重要的，可是你却不吃早餐；午餐的作用也很大，因为一般的公司下午的工作时间比上午要长，所以你应该尽量吃有营养的午餐，为下午的工作打基础；晚餐应该尽量少吃，因为晚上人们很少活动，需要的能量也少。

B：我也想吃得健康，可是现在我必须得全力工作，要不然永远都不能升职。

A：那你运动吗？我觉得你也没有时间运动。

B：哎！我知道运动对身体很重要，所以我办了一张我家附近的健身房的年卡，可是很惭愧啊，现在半年过去了，我只去过两次。

A：那你有时间放松吗？

B：不常常，但是每当项目成功完成的时候，我们都会一起去酒吧庆祝。我们在那儿喝酒、聊天儿、跳舞，玩儿到深夜或凌晨才回家，第二天睡一整天，好放松啊！

A：去酒吧喝酒，这的确是一种放松方式，但是对你的身体却没有任何好作用。酒吧里烟雾很重，空气不够流通，容易引发呼吸系统的疾病；还有，酒吧里太吵，对你的耳朵也很不好。哎！我真为你们这些工作狂的健康担心啊！

Breakfast: the Most Important Meal 早餐：最重要的一餐

Fasting overnight lowers the body's level of glucose, which is needed to produce the brain chemicals that keep us focused throughout the day. Breakfast brings those blood sugar levels back up to normal, and helps our bodies wake up so we don't feel sluggish. Those who eat breakfast report feeling more alert, less depressed, less irritable and less restless during the day. They are more productive at work in the morning, too.

一晚上的空腹使人体内的葡萄糖含量下降，葡萄糖是产生脑部化学物质使我们整天精力集中的必需物质。早餐使我们的血糖恢复正常，帮助我们的身体苏醒过来，不感到倦怠。那些吃早餐的人都说在白天他们感觉反应更加敏锐，较少沮丧、急躁和不安，上午的工作效率也更高。

Exercise Programme 健身计划

Recent research has revealed that the secret of sticking to an exercise programme is to select one that reflects the sort of person you are. If you are outgoing and like being with people, chances are you get bored quickly when exercising alone. Try aerobics. You need interaction, so working out with others motivates you to keep going. If you are well-organized and appreciate time to yourself, you might prefer to control your own exercise regime. Try jogging or working out at a gym. Set challenges that encourage you. If you push yourself to do well at work, you'll probably like competing against others. Try team sports. Matches will give your workouts a goal to work toward. If things are getting on top of you, choose an exercise routine that releases tension in the body. Try a yoga class. Stretching your muscles is a great way to relieve stored-up physical and emotional tension. Yoga's combination of stretching and strengthening is a great way to stay healthy, and it can also reduce the risk of injury during physical activity.

研究发现，一个人能否坚持其健身计划取决于它是否适合他的性格。如果你性格外向，喜欢与人交往，那么独自运动可能会使你很快感到乏味。试一试有氧健身法。你需要与他人互动，所以与他人一同运动会激励你坚持下去。如果你办事有条不紊，并愿意自己支配时间，你会喜欢能够自我调控的健身方式。那么，你可以尝试慢跑或在健身房进行健身。并设定有挑战性的目标来激励自己。如果你对工作很投入的话，你很可能会喜欢与人竞赛。试一试团体运动。球类比赛会使你的锻炼有目标性。如果你感到紧张、沮丧，不妨选择一项可以缓解体内压力的锻炼计划。试试参加一个瑜伽训练班。瑜伽的伸展和力量动作是缓解身心压力的非常好的办法，还可以减少因锻炼而受伤的危险性。

Enough Sleep 充足的睡眠

Experts say adults need at least 7 to 8 hours of sleep a night to function properly. When you get less sleep than that on two or more consecutive nights, you begin to accrue "sleep debt." As sleep debt increases functionality decreases and your body experiences a stress response and begins to release adrenaline. Now a vicious cycle has been created: you experience the feeling of being more and more tired, but your body is increasingly stimulated. "Power sleeping" for more hours on weekends is only a temporary solution. There is no substitute for getting a good night's sleep on a regular basis.

专家们说，要使身体机能运转正常，成人每晚至少需要 7 到 8 个小时的睡眠。如果你连续两晚或更多个晚上睡眠都少于这个时间，你就要开始负上"睡眠债"了。当睡眠债越积越多（同时身体机能减退），你的身体将做出压力反应，开始释放肾上腺素。这样就形成了一个恶性循环：你感觉越来越累，但你的身体受到的刺激越来越强。周末猛补几个小时的觉只是权宜之计。有规律地每晚睡一个好觉，这是不可替代的。

Exercises 练习

Answer these questions.

1. Why is it better to eat a small dinner?
2. What are some small ways to make your eating habits more healthy?
3. On average, how much sleep should a person get every night?

Translate these sentences into English.

1. 那些吃早餐的人都说他们在白天的工作效率更高。
2. 我昨晚睡得不好，所以今天有黑眼圈。
3. 你的饮食方式和营养学家提倡的恰好相反。
4. 每当项目成功完成的时候，我们都会一起去酒吧庆祝。
5. 伸展肌肉是一种缓解身心压力的非常好的办法。
6. 要使身体机能运转正常，成人每晚至少需要 7 到 8 个小时的睡眠。
7. 有规律地每晚睡一个好觉，这是不可替代的。

Complete the following paragraph with these words or phrases.

physically   applies   adequate   fall asleep   fatigued   unwind

Why is it so difficult to __1__ when you are overtired? There is no one answer that __2__ to every individual. It's possible to feel "tired" __3__ and still be unable to fall asleep, because while your body may be __4__, your mind is still racing. To fall asleep, you need __5__ time to __6__, even if you feel exhausted. It's not as easy as simply "turning off."

 Answers 答案

Translate these sentences into English.

1. Those who eat breakfast report they are more productive at work during the day.
2. I didn't sleep well last night, so I've got dark circles under my eyes.
3. Your diet is the exact opposite of what nutritionists advocate.
4. Every time we successfully complete a project, we all go out together to a bar and celebrate.
5. Stretching your muscles is a great way to relieve stored-up physical and emotional tension.
6. Adults need at least 7 to 8 hours of sleep a night to function properly.
7. There is no substitute for getting a good night's sleep on a regular basis.

Complete the following paragraph with these words or phrases.

1. fall asleep   2. applies   3. physically   4. fatigued
5. adequate   6. unwind

词 汇 表

nap
小睡；午觉
proposal
计划；提议
nutritionist
营养学家
embarrass
让人不好意思
circulate
循环；流通
come down with
感染上
respiratory
与呼吸有关的
infection
传染病
workaholic
工作狂
sluggish
懒怠的；呆滞的
alert
敏锐的
depressed
沮丧的
irritable
易怒的；急躁的
aerobics
有氧健身法
jog
慢跑
workout
锻炼；训练
get on top of
超出；过多
stretch
伸展
tension
紧张
function
机能；功能
consecutive
连续的
accrue
获得；积累
vicious cycle
恶性循环
stimulate
刺激

125

32. Public Recreation
大众健身

Dialogue

A: Hey! Where were you all morning?

B: I was in the park—I love going there in the morning to watch all the people dancing and practicing martial arts and everything. You never see anything like that in America. It's so amazing, this huge park is just filled with people who come together to do so many different kinds of things. There were even two different groups singing songs, one of them must have had over a hundred people!

A: Yeah, that's something that I never expected before I came to China, but it will be one of the things that I remember the most. People really use public spaces here; in the US, on the other hand, it seems like no one ever leaves their house.

B: I completely agree: when you're a kid you go to the public playgrounds, but for adults in the US leisure time is usually spent privately. And even when it's not, it tends to be more formally organized, and it's usually not free. People might take a dance or a yoga class, but they don't just congregate in public parks and have self-organized dance parties.

A: That's what I love the most: the dancing. There's something so great about the idea of coming to a park and dancing for a couple hours each night. I don't think Americans as a whole dance often enough. Maybe we'd all be happier if we just danced a little more.

B: That's an interesting theory! I think it's really true for elderly people though. It seems like so many old people in the US have such boring lives, they don't go out very much or spend much time with friends, but here senior citizens are always out and about, in the park dancing or playing cards or *majiang*, or just chatting. It just seems so much less lonely.

A: Elderly people in China are in much better shape than in the US, too. So many people, even in their 80's or 90's, go to the park every day and do exercises, or dance, or use the public exercise equipment. Staying flexible and getting even a little bit of regular

126

exercise is so important when you get older—otherwise it's really easy to get injured, and it can be incredibly hard to recover.

B: And it's free, too—the exercise equipment is there in the parks for anyone to use. In the US you'd have to pay a lot of money for a membership to a gym, and if you can't afford it there's no other option.

A: Some of the reasons that people spend more time in public parks are cultural, too. Take *taiji*, for example: lots of the people who go to parks go to practice *taiji*, which is a part of traditional Chinese culture.

B: Yeah, but Chinese culture is changing so fast, with economic development and more Western influence I hope this is one aspect that doesn't change!

对 话

A: 嗨！一整个早上你都在哪儿？

B: 在公园里，我喜欢早上去公园看人们跳舞和练武术等等。在美国，你从来也看不到这样的情景。太了不起了，那么大的公园，人满满的，他们一起做各种各样的活动。还有两组人在唱歌，其中一组有一百多人呢！

A: 是的，来中国以前，我从来也没想到过会有这样的情形，但是这是给我印象最深的事情之一。人们真的在利用公共空间，而在美国，好像没有人愿意离开自己的房子。

B: 我完全同意：美国的孩子会去公共的体育场玩儿，但是美国成年人的空闲时间通常都是自己做自己的事情，即使不是这样，也会组织得更正式，而且不是免费的。人们可能会去上舞蹈或瑜伽课，但是他们不在公园里聚集，也不会自发的组织舞会。

A: 我最喜欢的就是跳舞。每天晚上来公园跳几个小时的舞，这个想法太好了。我觉得美国人整体跳舞不够。如果我们多跳一点儿，可能我们会生活得更幸福。

B: 很有意思的说法！我觉得对老人来说很有用。好像美国老人的生活很无聊，他们不常常外出，也不见朋友；这儿的老人总是外出，在公园里跳舞或者玩儿扑克和打麻将，或者聊天儿。看起来不那么寂寞。

A: 中国老人的体形也比美国老人好。有很多老人，甚至八九十岁了，还每天去公园做运动，或跳舞，或用公共器械锻炼身体。人老的时候，保持灵活和做一些有规律的锻炼十分重要，要不然就很容易受伤，而且很难恢复。

B: 而且这是免费的，公园里的运动器械谁都可以用。在美国，你得付很多钱成为一个健身房的会员，如果你付不起，就没有别的选择。

A: 人们愿意去公园玩儿也有一些文化方面的原因。打太极拳，比如说，很多人去公园打太极拳，这是中国传统文化的一部分。

B: 是的，但是随着经济的发展和西方的影响，中国文化的变化非常快，我希望这个方面永远不会改变。

Background Reading 背景阅读

A Culture of Public Activity 公共活动文化

A culture in which people extensively utilize parks and public spaces has benefits for all members of society, but especially the elderly. Many of the activities that people participate in, such as dance and martial arts, are fun ways to exercise, which has extremely important benefits. Exercise decreases the risk of heart attacks, lowers blood pressure and cholesterol, enhances the immune system, decreases stress, and produces brain chemicals that improve mood and alertness. Exercise also improves strength and flexibility, which decreases the risk of broken bones and other injuries that are extremely hard to recover from at an advanced age.

人们广泛利用公园和公共空间，这种文化对所有的社会成员都有好处，尤其是对老人。人们参加的许多活动，比如舞蹈和武术，都是很有意思的锻炼方式，也有非常重要的好处。锻炼身体能降低心脏病发作的危险，降血压和降低胆固醇，增强免疫系统，降低压力，使大脑产生改善心情和知觉的化学物质。锻炼身体还能使人更有力量和灵活性，这可以降低老年人骨折或受到其它难以恢复的创伤的危险。

There are also many activities that take place in parks that aren't related to exercise, such as playing cards or majiang, practicing water calligraphy, singing or simply engaging others in conversation. These activities are important for their social aspect, which is especially valuable to older people who may have lost their spouse or some of their friends. In the US, 30% of people over 65 are widowed, which contributes to high rates of loneliness and depression among the elderly. Participating in public activities as often as the elderly do in China might help solve this problem. Even for those who are still married, doing things like going dancing together a couple nights a week can be a wonderful way to reignite the spark of romance after decades of being together.

公园里还有很多活动和锻炼身体没有关系，比如说打扑克或麻将，练书法、唱歌或只是聊天儿。对那些可能已经失去配偶或一些朋友的老人来说，这些活动是他们社交生活中很重要的一个方面。在美国，65岁以上的老人有30%都是丧偶的，这使感到孤独和沮丧的老年人的比例更高。就像中国老人一样，尽可能多的参加公共活动对解决这个问题很有帮助。即使是那些还有配偶的老人，一个星期一起出去跳几次舞也有可能在一起生活了几十年后再擦出浪漫的火花。

If the US wants to encourage a culture of public activity like there is in China, it is important to take note of the factors that have contributed to this phenomenon. First, the government can play a role. Public exercise equipment in parks is a valuable resource for people who can't afford to join a gym, especially seniors, many of whom have very limited sources of income. It is also important to have lots of smaller parks in different neighborhoods, because having a park close to home will encourage busy people or elderly people with limited mobility to get out and participate.

如果美国想提倡一种向中国一样的公共活动文化，把对这种现象有益的因素都记下来是很重要的。首先，政府可以起作用。对没有钱去健身房的人，尤其是收入有限的老人来说，公园里公共的健身设备是很有价值的资源。在不同的社区里建一些小公园也很重要，因为如果家附近有一个公园，这就会鼓励工作忙的人或行动能力有限的老人多出去参加活动。

Cultural differences between China and the US are inextricably related to the different ways in which people use public space in the two countries. Individualism and privacy are pillars of American culture, while in China group activities are often valued more highly than individual activities. In addition, in China the distinction between public and private activities and spaces isn't nearly as important to people as it is in the US. Finally, there is a history of government-organized public exercise and cultural activities in China, but not in the US. All of these factors contribute to the differing patterns of participation in public activities.

中美之间的文化差异和两国人民对公共空间的利用方式的不同是分不开的。个人主义和隐私是美国文化的柱石，但是在中国集体活动比个人活动更值得提倡。更进一步说，在中国，个人空间和公共空间的区别并没有像在美国那么重要。还有，在中国，由政府组织公共活动有很长的历史了，但是在美国没有。这些因素都是两个国家公共活动参与方式不同的原因。

Exercises 练习

Answer these questions.

1. In your opinion, what are the advantages of going to a park to exercise?
2. Do you prefer to exercise alone or with others? Why?
3. What is the one thing you most want to do when you're old?

Translate these sentences into English.

1. 很多中国人，尤其是老年人，喜欢早上去公园锻炼身体。
2. 美国成年人的空闲时间通常都是自己做自己的事情。
3. 中国老人看起来不那么寂寞。
4. 个人主义和隐私是美国文化的柱石。
5. 老年人想长寿的话，呼吸新鲜空气和进行体育锻炼相当有好处。
6. 晨练可以预防严重的疾病和受伤，从而延长寿命。
7. 现在中国人开始注意生活方式和习惯，并注重日常锻炼。

Complete the following paragraph with these words or phrases.

facilities classes public communities games nucleus alone

The social lives and activities of senior citizens in the US may not be as __1__ as those of elderly people in China, but that doesn't mean they're all sitting at home __2__. Many seniors live in retirement __3__ that offer a wide range of activities, from __4__ like bridge and bingo, to __5__ in painting or tap dance, to athletic __6__ and organized sports. Most towns and cities also have retirement centers that serve as a __7__ of the senior social scene.

 Answers 答案

Translate these sentences into English.

1. Many Chinese people, especially the elderly, enjoy going to the park in the morning to exercise.
2. American adults usually spend their leisure time privately.
3. It seems that Chinese elderly people are much less lonely.
4. Individualism and privacy are pillars of American culture.
5. For seniors who want to ensure a long life, fresh air and exercise can be very beneficial.
6. Morning exercise can prolong life by helping to prevent severe diseases and injuries.
7. Nowadays, Chinese people are beginning to pay more attention to their lifestyles and habits, and to attach great importance to regular exercise.

Complete the following paragraph with these words or phrases.

1. public   2. alone   3. communities   4. games
5. classes   6. facilities   7. nucleus

词 汇 表

martial arts	武术
amazing	令人惊奇的
congregate	集合；聚集
self-organized	自发组织的
a couple	几个；一些
theory	理论；学说
elderly	上了年纪的
boring	无聊的
equipment	设备
get injured	受伤
membership	会员资格
gym	健身房
extensively	广泛地
utilize	利用
decrease	降低
heart attack	心脏病发作
blood pressure	血压
cholesterol	胆固醇
enhance	提高；加强
immune system	免疫系统
mood	心情
strength	力量；力气
widowed	丧偶的
neighborhood	附近一带
pillar	柱石

33. Dealing with Stress
解 压

Dialogue

A: Do you think I'm an extrovert?

B: You? Totally, one hundred percent. Why do you ask?

A: Well I was out with some friends last Friday and one of them told me I should stop being so shy. I've never thought of myself as shy, but I guess I haven't left my comfort zone much lately and gone out to meet new people. I mostly hang out with people I already know and are comfortable with.

B: I don't think of myself as an introvert either, but I don't like to be around people all the time. I don't think wanting some time alone every once in a while makes you an introvert.

A: Right, everyone needs their personal space sometimes. If you're around people all the time, you can feel overwhelmed. I guess I've just been under a lot of stress lately, with this new job and everything. I always worry about making a good impression when I meet people for the first time, and it seems like I meet new people all the time at the office. I feel like after I've punched the clock, I'm on my own time, and I just want to be comfortable.

B: Nothing to be ashamed of. And there's nothing wrong with being an introvert either. I think some people just naturally prefer spending time with a few close friends to going out to parties and meeting new people every weekend. Sometimes I'd rather be at home reading a good book than out on the town.

A: Well, I know, I'm just worried about giving people the impression that I'm standoffish, cold, aloof, or just stuck up. I don't want people I haven't met yet to think I look down on them. It's just that sometimes I feel so drained, I don't have the energy to interact with strangers.

B: I completely understand, and I think they will too. You should take it easy, this new job sounds really stressful. Just don't work too hard, and you'll be back to your old self in no time.

A: Thanks! Sorry to unload on you, I know you must be busy too, didn't you just switch jobs?

B: Yeah, I did, and it's definitely been a change for the better. My new boss is sooooo much better than my old one, and my coworkers are friendlier too. The work is something I enjoy, and there aren't as many demands and deadlines. I feel like I won the lottery!

A: Well that's great! I'm so happy for you!

B: Thanks! I hope things will start to look up for you too!

对 话

A: 你觉得我是个外向的人吗?

B: 你? 百分之百是个外向的人。为什么问这个?

A: 上周五,我和一些朋友出去玩儿,其中一个人告诉我,我不应该那么害羞。我从来没觉得自己害羞,我觉得最近我总是表现得不自然,也没出去结识新朋友。我总是和那些我已经认识的人一起玩儿,和他们在一起很舒服。

B: 我也不认为自己是个内向的人,但是我不喜欢总是在人群中活动。我不认为偶尔喜欢独处的人就是内向的人。

A: 是的,有时候每个人都需要有自己的空间。如果你总是在人群中,你会受不了的。我觉得最近我正承受着很大的压力,因为新的工作和每件事情。我总是想在第一次见面时给对方留下好印象,但是好像我一直在办公室里认识新人。我很想下班以后,过自己的时间,我只想过得舒服一点儿。

B: 没有什么可不好意思的。不管怎么说,内向的人没有任何问题。我觉得一些人只是很自然地更喜欢每个周末和一些亲密的朋友在一起,而不是出去参加晚会并结识新朋友。有时候,比起出去玩儿,我更喜欢在家读一本好书。

A: 嗯,我知道,我只是担心给人留下不友好、冷淡,或者傲慢的印象。我不想让还不认识的人觉得我看不起他们。有时候我会觉得筋疲力尽,因为我实在没有力气去和陌生人打交道了。

B: 我完全理解你,我觉得他们也是一样。你应该放松,这个新工作好像压力很大,不要太辛苦了,很快你就会回到以前的状态。

A: 谢谢! 跟你说了那么多。我知道你最近一定也很忙,你不是刚刚换了工作吗?

B: 对! 是的,我觉得这是个很好的变化。我的新老板比以前的老板好多了,我的新同事们也比以前的友好。我比较喜欢这个工作,没有那么多要求和期限。我感觉好像中了彩票一样。

A: 那太好了! 我真为你感到高兴!

B: 希望你的情况也越来越好!

Background Reading 背景阅读

The Best Way to Deal with Stress 处理压力的最好办法

1. Relaxation really is the key. Everyone needs to set aside time to relax, either alone or with friends. Studies have shown that people who relax by socializing generally have lower stress levels than people who relax alone and both groups obviously have lower stress levels than people who do not relax enough. Bear in mind that humans are social creatures, interaction and communication are essential to our wellbeing! 2. Avoid other people who are stressed-out. Stress can be very contagious. Stressed-out people put a lot of pressure on those around them by being nervous, irrational, or mean, so their innocent victims begin to feel stressed themselves.

1. 放松真的很关键。每个人都需要给自己留一点儿时间放松，独处或者跟朋友在一起。研究显示，通过参加社交活动放松的人比那些自己放松的人的压力小，但是这两组人的压力明显都比那些放松不够的人低。别忘了，人类是社会的产物——和他人的交往和交流对我们的健康是非常重要的！2. 躲开那些紧张的人。压力是会蔓延的。紧张的人通常会通过表现得紧张、没有理性或者坏脾气把压力传递给他们周围的人，而那些无辜的牺牲者就会开始感到有压力。

A Difference Between Stress and Pressure Stress 和 Pressure 的区别

Pressure is an external condition that can accompany many circumstances with a sense of urgency and high tension. Pressure can be hard to take sometimes, but it can also be a powerful creative force, think of the pressures of competitive sports, for example, or the US and Russia's race to put a man on the moon. Stress is an internal response or reaction to the difficulties and pressures one faces in life. But it is much more than this, it is a destructive force that scrambles and paralyzes the mind when one needs to use it most urgently. In addition to being unpleasant and unproductive, however, stress can also be very bad for your health.

Pressure 是一个伴随很多紧急情况和高度紧张的事情而来的外在情况。有时候，Pressure 很难解决，但是它也可能是一个强大的创造性的力量，比如说来自体育竞争的压力，或者美国和苏联登月计划的比赛压力。Stress 是对生活中面对的困难和压力的内在的回应或反应。但是要比反应厉害的多，它是一个破坏性的力量，越是你要想问题的时候，它越会扰乱你的想法，或者使你丧失思考能力。除了使你不高兴和工作没有效率，压力对你的健康也非常有害。

Some Types of Stress 几种压力

There are many types of work-related stress. Some stress is the result of a heavy workload, some from competition for promotions, and some from interpersonal relationships at the office. Yet another type is the feeling that you are in a "dead-end job", "going nowhere", or are being kept down by a "glass ceiling". Some stress also results from a feeling that you are being discriminated against unfairly because of your gender, sexual orientation, or ethnicity.

有很多和工作有关系的压力。有些压力是由于工作负担太重，有些压力来源于竞争和升迁，有些压力来源于办公室里的人际关系。还有另一些压力来源于感觉工作没有前途、没地方可去、或者工作没有升迁的机会。还有一些人的压力来源于他们因性别、性取向或者种族而受到的歧视。

Exercises 练习

Answer these questions.

1. Do you like to spend time alone or hang out with other people? Why?
2. Where do you think pressure comes from?
3. When you feel under pressure what do you do?

Translate these sentences into English.

1. 我是一个外向的人，而我的男朋友却很内向。
2. 我不想给人留下冷淡和傲慢的印象。
3. 在现代社会，人们总是说他们生活在压力之下。
4. 我用逃避和对抗相结合的方式来缓解压力。
5. 很多事情都会让你产生压力，比如说恋爱关系、工作和重大的决定。
6. 通过参加社交活动来放松的人比那些自己放松的人的压力更小。
7. 由于要做的工作太多，他感到压力很大。

Complete the following paragraph with these words or phrases.

action   react   failures   saying   prevent   consensus
circumstances

Many Americans believe that one can avoid, __1__, or lessen stress by taking positive __2__. There is a __3__ that "10% of life is what happens to you and 90% is how you __4__ to it". The popular __5__ is that our successes as well as our __6__ are in large part the result of our own choices and efforts, rather than being determined by __7__ alone.

 Answers 答案

Translate these sentences into English.

1. I'm an extrovert, while my boyfriend is an introvert.
2. I don't want to give people the impression that I'm standoffish, or just stuck up.
3. Many people in modern society often feel stressed.
4. I deal with these pressures with a combination of evasion and confrontation.
5. Many things can cause stress, such as relationships, work, and big decisions.
6. People who relax by socializing generally have lower stress levels than people who relax alone.
7. He's stressed out because he has too much work to do.

Complete the following paragraph with these words or phrases.

1. prevent   2. action   3. saying   4. react
5. consensus   6. failures   7. circumstances

词 汇 表	
extrovert	外向的人
introvert	内向的人
overwhelmed	受不了
feel like	想要
ashamed	惭愧的；不好意思的
out on the town	出去玩儿
impression	印象
standoffish	不友好的
aloof	冷淡的
stuck up	傲慢的
drained	筋疲力尽
interact	相互影响
take it easy	放心吧
lottery	彩票
deadline	截止日期
unwind	放松；松弛
bear in mind	别忘了
innocent	天真的；无辜的
external	外在的
internal	内在的
destructive	毁灭性的
scramble	扰乱
paralyze	使…瘫痪
ethnicity	种族

34. Dieting and Healthy Eating

节食与健康饮食

Dialogue

A: Hey, do you think I should go on a diet? I really want to lose weight.

B: I dunno, what kind of diet?

A: Well there are lots. There are diets where you don't eat carbohydrates, diets where you don't eat meat...

B: Personally, I think you'll be better off if you were just healthy on a regular basis. Diets appeal to people because they seem like quick fixes, but in reality things like weight and health can't be changed in a single week.

A: Whatever, I've had a lot of friends who have gone on diets and seen real results! As long as you're committed to sticking it out, it can work!

B: That's dangerous! Cutting some kind of food completely out of your diet can be a real shock to your body!

A: Then what do you suggest?

B: Eat three good meals a day: an early breakfast that includes healthy food like fresh fruit, then a good lunch no McDonalds or fried foods! And then for dinner, try to eat a little less. The later you eat dinner, the more likely it's going to make you gain weight!

A: Hmmm, so maybe I should stop eating pizza right before I go to sleep...

B: That beer isn't helping either! Beer, pizza: these things are full of carbohydrates. The first step to being healthy is eating healthy. You should be eating more fruit and vegetables, especially when you're having a snack between meals.

A: That doesn't sound so bad. Anyway, it's a lot easier than giving up meat!

B: Well, I won't say giving up meat is essential for a healthy diet, but giving up fried meat is. So you still have to watch what you eat!

A: Yeah, I guess you're right. I always knew that it's easy to gain weight from eating fried foods, but I also heard the other day that it can cause cancer!

B: Also, eating less might make you get a little thinner, but if you want your body to look its best, or if you want to target a specific area, you can't just diet—you have to exercise too.

A: I got it, I got it well, thanks for the advice! I have to go, but I'll let you know how this works out.

B: No problem, see you!

对 话

A: 嗨，你觉得我应该节食吗？我很想减肥。

B: 我不懂，你想怎么节食？

A: 有很多种。比如说，完全不吃碳水化合物或者完全不吃肉等等。

B: 我个人觉得如果你很健康、生活有规律，你最好不要节食。节食很吸引人，因为人们想快点儿瘦下来，但是事实上，发胖和健康都不是一天两天能改变的。

A: 不管怎么样，我有很多朋友节食以后都看到了真正的效果！只要你保证能坚持，就有效！

B: 那很危险！从你的饮食中完全戒掉某些食物对你的身体来说是很大的伤害。

A: 那你有什么好主意？

B: 每天吃好三顿饭：一顿包括健康食物，比如说新鲜水果的早餐；一顿很好的午餐，别吃麦当劳或者油炸食品！晚餐要少吃一点儿。晚餐吃得越晚，越容易长肉！

A: 嗯，所以可能我应该改掉睡觉之前吃比萨饼的习惯。

B: 啤酒也没有好处！啤酒、比萨饼这些东西充满了碳水化合物。想要健康的第一步就是要吃得健康。你应该多吃水果和蔬菜，尤其是在两顿饭之间吃零食的时候。

A: 听起来不错。而且，比戒掉肉容易很多。

B: 嗯，我不能说不吃肉对健康饮食来说很重要，但是不吃油炸的肉的确很重要。所以你还得注意你吃的是什么！

A: 你说得对，我也知道吃油炸的东西容易发胖，而且我还听说油炸的东西容易导致癌症。

B: 还有，少吃饭可能会让你变得瘦一点儿，但是如果你想让你的体型看起来更漂亮，或者是想局部减肥，那光靠节食是不够的——最好的办法就是去做运动。

A: 我懂了，懂了，谢谢你的建议！我要走了，我会告诉你结果的。

B: 没问题，再见！

Background Reading 背景阅读

A Balanced Diet 均衡饮食

It's important to achieve a balance in one's diet. Nowadays we sometimes think too much about what we want to eat and not enough about what we should eat. While fried chicken, hamburgers, and ice cream may taste good, they can be high in fat and bad for you in general. It's best to try substituting healthier dishes with similar flavors, perhaps grilled chicken breast for the fried chicken and frozen yogurt for ice cream. These small substitutions can make a real difference.

The American Heart Association recommends that you include lots of fresh fruits and vegetables in your diet. These foods are a good source of vitamins, minerals, and fiber, but are not high in calories. However, be careful: canned vegetables sometimes have added sugar or fat, so it's best to buy fresh. Raw vegetables are good for snacks, and the ideal way of preparing vegetables is to steam or boil them. This way, there is no added fat or oil from cooking.

An increasing number of people are trying "crash diets": diets that are extreme in their restrictions but promise rapid results. Often these "crash diets" involve severely reducing or completely eliminating certain types of food from the diet. The goal of these diets is usually rapid weight loss; however, they are very unhealthy and rarely successful. If continued longer than a period of a few days or a week, "crash diets" can lead to malnutrition or more serious medical problems. However, to the great disappointment of the dieter, the moment one comes off of a "crash diet", regaining all the weight you lost—and then some—is almost inevitable. In short, "crash diets" aren't worth the effort!

Many American dieters are taking to heart the Chinese saying, "at breakfast eat well; at lunch eat until full; at dinner eat just a little." Still, although research has proven that eating late in the evening is more likely to make one gain weight, dinner is the main meal of the day for many Americans. In American restaurants, portions are often sizably bigger for dinner and patrons are more likely to order desert. Dinner is also considered more formal, and many restaurants with no dress code during lunch may require patrons to dress more formally during the evening. There are typically two menus: a lunch menu, and a more expensive dinner menu. This emphasis on dinner as a larger, more formal meal began during the Industrial Revolution, when one or both of the parents in a household would leave home to work in the morning and not return until the evening. Since the family was only reunited at the end of the working day, they celebrated dinner as their meal together.

一个人的饮食平衡是很重要的。现在我们对想吃什么考虑得太多了，而对我们应该吃什么考虑得不够。炸鸡、汉堡、冰激凌的味道都不错，但是一般来说它们都热量很高而且对身体不好。最好试用口味相近的健康食品来替代它们，可以用烤鸡胸代替炸鸡；用冷冻的酸奶代替冰激凌。这些小的改变会带来真正的变化。

美国心脏协会建议你的饮食中应该包括大量的水果和蔬菜。这些食物是维生素、矿物质和纤维的很好的来源，而且热量不高。但是，小心：罐装蔬菜有时候放了糖或脂肪，所以最好买新鲜的。生蔬菜用来作点心很不错，但最理想的办法是蒸熟或水煮。这样，就不会在烹饪过程中放油或脂肪了。

越来越多的人在尝试"快速减肥"：一种限制很严格但是保证能很快见效的节食方式。"快速减肥"就是严格地减少或完全排除饮食中的某些食物。这种节食的目标通常是很快地减重；但是却极不健康而且几乎不能成功。如果坚持的时间比几天或者一个星期长一点儿，"快速减肥"可能会导致营养不良或更严重的疾病。但是令节食者极其失望的是，一旦他们终止"快速减肥"，减掉的体重都会再重新长回到身上来，这几乎是不可避免的。总之，"快速减肥"不值得人们去做。

很多美国的节食者都按照中国的这句话去做："早饭要吃好；午饭要吃饱；晚饭要吃少"。虽然研究证明吃饭吃得越晚越容易增重，但是，对很多美国人来说，晚饭仍然是一天中最重要的一餐。在美国饭馆，晚饭的一份食物常常量很大，而且客人们很喜欢点甜点。晚饭也被认为更正式，很多饭馆在午饭时间没有穿衣准则，但是在晚上可能会要求客人穿得更正式一点儿。通常有两种菜单：一份午餐菜单和一份更贵的晚餐菜单。把晚餐看得更大、更正式，这种对晚餐的重视始于工业革命，从那时开始，一个家庭中的父母都早出晚归去工作。由于工作了一天以后，一家人才能聚在一起，所以他们把晚餐看作是他们共同的吃饭时间。

136

Exercises 练习

Answer these questions.

1. Have you ever been stressed out about losing weight?
2. What do you think is the best way to lose weight?
3. How is Chinese and American food different? Which do you think is healthier and why?

Translate these sentences into English.

1. 吃合适的东西对健康很重要。
2. 快速减肥是一种没有效果并且不健康的减肥方法。
3. "早饭要吃好；午饭要吃饱；晚饭要吃少。"
4. 比起完全戒掉某种食物，用健康的食品来代替更好，比如说，用蔬菜代替糖果。
5. 大部分美国人觉得晚餐是一天中最重要的一顿饭。
6. 一些人可能天生就比别人重，找到对你来说最健康的体重最重要。
7. 吃得少可能会帮你减肥，但你还得注意你吃的是什么。

Complete the following paragraph with these words or phrases.

> whole-wheat   include   encourages   avoided   balanced
> rich   substitute

The American Heart Association __1__ everyone to eat a healthy, __2__ diet. Such a diet should __3__ fresh fruit and vegetables, brown rice or __4__ bread, and foods that are __5__ in vitamins and minerals. Foods that are high in fat or sodium should be __6__ and used sparingly. Remember, a crash diet is no __7__ for regularly eating right! The greatest changes come gradually.

 Answers 答案

Translate these sentences into English.

1. Eating right is an important part of good health.
2. Crash diets are an ineffective and unhealthy way to lose weight.
3. "At breakfast eat well; at lunch eat until full; at dinner eat just a little."
4. Rather than cutting out snacks altogether, just substitute healthy foods like vegetables, for unhealthy foods, like candy bars.
5. Most Americans feel that dinner is the most important meal of the day.
6. Some people are naturally heavier than others; what's important is finding the body weight that is healthiest for you.
7. Eating small portions can help you lose weight, but you still have to watch what you're eating.

Complete the following paragraph with these words or phrases.

1. encourages   2. balanced   3. include   4. whole-wheat
5. rich   6. avoided   7. substitute

词 汇 表

diet	
	节食
staple food	
	主食
appeal	
	吸引
fried food	
	油炸食品
carbohydrate	
	碳水化合物
snack	
	小吃；零食
essential	
	必需的；必要的
balance	
	平衡
substitute	
	代替
flavor	
	味道
grill	
	烤
breast	
	胸
frozen	
	冷冻的
yogurt	
	酸奶
recommend	
	推荐
mineral	
	矿物质
steam	
	蒸
severe	
	严格的；苛刻的
eliminate	
	排除；消灭
promise	
	允诺；确保
rapid	
	快的；迅速的
malnutrition	
	营养不良
take... to heart	
	认真对待…
code	
	准则；规则

35. Swing Dancing

摇摆舞

Dialogue

A: You'll never guess what I did last night!

B: What?

A: I went to a swing dance class!

B: Really? That's awesome! I love swing dancing! Was it your first time?

A: Yup. I've been thinking about going for a while but I was scared because I don't know how to dance at all.

B: Well that's what the class is for! Did you like it?

A: It was hard, and I probably made a total fool of myself, but it was tons of fun. The teachers are great.

B: I'm so glad you enjoyed it! What got you interested in taking the class?

A: I've always kind of had this irrational refusal to learn how to dance, but lately I've been feeling like it's time to get over it. Then I heard you talking about swing dancing, and I saw you dance that one time, and it just looked like so much fun. My friend was interested in going too, so we went together. I'm looking forward to going back next week, but I feel like it will be forever before I'm good enough to dance for real.

B: That's not true at all. Just getting out there and dancing is actually the best way to learn. Dancing with people who are better than you is so important, because you'll pick up tons of new moves, and you'll get a better hang of the basics. Dancing with another beginner is really hard, because they don't know what they're doing either.

A: I suppose you're right, but I just feel self-conscious as a leader, because I hardly know any moves.

B: Don't worry about it! The most important thing is having a good feel for the music. I would much rather dance with a guy who only knows three moves but who can stay on the beat, than with someone who's doing all sorts of fancy stuff but isn't following the music.

138

A: I guess that's a little bit reassuring.

B: I tell you what: I'll make you a CD of swing music, and that way you can practice at home between lessons. Even listening to the CD while you're on the subway or at work will make you a better dancer, because if you have a really good feel for the music then dancing comes almost naturally.

A: Ok. Will you help me practice, too?

B: Of course, I would love to!

A: Great, thanks a lot—I'm going to need all the help I can get.

B: Nonsense! You'll be tearing up the floor in no time, I promise!

对 话

A: 你一定猜不到我昨晚做什么了!

B: 你做什么了?

A: 我去上摇摆舞课了!

B: 真的吗? 你太厉害了! 我喜欢摇摆舞! 你是第一次去吗?

A: 是啊。我早就想去了,但是一直都不敢去,因为我一点儿都不会跳。

B: 所以才会有舞蹈课啊! 你喜欢那个课吗?

A: 很难,而且我肯定出了很大的丑,但是非常有意思。老师很棒。

B: 我真高兴你喜欢这个舞蹈课! 是什么让你对上舞蹈课产生兴趣的?

A: 我对学跳舞总是有一些抵触,但是最近我觉得我应该克服这种抵触情绪。再后来听你说起摇摆舞,又看你跳过一次,看起来很有意思。我的一个朋友也想去,所以我们就一起去了。我正期待下周再去,但是我觉得自己离跳得好还差很远很远。

B: 不是那样的。你只要去那儿然后跳舞就是学舞蹈的最好的办法。和比你跳得好的人一起跳舞是很重要的,因为你会学到很多新的动作,并且可以掌握一些基本技巧。而和另一个初学者一起跳舞就会很难,因为他也不知道该做什么。

A: 我觉得你说的对,但是如果我是起主要作用的人,我会觉得很不自然,因为我几乎什么动作都不会。

B: 不要着急! 最重要的是有好的乐感。我宁愿和一个虽然只会三个动作但可以踩到乐点上的人跳舞,也不愿意和一个各种花样动作都会却跟不上音乐节奏的人跳。

A: 这样我就放心些了……

B: 我告诉你:我会给你做一张摇摆舞音乐的 CD,这样没有课的时候你就可以在家练习了。即使你只是在地铁里或者工作的时候听听这张 CD,你也有可能跳得更好,因为如果你有很好的乐感,那你自然就能跳出来。

A: 好的。你可以帮我练习吗?

B: 当然,我很愿意啊!

A: 太好了,非常感谢——我需要能得到的所有帮助。

B: 不要这么说! 你很快就会跳得很好的,我保证!

Let's Swing！ 摇起来！

Swing dancing was invented in the United States alongside the development of jazz music in the first half of the 20th century. Swing dance is done to swing music, which is a particular style of jazz that features a syncopated rhythm and a range of tempos suitable for dancing. Swing music evolved from earlier forms of jazz; swing dancing likewise evolved from earlier styles of dance. Swing is mostly a partner dance, with one leader and one follower dancing together. It is a very energetic type of dance, characterized by lots of kicking, jumping and spinning. It is much more improvisational and free-spirited than other Western styles of partner dancing such as tango or waltz.

摇摆舞是20世纪前半期伴随着爵士乐的发展而在美国产生的。摇摆音乐就是跳摇摆舞时演奏的音乐，这是一种很特别的爵士乐，它具有很特别的韵律和变化很大的节拍，所以很适合跳舞。摇摆音乐是从早期的爵士乐逐步发展而来的；同样，摇摆舞也是从早期形式的舞蹈发展来的。摇摆舞通常是双人舞蹈，一个人起主要作用，另一个人跟着他跳。它是一种充满活力的舞蹈类型，特点是有很多的踢腿、跳跃和旋转的动作。它比其它的西式双人舞蹈，比如说探戈和华尔兹随意和放松得多。

"Big Band" swing music was hugely popular in the US and all over the world in the 1930s and 40s; the groups that played this type of music were literally "big bands", with many trumpets, saxophones and trombones in addition to the piano, bass, drums and guitar that are the foundation of most jazz ensembles. Vocalists, both female and male, were also extremely popular, and many were skilled at vocal improvisation, called "scat singing", where the singer improvises a melody and sings nonsense words instead of lyrics.

"Big Band" 摇摆音乐在20世纪30年代和40年代风靡美国和全世界；演奏这种音乐的人就是真正的"大乐队"，他们除了有钢琴、贝斯、鼓和吉他这些爵士乐队的基础乐器以外，还有很多喇叭、萨克斯管和长号。男女歌唱家也都特别受欢迎，而且他们很善于即兴演唱，被称作"疯狂演唱"，歌手们即兴谱曲然后随便乱唱，而不是唱事先写好的歌词。

In the heyday of swing there were huge ballrooms where the most popular bands of the day would play and the floor would be completely packed with dancers. However, starting in the 1950s swing began to lose popularity. The new direction in jazz music was be-bop, which was usually played too fast to dance to, while rock and roll was replacing swing as the most popular kind of music in America. Swing never went away, however, and actually had a big revival in the 1990s, when a few new swing bands topped the charts and millions of people took swing dancing lessons. Ever since the 1920s, swing dancing has been popular all over the world, and it still is today—even some Chinese cities have swing dance clubs!

在摇摆舞的全盛时期，最流行的乐队会在很多大舞厅演奏，大厅里常常站满了跳舞的人。然而，从20世纪50年代开始，摇摆舞开始失去了光彩。爵士乐的新方向是 be-bop，这种音乐通常演奏得太快而不能跳舞，然后摇滚乐取代了摇摆音乐成了美国最流行的音乐。但是，摇摆音乐从来没有离去，在90年代，它又得到了大规模的复苏，当时，一些新的摇摆乐队又流行起来，上百万人去上摇摆舞的课。自从20世纪20年代，摇摆舞就风靡全世界，直到今天——甚至一些中国城市里都有摇摆舞俱乐部！

"Swing Beijing" was started in 2003 by an American named Adam Lee. Adam had been a passionate swing dancer and teacher for several years when he moved to Beijing. After spending two years wishing that he had more opportunities to swing dance in Beijing, he decided to take matters into his own hands, and "Swing Beijing" was born. "Swing Beijing" is a loosely-organized group of people that meets a couple times each week for lessons and open dances. New people are joining every week, and although swing dance is just starting to catch on in the Chinese capital, the future looks very bright.

"摇摆北京"是由一个叫亚当·李的美国人在2003年创办的。他是一个有激情的摇摆舞者，在北京生活的时候，他也当过几年老师。等待了两年以后，他终于有了更多的机会在北京跳摇摆舞，他决定靠自己开始这项事业，然后就有了"摇摆北京"。"摇摆北京"是一个很松散的组织，人们每周会为了上课和跳舞见面。每周都有新人加入，尽管摇摆舞刚刚在北京开始流行，但前途很明朗。

Exercises 练习

Answer these questions.
1. What's your favorite kind of dance? Why?
2. What instruments are found in a swing band?
3. Why did swing music lose popularity in the 1950s?

Translate these sentences into English.
1. 我怕出丑，所以我一直不敢学跳舞。
2. 我跳舞的时候总是跟不上节奏。
3. 跳舞最重要的就是要有乐感。
4. 如果你有很好的乐感，那你自然就能跳出来。
5. 摇摆舞通常是一个双人舞蹈，一个人起主要作用，另一个人跟着他跳。
6. 摇摆舞比其它的西式双人舞蹈，比如说探戈和华尔兹随意和放松得多。
7. 在90年代，摇摆舞得到了大规模的复苏。

Complete the following paragraph with these words or phrases.

exercise reasons steps exhausted spirits foremost

Why swing? There are many __1__ why people love swing dancing. First and __2__, it's tons of fun! The upbeat music and energetic __3__ are sure to lift even the gloomiest of __4__. But swing dancing isn't just fun, it's great __5__ too! Just look around at the end of a dance—everyone will be sweaty and __6__, but they'll surely have a big smile on their face.

 Answers 答案

Translate these sentences into English.
1. I'm afraid of making a fool of myself, so I never dared to learn how to dance.
2. I can't stay on the beat when I'm dancing.
3. The most important thing when you're dancing is having a good feel for the music.
4. If you have a really good feel for the music then dancing comes almost naturally.
5. Swing is mostly a partner dance, with one leader and one follower dancing together.
6. Swing is much more improvisational and free-spirited than other Western styles of partner dancing such as tango or waltz.
7. Swing had a big revival in the 1990s.

Complete the following paragraph with these words or phrases.
1. reasons 2. foremost 3. steps 4. spirits
5. exercise 6. exhausted

词 汇 表

awesome
　　　　令人敬畏的
make a fool of oneself
　　　　出丑
irrational
　　　　不合理的；荒谬的
refusal
　　　　拒绝；推却
get over
　　　　战胜；克服
looking forward to
　　　　期待
pick up
　　　　学会；得到；获得
get a hang of
　　　　懂得…的技巧
self-conscious
　　　　不自然的
beat
　　　　鼓声；节拍
invent
　　　　发明；创造
alongside
　　　　随着
rhythm
　　　　韵律
tempo
　　　　拍子；速度
evolve
　　　　演化；进化；发展
spin
　　　　旋转
improvisational
　　　　随意的
band
　　　　乐队
trumpet
　　　　喇叭
ensemble
　　　　小乐队；文工团
instrument
　　　　乐器
era
　　　　时代；年代
vocalist
　　　　歌唱家；演唱者
ballroom
　　　　舞厅
catch on
　　　　变得流行

36. Having Fun

玩乐篇

Dialogue

A: Got any plans for the weekend?

B: Yeah, on Saturday night I'm hanging out with a
few of my friends from school.

A: What do you guys usually do for fun?

B: We go out for dinner, or sing karaoke. Do Americans do those things?

A: Not really. Going out to dinner is much more expensive in the US than it is in China, so
college students more often meet their friends at the university dining hall or at someone's
house to have dinner. When I moved off campus my roommate and I would have friends
over for dinner at least once a week.

B: What about karaoke?

A: Karaoke isn't nearly as popular in the West as it is in Asia. Also, it's set up differently.
Mostly in the West karaoke bars will be just like a regular club with one TV screen and
one microphone in the main room, so you have to pick one song at a time and sign up
and wait your turn. At most karaoke places in China it's all private rooms, so you and
your friends can sing the entire time. I think it's much more fun that way. Also, I think
Chinese people in general are much less shy about singing. In America there's kind of a
sense that you should only sing if you're a good singer, but in China everybody sings.

B: So what do American college students do on the weekends?

A: For better or worse, a lot of what American college students do on a Friday or Saturday
night centers around drinking.

B: Like going out to bars and clubs?

A: Yes, and house parties too, especially if you go to school in a smaller town that doesn't have a lot of clubs.

B： What else do you do besides drink?

A： Haha, I don't want to make it sound like we're all alcoholics or something. There are plenty of people who don't drink, and even for those who do, going to bars or parties is more about hanging out with your friends or meeting new people. I also love going out to see live music, whether it's a big concert or a smaller show at a bar or a coffee shop. When I was a freshman in college my friends and I would go out dancing at this one club every Saturday night.

B： Well, if you don't have any plans for this Saturday night you should come out with my friends and me!

A： Sure, I would love to!

对 话

A： 这个周末你有计划吗？

B： 有啊，星期六晚上，我要和学校的一些朋友出去玩儿。

A： 你们出去玩儿的时候通常做什么？

B： 我们出去吃晚饭，或者唱卡拉 OK。美国人也这样玩儿吗？

A： 不是，在美国，出去吃晚饭比在中国贵得多，所以大学生们常常在大学的食堂或在某个人的家里一起吃饭。我从学校搬出来以后，我的同屋和我每周至少会请朋友来吃一次饭。

B： 卡拉 OK 呢？

A： 卡拉 OK 在西方并没有在亚洲那么流行。而且，卡拉 OK 厅的布局也不同。在西方，大部分卡拉 OK 就像一般的酒吧一样，只是有一个电视屏幕和一个麦克风在大厅中间，所以一次你只能点一首歌，还要签名，然后等轮到你的时候再唱。在中国，大部分的卡拉 OK 都是单独的小房间，所以你和你的朋友可以一直唱歌，我觉得那样更有意思。还有，我觉得一般来说，中国人唱歌的时候不会不好意思，在美国，我们总是觉得只有在你唱得好的情况下你才能唱歌，但是在中国，每个人都可以唱。

B： 那么美国大学生周末的时候都做什么呢？

A： 不管怎么说，很多美国大学生周五或周六晚上做的事情都和喝酒有关。

B： 去酒吧和俱乐部吗？

A： 对，还有家庭晚会，尤其是当你的学校在一个没有太多酒吧的小镇的时候。

B： 除了喝酒，你们还做什么？

A： 哈哈，我不想让你听起来觉得我们都是酒鬼什么的。有很多人不喝酒，那些喝酒的人去酒吧或晚会也只是为了和朋友一起玩儿或者认识新朋友。我也喜欢去看现场的音乐表演，不管是大型的音乐会还是在酒吧或咖啡馆的小表演。我上大一的时候，每个星期六的晚上都和朋友去一个酒吧跳舞。

B： 如果这个周六晚上你没有什么事的话就跟我和我的朋友们一起出来玩儿吧！

A： 好啊，我很想去！

Background Reading 背景阅读

Parties and Drinking 晚会与喝酒

American students, both graduates and undergraduates, often socialize at parties. The typical American party consists of people talking in small groups or pairs while drinking alcoholic beverages and perhaps eating some snacks. There is often music playing, and at some parties people dance, but games or other organized activities are rare. It is also common for universities to have a reception following a lecture, concert or other event. Many of the people at a party may be strangers to each other. When invited to a party, Americans are relatively unlikely to ask, "Who will be there?" Because they are accustomed to meeting strangers and starting conversations with them; indeed, the opportunity to meet new people is one of the reasons Americans enjoy going to parties.

美国大学的本科生和研究生都通过参加晚会来进行社交活动。典型的美国晚会是这样的：几个人或者两个人围在一起边喝酒边聊天儿，还有一些零食。晚会上通常会放音乐，有些还会跳舞，但是游戏和其它有组织的活动却很少见。在讲座、音乐会或别的大事完了以后，大学院系举办的招待会也很常见。参加这种晚会的许多人可能都是陌生人。当被邀请去参加一个晚会时，美国人不太可能会问"都有谁啊?"他们习惯于在晚会上认识陌生人并开始跟他们聊天儿。美国人喜欢参加这种晚会的一个原因就是这的确是他们认识新朋友的机会。

In the US, the legal drinking age is 21. Bartenders and liquor stores are supposed to check everyone's driver's license, and if you're not 21 they can't serve or sell you alcohol. Many bars and clubs check IDs at the door, and refuse to let underage people come in. Sometimes they let everyone in, but if you're under 21 they might give you a stamp or an X on your hands so the bartender knows not to serve you. If the police catch them serving someone under 21, the bar will get fined or even have their liquor license revoked. Most people turn 21 during their junior year of college, but underage drinking is very common on American college campuses, because students go to house parties, where no one checks ID.

在美国，可以喝酒的合法年龄是21岁。酒吧侍者和卖酒的商店都得检查每个人的驾照，如果你不到21岁，他们就不能卖酒给你。很多酒吧和俱乐部都会在门口检查身份证，拒绝不够年龄的人进入。有时候，他们让每个人都进来，但是如果你不满21岁，他们会在你的手上做一个标记或一个X，所以酒吧侍者就不会给你服务了。如果警察抓到他们向不到21岁的人卖酒，这个酒吧就会被罚款，甚至撤销他们卖酒的执照。很多人都是上大学三年级的时候才满21岁的，但是在美国大学校园里，不到年龄就喝酒是很普遍的，因为学生们常常去参加晚会，在那儿没有人检查身份证。

Drinking alcohol is not very common among Chinese students. Someone who drinks once a week is considered a frequent drinker, while in the US, drinking once a week is about average. In America, drinking is a part of typical Friday or Saturday night activities, but in China, drinking is only common on certain situations, some happy (graduation or finishing a big exam), some sad (breaking up with a boyfriend or girlfriend). In the US, college students and adults often drink alcohol at parties, but in China this is very rare.

中国学生喝酒的现象不太普遍。每个星期喝一次酒的人就会被认为是一个常常喝酒的人，但是在美国，每个星期喝一次酒是很一般的情况。在美国，喝酒是典型的周五或周六晚上活动的一部分，但是在中国，只有在一些特殊的场合下，喝酒才很常见，比如一些令人高兴的事情（毕业或者考完一个大考试），或一些令人伤心的事情（和男女朋友分手）。在美国，大学生和成人常常在晚会上喝酒，但是在中国很少见。

Drinking patterns don't differ much between men and women in the US, but the situation in China is different. Female students in China don't drink as often or as much as male students. Even if a large group of students go out to dinner together, the girls will often drink just one glass or none at all. Female students also choose not to drink because it is considered less socially acceptable for women to drink; a potential boyfriend might get turned off by a girl who drinks alcohol, or parents might not allow their daughter to drink.

在美国，男人和女人喝酒的方式没什么不同，但是在中国是有区别的。在中国，女生喝酒的次数和酒量都没有男生多。即使是一大群学生一起出去吃晚饭，女孩子们通常只喝一杯酒或完全不喝。女生选择不喝酒是因为女孩子喝酒不太被社会接受；她未来的男朋友可能会讨厌一个喝酒的女孩子，或者父母们可能不允许他们的女儿喝酒。

Exercises 练习

Answer these questions.

1. What do you usually do for fun?
2. Do you think there should be differences between men and women when it comes to drinking alcohol?

Translate these sentences into English.

1. 美国学生通常都在周末进行社交活动和玩乐。
2. 喝酒，无论是去酒吧还是参加晚会，都是美国本科生经常参加的一项重要社交活动。
3. 卡拉 OK 在西方并没有在亚洲那么流行。
4. 去酒吧或晚会只是为了和朋友一起玩儿并认识新朋友。
5. 在美国，可以喝酒的合法年龄是 21 岁。
6. 如果某个酒吧向不到 21 岁的人卖酒，这个酒吧就会被罚款，甚至被撤销他们卖酒的执照。
7. 在中国，女生喝酒的次数和酒量都没有男生多。

Complete the following paragraph with these words or phrases.

lowering opportunity cut down concern undergraduates responsible

Underage and irresponsible drinking on American campuses is a major __1__ of educators and health officials. Many __2__ , especially freshmen, get carried away with their newfound freedom from their parents' watchful eyes by drinking too often or too much. Some people argue that __3__ the legal drinking age would actually __4__ on binge drinking on college campuses, by giving young people an __5__ to learn __6__ drinking habits before they go off to college.

 Answers 答案

Translate these sentences into English.

1. American students like to spend their weekends socializing and having fun.
2. Drinking alcohol, whether at a bar or a party, is a frequent component of American undergraduates' social life.
3. Karaoke isn't nearly as popular in the West as it is in Asia.
4. Going to bars or parties is about hanging out with your friends and meeting new people.
5. In the US, the legal drinking age is 21.
6. If a bar serves someone under 21, the bar will get fined or even have their liquor license revoked.
7. Female students in China don't drink as often or as much as male students.

Complete the following paragraph with these words or phrases.

1. concern 2. undergraduates 3. lowering 4. cut down
5. opportunity 6. responsible

词 汇 表

set up
　　　　布局
regular
　　　　一般的
private
　　　　私人的
alcoholic
　　酒鬼；含酒精的
live
　　　　现场
unstated
　　　　未明说的
entail
　　　必需；需要
participating in
　　　　参与
recreational
　　　　娱乐的
refers to
　　　　指
beverages
　　　　饮料
socialize
　　　　交际
liquor
　　　酒；烈性酒
be supposed to
　　　理应；应该
driver's license
　　　　驾驶执照
ID
　　　　身份证
stamp
　　　　标记
revoke
　　　　撤销
throw
　　　　举行
typical
　　　　典型的
certain
　　　　特定的
break up
　　　与男/女朋友分手
turn off
　　　厌烦；讨厌

37. Working

工作篇

Dialogue

A: Hi! How have you been? I haven't talked to you in ages!

B: I know, I've just been so busy between school and working part-time that I haven't had time to keep in touch with any of my friends in China.

A: I didn't know you had a part-time job. What do you do?

B: I just work at a coffee shop on campus. It's nothing special, but I enjoy it because it seems like everyone I know comes in to get coffee, so I can say hi to people I might not otherwise run into that much.

A: Is it very common for Americans to work while they're in college?

B: Definitely. Going to college in the US is really expensive, so a lot of students work part-time to help pay for their tuition. Also, a lot of students who receive financial aid from the government or from their university are actually required to contribute a certain amount each year. But some students get a job just so they have some extra spending money, or save money to travel during summer vacation.

A: What kinds of jobs are most common?

B: Working in a coffee shop or a restaurant is pretty typical, but lots of students get jobs on campus too, like working in the library, the dining hall, or an office. Some students also work for professors as research assistants.

A: How many hours a week do you work?

B: Usually about 15. I think the average is 10 or 15 hours a week—definitely no more than 20. Lots of students work full time over the summer, although it's also really common to do an unpaid internship as a way to gain experience for your future career, or to help you decide if a certain career path is right for you.

A: It's probably a good opportunity to get to know people and make connections, too.

B: Absolutely. What about in China? Do lots of students work during college?

A: It actually isn't very common for Chinese students to have a job. Some work as tutors, but that's about it.

B: Why do you think that is?

A: Well, tuition at Chinese universities isn't as expensive as it is in the US, but I think the main reason is just that most students want to focus all their attention on their studies.

B: That's good too. I know plenty of people who could definitely afford to be a little more focused!

对 话

A: 嗨！你怎么样？好久没跟你聊天儿了！

B: 我知道，最近我一直忙于学习和打工，所以我没有时间和在中国的朋友联系。

A: 我不知道你在做兼职，你做什么工作啊？

B: 我在学校里的一个咖啡店工作，没什么特别的，但是我喜欢这个工作，因为差不多每个我认识的人都会来这儿买咖啡，所以我可以跟他们打招呼，要不然没那么多机会见面的。

A: 美国人上大学的时候打工，这种现象很普遍吗？

B: 当然。在美国上大学非常贵，所以很多学生都做兼职工作，帮助付学费。还有，很多学生会从政府或大学得到经济帮助，条件是他们每年也得做一定量的工作。当然，也有一些学生打工只是想挣点儿零花钱，或者攒钱留着暑假的时候去旅行。

A: 什么样的工作最普遍呢？

B: 最典型的工作就是在咖啡馆或饭馆里工作，但是很多学生也在学校里工作，比如说在学校的图书馆、食堂或办公室工作。还有一些学生给教授当研究助手。

A: 你们一周工作几个小时？

B: 通常是 15 个小时。我想是每周平均 10 到 15 个小时——绝对不超过 20 个小时。很多学生夏天的时候会做全职工作，当然也有很多人去不给钱的地方实习，为将来的工作积累经验，或者是想看看某种工作适合不适合自己做。

A: 这也是一个认识别人并建立关系的好机会。

B: 没错。在中国怎么样？在大学里有很多学生打工吗？

A: 事实上中国的学生打工并不普遍。有些人做家教，仅此而已。

B: 你觉得那是为什么呢？

A: 嗯，中国大学的学费没有美国大学的学费那么贵，但是我觉得中国大学生不打工的最主要的原因是他们想集中精力学习。

B: 那也很好。我认识很多人可以更集中精力学习的。

Work Part-Time 兼职工作

There are many reasons in addition to having some extra money in your pocket that make working part-time during college a smart decision.

上大学时做兼职工作是个明智的决定，这不仅是因为这样做可以挣点儿零花钱，还有很多原因。

Learn New Skills 学习新技能

Some jobs you do just for the money, or just because they're fun, but other jobs can provide important building blocks for your future. Many students who plan to become lawyers will get a summer job during college working at a law firm. Young people who want to become doctors can get certified as emergency rescue workers and spend their Sunday nights saving lives. Even that restaurant job can help you decide if you really want to become a chef—and if you do, you'll already know a lot about the business.

有些工作你做只是为了赚钱，或者那些工作很好玩儿，但是还有一些工作可以为你的将来提供很重要的经验。很多想当律师的学生可以在大学期间在律师事务所工作一个夏天。想当医生的年轻人可以取得急救人员的资格并可以在周日晚上救人。就算在饭馆工作也可以帮助你决定你将来是不是想当一个厨师，如果你真的想，那么你已经知道了很多。

Build Experience, Build Your Resumé 丰富你的经历，丰富你的简历

Even if your part-time job has nothing to do with your future career, potential employers will be more impressed with a resumé that has something on it besides chess club. Even if you've just been working at the mall, having a job shows that you're responsible, that your time-management skills are good enough to juggle work and school, and that you can handle yourself professionally. A good reference from a former boss shows the person who is considering hiring you that you're good at something besides studying.

即使你的兼职工作和你未来的职业没有任何关系，如果你的简历上除了你曾经参加过棋类俱乐部以外还有点儿别的东西的话，这也会给有可能成为你老板的人留下更深的印象。哪怕你只是在商场里工作过，有工作就意味着你负责任，你管理时间的技巧足够好，因为你可以同时应付工作和学习，而且你可以管好你自己。以前的老板给你的很好的评语可以告诉正在考虑雇用你的人，除了学习，你还擅长做别的事情。

Get a Taste of the "Real World" 经历一下"真正的世界"

For many students who went to college straight after graduating high school, the prospect of finishing school and being dumped out into the real world is terrifying. Getting a job while in college can help prepare you for the transition. Also, when you get a job, you may find that the real world isn't scary after all! You'll realize that supporting yourself financially isn't as hard as you thought, even if you don't get that dream job right away. Finally, spending some of your time on other things can make the time you spend on your studies more focused and efficient, and give you perspective on why you're in college.

很多学生都是高中毕业以后就直接上大学了，完成学业以后就直接被抛到现实世界中，这种前景很可怕。在大学里有一份工作有助于你的转变。还有，当你有了工作，你可能会发现现实世界一点儿也不可怕！就算你没得到理想的工作，你也会发现养活自己并不像你想像的那么难。最后，用你的一部分时间多做点儿别的事情可以使你学习的时候更集中、更高效，让你想清楚为什么要上大学。

Earn Money! 赚钱!

While there are many other good reasons for working part time, you shouldn't overlook the importance of that extra money in your pocket. Earning and spending your own money teaches you financial management skills that you'll use throughout your life. Furthermore, you can use your hard-earned cash for many things that are more meaningful than that new pair of sneakers you've been eyeing. Travel is one thing that many American students spend their money on. Seeing the world and learning about different cultures are as much a part of becoming an educated person as burying your nose in a book.

做兼职有很多好处，但是你最不应该忽视的就是挣零花钱的重要性。挣自己的钱、花自己的钱可以让你学会理财的技巧，这些技巧会使你受用一生。更进一步说，你可以用自己辛辛苦苦赚来的钱买很多东西，这些都比一双你看上很久的帆布运动鞋更有意义。很多美国学生常把钱花在旅行上。看看世界和学学不同的文化同埋头读书一样都会使你受益匪浅。

Exercises 练习

Answer these questions.

1. Did you have a part-time job when you were in college?
2. What are the advantages of working part-time during college?
3. Do you think having a part-time job will affect your studies?

Translate these sentences into English.

1. 最近我一直忙于学习和打工。
2. 美国人上大学的时候打工，这种现象很普遍。
3. 我做兼职是想挣点儿零花钱。
4. 我做兼职是想攒钱留着暑假的时候去旅行。
5. 做兼职也是一个认识别人并建立关系的好机会。
6. 中国大学生上学期间不打工的原因是他们想集中全部精力学习。
7. 上大学时做兼职工作是个明智的决定。

Complete the following paragraph with these words or phrases.

in particular   perk   opportunity   on campus   break   provide

Another __1__ of a part-time job is the opportunity to meet new people. Whether your job is __2__ or off, working will give you an __3__ to meet people you might not otherwise have gotten to know. __4__ , working off campus can __5__ a much-needed __6__ from the self-contained bubble of college life.

 Answers 答案

Translate these sentences into English.

1. Lately I've just been so busy between school and working part-time.
2. It's very common for Americans to work while they're in college.
3. I got a part-time job to make some extra spending money.
4. I got a part-time job to save money so I can travel during summer vacation.
5. Working part-time is also a good opportunity to get to know people and make connections.
6. Most Chinese students don't work during college because they want to focus all their attention on their studies.
7. Working part-time during college is a smart decision.

Complete the following paragraph with these words or phrases.

1. perk 2. on campus 3. opportunity 4. In particular
5. provide 6. break

词 汇 表

keep in touch
　　　　　保持联系
part-time job
　　　　　兼职工作
run into
　　　　　偶然碰到
definitely
　　　当然；无疑地
financial aid
　　　　　经济援助
contribute
　　　　　出力协助
typical
　　　　　典型的
average
　　　　　平均的
internship
　　　　　实习
gain
　　　　获得；获益
tutor
　　　　　家庭教师
focus on
　　　　　集中
afford
　　　　　负担得起
certify
　　　　　证明
emergency
　　　　　突发事件
rescue
　　　　援救；营救
chef
　　　　　厨师
resumé
　　　　　简历
mall
　　　　　百货商店
juggle
　　　　　玩杂耍
handle
　　　　　处理
transition
　　　　　转变
scary
　　　　令人害怕的
efficient
　　　　　效率高的

38. Dormitories

宿舍篇

Dialogue

A: I went to my friend's dorm today and you wouldn't believe it. All of their dorms have 6 or 8 people in a room! And my friend is a senior!

B: Wow, that's crazy! Are all Chinese universities like that?

A: I think so.

B: Did it seem really crowded?

A: Actually it was pretty nice, but only a couple of her roommates were there. I imagine when all 8 girls are there at once it feels very different.

B: Can you imagine if an American university tried to make its students live in a dorm with 7 other people?! The students would all have a fit!

A: That's for sure. But I think it just depends on what you're used to. Independence and personal freedom are very important to Americans, so they believe that a person should have their own space, and that other people shouldn't interfere in their personal business. Chinese people are very different: contact with family and friends is extremely important, and they like to live as part of a larger group.

B: That makes a lot of sense.

A: For example, that friend of mine that I mentioned, she really likes living with all 7 of her roommates. They do everything together: they go to class together, they eat together, they go shopping together, and so on. She especially loves each night before going to sleep when they all lie on their beds chatting, telling each other about what's on their minds, or sharing secrets—just what Americans call their private business.

B: Haha, that's so interesting! Do most Chinese college students live in dorms all four years?

A: I think they live in dorms if they go to college away from home, but if they stay in their

150

hometown I think lots of students continue living with their families. It's not like in America where most students live in the dorms for their first couple of years but then move into an apartment or a house off campus, regardless of whether their parents live in the same city or not.

B: Yeah, I moved off campus as soon as they would let me.

A: Me too.

B: It seems like college life in China and America are really very different! I would really like to experience Chinese college life, but I'd be worried that I wouldn't be able to adjust.

A: Same here. It's probably really hard for Chinese students to adjust when they come to America, too. But now I can see the merits of both types of situations.

对 话

A: 今天我去了我朋友的宿舍，你简直不能相信。她们所有的宿舍都是一个房间住6个人或者8个人！还有，我的朋友已经上大四了！

B: 哇，疯了。所有的中国大学都是这样吗？

A: 我觉得是。

B: 她们的宿舍看起来很挤吗？

A: 事实上，她们的宿舍很好，但是只有两三个室友在那儿。我能想像如果8个女孩都在，感觉肯定很不一样。

B: 你能想像如果一个美国大学让它的学生跟另外7个人住在一起吗？学生们肯定气死了。

A: 一定会。但是我觉得那得看你习惯怎么住。隐私的概念是美国文化中一个非常大的部分，美国人看重独立和自由，他们觉得一个人一定得有自己的私人空间，个人的私事不能受到别人的干涉。但是中国人却不一样，中国人特别看重和家人、朋友的联系，他们喜欢生活在群体之中。

B: 你说的有道理。

A: 比如说，我的那个朋友，她就特别喜欢跟她的另外7个室友住在一起，她们常常一起去上课、吃饭、买东西等等。最让她们兴奋的是每天晚上入睡之前躺在床上聊天，分享自己的心事和小秘密——就是美国人所谓的隐私。

B: 哈哈，太有意思了！大部分中国大学生四年都要住在宿舍里吗？

A: 我觉得如果他们离家上大学，他们就住在宿舍里，但是如果在家乡上大学，他们就可能住在家里。这和美国不一样，大部分美国大学生在上大学的头两年都住在宿舍，之后可能搬到校外的公寓或房子里，而不管他们的父母是不是住在同一个城市里。

B: 是的，学校允许我们搬出去的时候，我马上就搬走了。

A: 我也是。

B: 看来中国的大学生活跟美国的大学生活真是大不相同！我很想体验一下中国的大学生活，但是我又担心自己适应不了。

A: 我也是。可能中国学生到了美国也很难适应。不过，现在我觉得这两种情况各有优点。

Background Reading 背景阅读

Living in Dorm 住宿舍

Where a Chinese student might have 3, 5 or even 7 roommates, Americans tend to live with one roommate or in a room by themselves. Americans often change housing three or four times during college, but Chinese students often stay in the same dorm for all four years. Among American students there are different kinds of living arrangements. Some students live on campus all four years; some live in off-campus apartments, and some, though not many, commute from home. Dorms these days are rarely segregated by gender; male and female students may live on different floors, but more commonly they live next door to each other.

中国大学生一般有3或5个甚至7个室友，美国大学生一般只有一个室友或自己住一个房间。上大学的时候，美国学生一般要换三四次宿舍，但是中国学生却4年住在同一个房间里。在美国学生中，也有不一样的住宿安排。一些学生4年都住在学校里，一些学生住在校外的公寓里，还有一些，虽然不太多，住在家里，每天往返于学校和家之间。现在的宿舍已经很少用性别来区分了，男生和女生可能住在一栋楼的不同楼层，住在相邻的宿舍更常见。

Common Rooms 公用房间

Almost all American dormitories have shared kitchens, but students, especially freshmen, don't do much cooking. They mostly use the kitchens to store food in the refrigerator or heat things up in the microwave. College dorms in America also usually have common rooms, which are used by students to study or hang out with their friends. Common rooms often have televisions, and VCRs or DVD players for students to watch movies. Ping-pong tables are another typical feature of common rooms in American dorms, but at Chinese universities ping-pong equipment is usually found in the athletic facilities.

几乎所有的美国大学宿舍都有公用的厨房，但是学生们，尤其是大一新生，很少做饭。他们通常只是用厨房里的冰箱来储存东西或者用微波炉来加热东西。美国的大学宿舍通常也有一些公用的房间，学生们可以在这些房间里学习或者跟朋友一起玩儿。这些公用的房间里一般有电视、录像机或者DVD机，学生们可以用来看电影。这些房间里还有乒乓球桌，这是这些美国大学宿舍公用房间的另外一个特征。但是在中国大学里，乒乓球设备通常在体育馆里才能找到。

Living on Campus 住在校内

If you live on campus, you can easily walk to classes, libraries, computer labs, etc., so you can save time and money on going to and from school. Also, you don't have to cook if you eat at the students' dining hall, and you don't have to worry about monthly rent and utility bills. In addition, living on campus will allow you to meet more people and establish more friendships than if you live off campus. However, the close living space means little privacy; at most colleges, the dorm rooms are tiny and crowded. Also, because dorm life is very social, your grades may be affected in a negative way.

如果你住在校内，你可以很容易走路去上课、去图书馆和计算机房等等，这可以节省上学的路费和时间；你可以在学校食堂吃饭，不用自己做饭，也不需要操心每个月付房租和各种费用；此外，住学校宿舍比在校外租房有更多机会结识他人，成为朋友。但是，非常近的居住空间意味着没有隐私；大部分的大学宿舍都很小很拥挤；还有，因为宿舍生活丰富多彩，所以你的成绩可能会受到负面的影响。

Living off Campus 住在校外

Living off campus will give you more freedom and you don't have to follow the rules of students' dorms; you can have a place to call your own and time to yourself to do your own things. Living off campus will help you be more responsible, you will be in charge of paying bills, cleaning house, grocery shopping, and cooking. However, living off campus could be more expensive, and if you have to drive to campus, traffic can also be an issue. Finally, you may be less involved with campus activities, and this could cause you to feel somewhat detached from your college.

住在校外给你更多的自由，而且你不必遵守宿舍的规定；有空间和时间做自己的事情；会使你更有责任感，因为你得负责付账单、打扫房间、买东西和做饭。但是，住在校外花销更大，如果你开车上学，那么交通费也是一笔花销；你可能不常常参加学校活动，这会使你有远离学校的感觉。

Exercises 练习

Answer these questions.

1. Do you like living alone or with other people? Why?
2. What are the advantages and disadvantages of living on campus vs. off campus?

Translate these sentences into English.

1. 如果一个美国大学让学生跟另外7个人住在一起，学生们肯定气死了。
2. 大部分美国大学生在上大学的头两年都住在宿舍，之后可能搬到校外的公寓或房子里。
3. 我很想体验一下中国的大学生活，但是又担心自己适应不了。
4. 住学校宿舍比在校外租房有更多机会结识他人，成为朋友。
5. 因为宿舍生活丰富多彩，所以你的成绩可能会受到负面的影响。
6. 住在校外给你更多的自由，而且你不必遵守宿舍的规定。

Complete the following paragraph with these words or phrases.

duration commuting arrangements while either vary

__1__ Chinese students usually live in the same room for all four years of university, American students usually change living __2__ each year. Specific living arrangements __3__ from school to school. At some schools almost all students live in campus dorms for the __4__ of their time at the school; at others, students live off campus for all or part of their college years, __5__ renting an apartment or __6__ from home if their parents live near their university.

Answers 答案

Translate these sentences into English.

1. If an American university tried to make its students live in a dorm room with 7 other people, the students would all have a fit!
2. Most American students live in the dorms for their first couple years but then move into an apartment or a house off campus.
3. I would really like to experience Chinese college life, but I'd be worried that I wouldn't be able to adjust.
4. Living on campus will allow you to meet more people and establish more friendships than you could if you live off campus.
5. Because dorm life is very social, your grades may be affected in a negative way.
6. Living off campus will give you more freedom and you won't have to follow the rules of students' dorms.

Complete the following paragraph with these words or phrases.

1. While   2. arrangements   3. vary   4. duration
5. either   6. commuting

词 汇 表

senior
　　　　大四学生
crowded
　　　　拥挤的；挤满的
roommate
　　　　室友；同屋
imagine
　　　　　想像
have a fit
　　　　非常愤怒
interfere
　　　　　干涉
contact with
　　　　与…联系
extremely
　　　　极其；特别
apartment
　　　　　公寓
adjust
　　　　　适应
merit
　　　　优点；长处
commute
　　　　来往；往返
segregate
　　　　分开；隔离
gender
　　　　　性别
store
　　　　　储存
heat
　　　　　加热
athletic
　　　运动的；体育的
establish
　　　　　建立
affect
　　　　　影响
rule
　　　　规则；规定
in charge of
　　　　　负责
expense
　　　　　开销
be involved with
　　　　　参与

39. Dating

爱情篇

Dialogue

A: Fangqi and his girlfriend are so cute! Do you know how long they've been together?

B: Three and a half years. They started dating our second year at university.

A: Wow, that's a long time. Did you have a boyfriend in college?

B: No. There were a couple guys who kind of pursued me but I was never really interested. A lot of my friends never dated in college either. It's much less common for Chinese college students to date than it is for Americans.

A: Why do you think that is?

B: Well for one thing it's strongly discouraged by parents and professors, because it's seen as a distraction from your studies.

A: Do students really care about that?

B: Some do. But another reason people don't date as much is that they approach relationships more seriously—Chinese people our age don't date a different person every six months just for fun, they think of relationships as potentially leading to marriage.

A: Yeah, that's really different from Americans. I mean, I'm not saying we're all a bunch of sluts! I know plenty of people who are in really serious relationships, and lots of people end up marrying someone they met in college. But I think the difference is that Americans don't go into a relationship thinking about marriage until they're older.

B: There are different attitudes about sex, too. Isn't it very common for Americans to sleep with someone they're dating while they're in college?

A: Yeah. There are certainly people who won't have sex even if they're in a serious relationship, but I think that's much more common among Chinese students.

B： There are also lots of external factors in Chinese students' decision not to have sex: their parents would probably get really angry if they found out, and it's also just impossible to get any privacy if you have six roommates.

A： That's for sure! One of my friends said that there are certain places on campus, like an out-of-the-way stairwell, where some students go to make out with their boyfriend or girlfriend.

B： I guess some people are really motivated. . .

A： Of course! Who wouldn't be?

对 话

A： 方起和他的女朋友那么可爱！你知道他们在一起多长时间了吗？

B： 三年半了。他们是从大学二年级开始交往的。

A： 哇，那么长时间。你上大学的时候有男朋友吗？

B： 没有。有几个男孩子追求过我，但是我从来没动过心。我的很多朋友在上大学的时候也没谈过恋爱。在中国，谈恋爱的大学生比在美国少。

A： 你为什么这么想呢？

B： 嗯，一个原因是中国的父母和老师都不鼓励学生谈恋爱，谈恋爱被看作是对学习的分心行为。

A： 学生们真的在乎那些吗？

B： 一些人在乎。但是他们不谈恋爱的另一个原因是他们处理恋爱关系的态度更严肃——像我们一样大的中国人不会只是为了玩一玩而每6个月和不同的人约会，他们认为恋爱关系应该向婚姻的方向发展。

A： 是的，那真是和美国人有很大的差异。我的意思是，我们并不是一些很随便的女孩！我知道很多人都很严肃地对待恋爱关系，而且很多人也都和他们大学时认识的对象结婚了。但是我觉得这个差异是美国人不到一定的年龄是不会为考虑结婚而谈恋爱的。

B： 对待性，他们的态度也不同。对美国人来说，和他们大学时的交往对象上床是很普遍的事情，不是吗？

A： 是的。当然也有人确定关系以后也不会发生性关系，但是我想这种现象在中国学生中更普遍。

B： 中国学生决定不发生性关系还有很多外在的原因：如果父母发现了会非常生气，还有就是如果你有6个同屋的话，那你也没有私人空间做这件事。

A： 那肯定是！我一个朋友说在校园里有一些地方，比如说人少、僻静地方的楼梯间，有很多大学生和他们的男女朋友在那儿接吻。

B： 我觉得有的人真的很想……

A： 当然！谁不想呢？

Background Reading 背景阅读

Male-female Relationships 男女关系

Dating is very common among American college students. However, this does not mean that all young Americans have a casual approach toward sexual activity, as the media sometimes imply, although an estimated 75 per cent of American undergraduates are sexually active.

美国大学的男生和女生交朋友很随便。然而，虽然就像媒体有时候报道的一样，据估计75%的美国大学生都有过性经历，但这并不意味着他们都对性有很随便的想法。

Friendships between members of the opposite sex are also extremely common among American college students; indeed, it is very rare for a student not to have close friends of both sexes. When large groups of students socialize together, there are always both men and women included, and male and female students frequently live together in the same dormitory or off-campus house. While most of these friendships remain platonic, it is not uncommon for friends of the opposite sex to begin dating. Due to the enclosed nature of college life, romantic relationships often form between two people who were already friends, rather than between two people who started dating right after they met.

在美国大学生中，异性间的友谊也很普遍，如果一个学生没有同性和异性的朋友，这的确很少见。很多学生一起玩儿的时候，通常是男女生都有，而且不管是在宿舍里还是在校外租房子，男女生都常常住在一起。他们的关系都是柏拉图式的，但是如果他们开始交往，这也很正常。由于大学生活使他们经常在一起，爱情常常发生在已经是朋友的两个人中间，而不是两个人第一次见面就开始交往。

They do not always clearly define their dating relationships as a monogamous couple relationship, even if they are sexually active together. They might have a friend with whom they have sex even though they are not in a romantic relationship, calling them a "friend with benefits". If asked about their availability for dating, they might say they are "seeing someone"; this vague phrase can mean they are monogamously involved, casually dating a "friend with benefits", or regularly but not exclusively dating someone whom they are not sleeping with. However, there is a lot of diversity among American college students, so there are also many who have more traditional values, and prefer to define their relationships more clearly.

美国学生对"朋友"的概念定义非常广泛。他们不总是把自己的约会对象清楚地定义为一对一的情侣关系，尽管他们已经发生了性关系。在没有爱情的情况下，他们也可能跟一个人发生性关系，他们把这样的朋友称为"有好处的朋友"。当被问及是否有空约会时，美国学生可能会说他们在"见某人"，这是一个模糊的说法：可以指与某个人有认真的专一关系；或者指与一个"有好处的朋友"随便交往；或者在与某人定期约会，但彼此关系并非专一而且也不发生性关系。总之，在美国学生中，有各种各样的情况，也有些人有更传统的价值观，希望把他们的关系定义得更清楚一些。

It is evident that today's young people in China are more open-minded about sex. An online survey indicates that the rate of premarital sex in Guangzhou is as high as 80%, while the rate in Shanghai nears 70%. Chinese people's view on sex is becoming more open, and traditional opinions on virginity and other issues have changed dramatically. A modern, human-oriented view of love and sex is based on what is appropriate for the people involved, and is accepting of diversity. Premarital sex is no longer a no-go zone for students. There are even those that rent apartments off campus specifically to cohabitate. Such cases, while frowned upon by some, are usually open secrets.

在中国，现在年轻人对性的看法明显越来越开放了。一项在线调查显示在广州，发生婚前性行为的比例已高达80%，在上海也将近70%。中国人对性的看法比以前开放了，传统的对贞操的看法和其它的一些观点已经发生了戏剧性的改变。对身处爱河的人来说，现代的、以人为本的对爱和性的看法是最合适的，还有，应该接受爱情的多样化。对学生来说，婚前性行为也不再是不能进入的地带了。有些学生甚至在校外租房，就是为了同居。这样的事情，虽然有些人不赞成，但已经是公开的秘密了。

Exercises 练习

词 汇 表

Answer these questions.
1. Do you think dating in college can influence your studies?
2. Around what age do you think it's appropriate to start dating?
3. Do you support cohabitation before marriage?

Translate these sentences into English.
1. 他们是从大学二年级开始交往的。
2. 有几个男孩子追求过我，但是我从来没动过心。
3. 中国的父母和老师都不鼓励学生上大学时谈恋爱，谈恋爱被看作是对学习的分心行为。
4. 大部分中国人认为恋爱关系应该向婚姻的方向发展。
5. 美国人不到一定的年龄是不会为考虑结婚而谈恋爱的。
6. 美国大学的男生和女生交朋友相当随便。
7. 最合适的看待爱和性的方式就是以人为本。

Complete the following paragraph with these words or phrases.

influenced   premarital sex   increased   punished
forbidden fruit   particularly   traditional

During the first 30 years of the People's Republic, __1__ was a social taboo. Campus sex was __2__ and those students involved in campus sex would be __3__ for immoral behavior and sexual misconduct. Since 1978, however, and __4__ since the 1990s, __5__ Chinese attitudes towards sex have been challenged and __6__ by the West. Sexual relationships among university students have __7__ in recent years.

Answers 答案

Translate these sentences into English.
1. They started dating our second year at university.
2. There were a couple guys who kind of pursued me but I was never really interested.
3. Dating in college is strongly discouraged by parents and professors, because it's seen as a distraction from your studies.
4. Most Chinese think of relationships as potentially leading to marriage.
5. Americans don't go into a relationship thinking about marriage until they're older.
6. Male and female American students associate with each other rather freely.
7. A human-oriented view of love and sex is based on what is appropriate for the people involved.

Complete the following paragraph with these words or phrases.
1. pre-marital sex 2. forbidden fruit 3. punished 4. particularly
5. traditional 6. influenced 7. increased

date
交往
pursue
追求
discourage
劝阻；阻拦
distraction
分心
approach
态度；处理办法
marriage
婚姻
slut
放荡的女子
motivated
有动机的
associate
结交
estimate
估计
be acquainted with
结识
loosely
松散的
be consists of
由…组成
reception
招待会
feature
以…为特征
relatively
相当地；相对地
unlikely
未必的；不大可能
be accustomed to
习惯于
interaction
互动
evident
明显的
premarital
婚前的
virginity
贞操
appropriate
合适的
human-oriented
以人为本
cohabitate
未婚同居

40. Studying Abroad

留学篇

Dialogue

A: Hi! I haven't seen you in ages!

B: I know, I just got back to the States a few weeks ago.

A: You were in China last semester, right?

B: Yeah, I was in Beijing.

A: It must have been incredible... Is it hard being back? I know when I went to Mexico last summer I had a much easier time adjusting to life there than I did readjusting when I got back to the US.

B: This first week of school has been pretty overwhelming, but at the same time I'm excited about this semester. Before I went to China I was getting kind of burnt out—I was sick of reading all the time, and writing papers was such a struggle. But because I was only taking language classes while I was in China, it was a totally different kind of studying, using different skills and a different part of my brain.

A: So even though you were still in school it was like you were taking a break.

B: Exactly. After a while I actually started to miss non-language classes, and reading, and even papers! So now I'm reinvigorated and ready to jump back into the college routine.

A: Did you live with a host family while you were there?

B: No, in my program we lived in a dorm, but we all had Chinese roommates who were students at other universities around Beijing. Cultural immersion is really important, but whether you prefer to live with a family or with other students I think is just a matter of personal opinion. I really enjoyed living in the dorm, because it gave me an opportunity to make lots of Chinese friends of my own age.

A: That sounds like fun. What was your favorite thing to do with your Chinese friends?

B: Definitely karaoke! We'd go in a huge group of twenty or thirty people and rent a room and sing until the wee hours of the morning.

A: Did you sing songs in English or Chinese?

B: Some of both. But it was educational, too—learning how to sing songs is actually a really good way to learn a language! And karaoke makes it easier because you can read the characters at the same time.

A: Haha, you should've asked for extra credit! But overall, are you glad you decided to spend a semester abroad? Would you recommend studying abroad to other students?

B: Absolutely. Even though I missed out on things here while I was gone, spending a semester in China was a once-in-a-lifetime experience.

A: Sure sounds like it. But it's nice to have you back.

B: Yeah, reuniting with all my friends makes me happy to be back too.

对 话

A: 嗨！好久不见了！

B: 我知道，我刚回美国几个星期。

A: 上个学期你在中国，对吧？

B: 对，我在北京。

A: 真让人难以置信……回来以后很难适应吧？去年夏天我去墨西哥的时候很快就适应了，但回美国以后却很难适应。

B: 回学校的第一个星期真的感觉很不同，但是同时对于这个学期我也感到很兴奋。我去中国之前，真是累死了——我一直不喜欢阅读，还有写文章，简直就是挣扎。但是因为我在中国只学语言，和我以前是完全不一样的学习，用不一样的学习方法，而且用我大脑的另一部分。

A: 所以尽管你还在学校，但是觉得好像放假一样。

B: 没错。过了一段时间，我开始想念那些非语言的课程，还有阅读、甚至写论文！所以现在我又有精力回到这些大学的常规课程上来了。

A: 你在那儿的时候住在中国人家里吗？

B: 不，根据我的项目，我们住宿舍，但是我们都有中国同屋，他们都是北京另一些大学的学生。沉浸在当地的文化之中非常重要，不过不管和一个家庭一起住还是和别的学生一起住，我觉得只是个人观点的不同。我很喜欢住宿舍，因为这样我有机会交到和我年龄差不多的中国朋友。

A: 听起来很有意思。你和中国朋友在一起的时候，最喜欢做什么？

B: 当然是唱卡拉OK！我们常常是二三十人一起去，包一个房间，一直唱到早上。

A: 你们唱英文歌还是中文歌？

B: 都唱一些。这也是一种学习——学唱歌实际上是学习语言的一个很好的办法！而且唱卡拉OK使学汉语更容易，因为你可以同时看汉字。

A: 哈哈，你该多向老师要几个学分的。但是总的来说，你决定出去过一个学期，你高兴吗？你会向其他学生推荐出国留学吗？

B: 当然。尽管我不在的时候错过了一些东西，但是在中国度过一个学期是一生中只有一次的经历。

A: 当然是。但是很高兴你回来了。

B: 是的，和朋友重新聚在一起也让我觉得回来很高兴。

Background Reading 背景阅读

Why Study Abroad? 为什么要留学？

Learn a Language 学习一种语言

In today's ever more interconnected and globalized world, being able to speak multiple languages is an extremely valuable skill. The best (and easiest, and most fun) way to learn a language is to go to the country where it's spoken. What might take you years of study to learn in your home country, you can learn in one semester in the country where it's the native tongue. Even more importantly, while you can learn a lot from books, you can never really learn the way people authentically speak until you are immersed in the language environment. Finally, the key to learning a language is practice: speaking it all the time, and in lots of different contexts. This is impossible to do in your home country, but it's almost impossible to avoid when you're abroad!

在今天这个联系更紧密、更全球化的世界，能讲多种语言是极有价值的技能。学习语言的最好的（也是最容易的、最有意思的）办法就是去讲那种语言的国家。在你自己的国家可能要花几年才能学到的东西，在那个母语国家花一个学期就能学到。更重要的是，尽管你能从书本上学到语言，但是直到你沉浸在语言环境中时，你才能真正学到人们是怎么说话的。最后，学习语言的关键是练习：一直说，而且在不同的情景中说。这在你自己的国家几乎是不可能的，但是当你在国外的时候却是不可避免的。

Learn About a Different Culture 了解不同的文化

Even in the 21st century, when some things like MacDonald's and Starbucks can be found anywhere in the world, there are still millions of ways that every culture is unique. Studying abroad is a great way to experience some of these things, from language, to food, to history, to music and dance. By learning to cook or to play a foreign instrument you can even bring some of the foreign culture home with you.

尽管是在21世纪，像麦当劳和星巴克一样的东西在世界各地都能找到，但是每种文化还都有它的独特之处。留学就是去经历这些独到之处的一种很好的方式，从语言到食物、历史、音乐和舞蹈。通过学习烹饪和一种外国的乐器，你甚至可以把外国的文化带回家去。

Gain a New Perspective on Your Home Country 从一个新的视角审视你的祖国

Students studying abroad will constantly be asked about their home country, and often asked to defend it. Comparing cultures and trying to explain your home country to people who have never been there can show you things you never thought of before about yourself and where you come from. You also get an intimate perspective on how your country is viewed by others, including the ways it is idealized, criticized or just plain misunderstood.

留学生经常会被问到关于自己国家的事情，而且经常得为自己的国家辩护。比较文化和试着向从来没去过那儿的人们描述你的祖国可以告诉你一些你从来没想过的关于你自己和你的国家的事情。你也可以知道别人如何看待你的国家，包括被理想化的、被批评的或者就是一般被误解的。

Different Opportunities 不同的机会

Students from different countries have different opportunities for studying abroad. American and European students generally have the most freedom, financially and with respect to visas, to study wherever they choose. However, not all students around the world are in the same situation. Many students from developing countries wish to study abroad because the quality or diversity of higher education may be better in another country. However, it is precisely these students who face the biggest barriers to study abroad, such as travel restrictions from their home country or the country they wish to visit, or prohibitive cost.

来自不同国家的学生有不同的留学机会。美国人和欧洲人一般有最大的自由，在经济上和签证上都没问题，他们可以随便选择去哪儿留学。然而，并不是世界上所有的学生都是这样的。很多来自发展中国家的学生希望能出国留学，因为别的国家高等教育的质量或多样性可能更好。然而，恰恰就是这些学生，面临着出国留学的最大障碍，比如说，来自祖国或者他们想去的国家的旅行限制或者承担不起的费用。

Exercises 练习

Answer these questions.

1. What are the academic advantages of studying abroad?
2. What are the non-academic advantages of studying abroad?
3. Why is it easier to learn a language by studying abroad?

Translate these sentences into English.

1. 我一直不喜欢阅读，还有写文章，简直就是挣扎。
2. 沉浸在当地的文化之中对学习一种语言非常重要。
3. 学唱歌实际上是学习语言的一个很好的办法。
4. 在中国度过一个学期是一生中只有一次的经历。
5. 学习语言的最好的（也是最容易的、最有意思的）办法就是去讲那种语言的国家。
6. 直到你沉浸在语言环境中时，你才能真正学到人们是怎么说话的。
7. 留学生经常会被问到关于自己国家的事情。

Complete the following paragraph with these words or phrases.

approaching report worldview focus refreshed energy

Many students who have studied abroad __1__ that they come back feeling __2__ and invigorated from their experience, __3__ their remaining studies with new __4__ and a broadened __5__ . They may develop new academic interests, change directions or bring a new __6__ to their studies and their lives.

 Answers 答案

Translate these sentences into English.

1. I was sick of reading all the time, and writing papers was such a struggle.
2. Cultural immersion is really important for learning a language.
3. Learning how to sing songs is actually a really good way to learn a language.
4. Spending a semester in China was a once-in-a-lifetime experience.
5. The best (and easiest, and most fun) way to learn a language is to go to the country where it's spoken.
6. You can never really learn the way people authentically speak until you are immersed in the language environment.
7. Students studying abroad will constantly be asked about their home country.

Complete the following paragraph with these words or phrases.

1. report 2. refreshed 3. approaching 4. energy
5. worldview 6. focus

词汇表

ages	
	很长一段时间
semester	
	学期
adjust	
	适应
burn out	
	精力耗尽
be sick of...	
	对…厌倦
struggle	
	挣扎；搏斗
skill	
	技能；技巧
brain	
	大脑
take a break	
	休息
reinvigorated	
	使恢复精力
routine	
	常规；惯例
immersion	
	沉浸
credit	
	学分
overall	
	总的来说
recommend	
	推荐
reunite	
	重新相聚
globalized	
	全球化的
multiple	
	多种的
authentically	
	真正地
context	
	情景；上下文
unique	
	独特的
intimate	
	个人的；私人的
with respect to	
	关于
prohibitive	
	禁止的；抑制的

41. Dining Out

外出就餐

A: Can you believe it's already been 6 months since I came to China?

B: Really? Time flies!

A: I know, it seems like just yesterday I was wandering around in a daze because everything was so different and unfamiliar—even little things, like going out to a restaurant for dinner.

B: How's that so different from in America?

A: Oh, there are a million little differences. Like in the US, everyone orders their own dish, but in China one person orders a bunch of dishes for the table and then everyone shares. Of course it partly has to do with the different ways of preparing food: Chinese food is all prepared by cutting everything into small pieces, so it's easy to share.

B: So which way to you like better?

A: I like the Chinese way better, because you get to try a little bit of a lot of different things. Also, if you're eating at a Western restaurant and you don't end up liking what you ordered then you're stuck, but at a Chinese restaurant if you don't like one of the dishes there are always plenty of other ones to choose from.

B: You know what else is different? I've heard that Americans like to split the bill evenly, but in China one person takes care of the whole bill, and then the other people return the favor the next time.

A: That's true: if there are a lot of people, Americans always split the bill. But if it's a smaller group, like two friends or two families, it's not uncommon for one person to offer to treat. But the other person always tries to refuse the offer and pay the bill themselves, just like in China.

B: Are there other situations where Americans don't split the bill?

A: Definitely! One situation where Americans almost never split the bill is if they're out on a date. Then the guy usually pays, especially if they don't know each other very well yet. In fact, if it's the first or second date, and the guy doesn't offer to treat or the girl wants to split the check, he or she is kind of sending a signal that they don't consider it a romantic date, and they just want to be friends.

B: That's so interesting! But all this talk of going out to eat is making me hungry! Do you want to go get lunch?

A: Sure! But only if you let me treat!

B: Haha, ok!

对 话

A: 你能相信吗? 我来中国已经6个月了。

B: 真的吗? 时光飞逝啊!

A: 对啊, 好像昨天我还茫然地在街上徘徊, 因为所有的东西对我来说都是不同的和不熟悉的——甚至非常小的事情, 比如说去饭馆吃饭。

B: 在中国饭馆吃饭和在美国饭馆吃饭有多么不同呢?

A: 哦, 那些细微的差别多得数不过来。比如说, 在美国, 每个人点自己的菜, 但是在中国, 一个人为吃饭的所有人点很多菜, 然后大家一起吃。当然这和两个国家准备食物的方式不同有关: 中国菜都是被切成小小的部分, 所以大家很容易一起分食。

B: 那么你觉得哪种方式更好?

A: 我喜欢中国的方式, 因为不同的菜你每一样都可以尝到一点儿。还有, 如果你在一个西餐馆吃饭, 如果你不喜欢吃自己点的菜, 你就没办法, 但是在中国饭馆吃饭, 如果你不喜欢某一个菜, 你还可以吃别的菜。

B: 你还知道别的不同吗? 我听说美国人喜欢平均分摊账单, 但在中国, 常常是一个人付所有的钱, 然后下次可能是别的人请客来回报他的好意。

A: 是真的: 如果很多人一起吃饭, 美国人常常分摊账单。但是如果吃饭的人很少, 比如说两个朋友或两个家庭, 一方要请客也不奇怪。但是另一方通常会拒绝, 然后自己付钱, 就像在中国一样。

B: 还有别的情况吗?

A: 有啊! 美国人从来不分摊账单的唯一情况就是约会的时候, 这时候通常由男方付钱, 尤其是他们还不太了解对方的时候。事实上, 如果是第一次或第二次约会, 如果男方不为女方付钱或者女方想要分摊账单, 那他们实际上是在传递一种信号: 他们不觉得这是一个浪漫的约会, 他们只是想做朋友而已。

B: 太有意思了! 我们聊的都是和吃饭有关的话题, 都让我觉得饿了。你想去吃午饭吗?

A: 当然, 但是你得让我请客!

B: 哈哈, 好吧!

Background Reading 背景阅读

What's on the Table 桌上的东西

Eating is a huge part of culture, and there are endless differences in how people around the world take their meals. One set of differences between restaurants in China and the US is simply what's on the table. In China, common things to be found on the table are vinegar, chili oil, and soy sauce. In the US, all restaurants have salt and pepper at each table, and some also have sugar or ketchup. Large tables at Chinese restaurants will have a "Lazy Susan" (a circular piece of glass that rotates) to make it easier to pass dishes around a crowded table. American restaurants never have Lazy Susans, because food is seldom shared. Many Chinese restaurants have ashtrays on the table, as do some in the US, but in the UK and several states in the US it is illegal to smoke in restaurants.

吃是文化中很大的一个部分，世界各国的人们在吃饭上有数不过来的不同。美国饭馆和中国饭馆之间许多不同中的一个方面就是桌子上放的东西。在中国，一般在桌子上你会发现醋、辣椒油和酱油。在美国，所有的饭馆都有盐和辣椒粉，一些饭馆有糖和番茄酱。中国饭馆里的大桌子上会有转盘，这样菜可以方便地转到每个客人的面前。美国的饭馆从来没有这样的转盘，因为食物常常不会被共享。很多中国饭馆的桌子上有烟灰缸，有的美国饭馆也有，但是在英国和美国的一些州，在饭馆里吸烟是违法的。

Differences in Service 服务的不同

In China, waiters and waitresses will stand beside your table until you're ready to order, while in the US, they'll give you the menu and then come back a few minutes later to take your order. If you need something from the server in a Chinese restaurant, you simply call out to her and she'll come over. In the US, however, calling a server loudly is considered impolite, so you should wait until she comes near your table to catch her eye or call her more quietly. Servers in American restaurants will usually periodically come around to each of their tables to check if anyone needs anything. In the US, your server will wait until they see that you've finished your meal, and then they'll bring the check. It's also perfectly acceptable to ask them to bring the check. In China, on the other hand, the server will always wait until you ask them to bring the check.

在中国，服务员会一直站在桌边等着你开始点菜，但是在美国，他们会先给你菜单，然后离开一会儿，再回来为你点菜。在中国饭馆，如果你需要服务，你直接喊服务员就行了，然后他就会过来。但是在美国，大声地喊服务员被认为是不礼貌的，所以你应该等他走到你桌子的附近，给他一个眼神或者轻轻地叫他一下。美国饭馆的服务员会在他服务的几个桌子附近来回走动，以备客人有需要。在美国，服务员会等到你们吃完饭，然后给你们出示账单，让服务员拿账单过来也是完全可以的。而在中国，服务员通常要等你叫他，他才会来结账。

Dessert 甜点

Dessert is not part of a traditional Chinese meal. As a result of the influence of Western culture, the custom of eating something sweet at the end of a meal is starting to gain a little bit of popularity, but restaurants will usually offer fresh fruit rather than pastries. Western-style sweets are very popular in China, but they are very rarely eaten in restaurants. Chinese cuisine has traditionally included sweets, but there is not such a strong distinction between these foods and more savory dishes, like there is in the West. Still, even though Americans and other Westerners enjoy eating dessert, most people don't have dessert with every meal. In America eating dessert is more common at restaurants or on special occasions; most Americans don't usually have dessert at home.

甜点并不是中国传统食物里的一部分，受西方文化的影响，在饭后吃一点儿甜的东西也开始流行起来，但是饭店常常提供给客人新鲜的水果，而不是甜点。西方的甜点在中国很流行，但是却很少在饭馆里吃。中式烹饪里本来有甜食，但是甜品和不甜的食物并没有像西方那样大的区别。还有，虽然美国人和其他西方人喜欢吃甜点，但是大部分人并不是每顿饭都吃甜点。在美国，在饭馆里或特别的场合吃甜点更常见，美国人一般不在家里吃甜点。

Exercises 练习

Answer these questions.

1. What is a "Lazy Susan"?
2. When Americans go out to eat together, how do they usually pay?
3. When Chinese people go out to eat with friends, how do they usually pay?

Translate these sentences into English.

1. 在中国，饭后吃一点儿甜的东西也开始流行起来。
2. 在一些国家，在饭馆里吸烟是违法的。
3. 在美国，大声地喊服务员被认为是不礼貌的。
4. 在美国，每个人点自己的菜，但是在中国，一个人为吃饭的所有人点很多菜，然后大家一起吃。
5. 如果很多人一起吃饭，美国人常常分摊账单。
6. 美国人从来不分摊账单的唯一情况就是约会的时候，这时候通常由男方付钱。
7. 我点了几个开胃菜。

Complete the following paragraph with these words or phrases.

leftovers extra opinion waste feed imply enough

In China, taking the __1__ home from a restaurant (also called taking a "doggie bag") has in the past had a bit of a stigma, because it seems to __2__ that the person taking the food doesn't have __3__ at home to eat. However, for many people this view has been replaced by the __4__ (shared by most Americans) that it's better for the __5__ food not to go to __6__, even if you're just going to __7__ it to your dog.

 Answers 答案

Translate these sentences into English.

1. Eating something sweet at the end of a meal is starting to gain a little bit of popularity in China.
2. It is illegal to smoke in restaurants in some countries.
3. In the US, calling a server loudly is considered impolite.
4. In the US, everyone orders their own dish, but in China one person orders a bunch of dishes for the table and then everyone shares.
5. If there are a lot of people, Americans almost always split the bill.
6. The only time when Americans almost never split the bill is if they're out on a date, and then the guy usually pays.
7. I ordered a few appetizers.

Complete the following paragraph with these words or phrases.

1. leftovers 2. imply 3. enough 4. opinion
5. extra 6. waste 7. feed

词 汇 表

wander	漫步；闲逛
in a daze	茫然，迷乱
unfamiliar	不熟悉的
order	点菜
split	均分；分摊
favor	好意
treat	请客
refuse	拒绝
on a date	约会
signal	信号
endless	无尽的
vinegar	醋
chili oil	辣椒油
soy sauce	酱油
ketchup	番茄酱
seldom	几乎不
ashtray	烟灰缸
perfectly	完全地
acceptable	可接受的
dessert	甜点
influence	影响
cuisine	烹饪；烹饪法
distinction	区别
savory	咸味的
occasions	场合；时刻

165

42. Table Manners and Diet Customs

餐桌礼仪和饮食习俗

Dialogue

A: Last week I went as a guest to a Chinese friend's house, it was really an interesting experience. I felt a little bit of culture shock.

B: Really? So you discovered a few of China and America's different customs?

A: Definitely. First, Chinese and Americans have very different ways of accepting gifts. When I went to their house, I brought a bottle of wine as a small gift. I had originally thought we would drink it together as we ate, so I was surprised when the host put it aside and didn't open it. I really didn't understand, but I didn't say anything.

B: You shouldn't have worried, that's just the way Chinese people accept gifts—it's considered impolite to open something right when you receive it. The way Chinese people see it, opening a gift on the same occasion that you receive it seems to imply that you only want to see whether the gift is good or bad, and you don't care about the thought your friend put into it.

A: Oh, really? I guess it was just a misunderstanding then. Americans almost always open a gift right away, because then they can say something nice to show that they like what the person gave them.

B: When you were having dinner, did they keep encouraging you to eat and drink?

A: Yes! They were always saying, "Eat some more, take a bit more," and the moment there was a bit of space in my bowl, they immediately gave me another helping. That day I had four bowls of rice, ate I-don't-know-how-much food I ate so much I couldn't walk a straight line. In America, the host won't urge the guest to eat and drink more. The guest just eats however much they want to eat.

B: That's the Chinese way of being friendly and welcoming to one's guests. For Chinese people, making sure the guest eats their fill and eats well is the most important thing.

A: Also, they set out this an incredibly abundant table of food, but then they said, "There's nothing here to eat, it wasn't prepared very well" and other things like that. This seemed

166

even stranger to me. If they had prepared well, then how many dishes would they have had?

B: Haha, they were just being modest. Even if they had prepared more, they still would have said that. And Chinese hosts will always prepare a whole lot of dishes, because if there were a more meager selection the host would feel that he had lost face. Preparing a huge feast is a way of showing your respect for your guest.

A: Oh, Chinese customs are so complicated! I would never have understood if you hadn't told me.

B: Every culture has its own particular ways of doing things, though. There are some Western customs that Chinese people think are hard to understand.

A: I guess what I've learned is that when you study a language, you also have to understand the culture that's behind it, because otherwise it's easy to create misunderstandings and miscommunications.

B: I agree.

对 话

A: 上个周末，我去了一个中国朋友家做客，这真是一次很有意思的经历。我感受到了文化碰撞。

B: 是吗？你一定发现了很多中国和美国习俗的不同吧？

A: 当然，首先，在接受礼物方面，中国人和美国人的做法就很不同，我去他们家的时候，准备了一个小礼物，是一瓶葡萄酒，本来想我们吃饭的时候一起喝，可是没想到，主人却没有打开，而是把它放到了一边。我很不理解，但是我什么都没说。

B: 你不应该担心，那就是中国人接受礼物的方式——接受礼物就当场打开是不礼貌的。中国人认为，接受礼物当场打开意味着你只是想看看礼物好不好，而不在乎你朋友的心意。

A: 真的吗？我差点儿误会了。美国人收到礼物时一定要当场打开，还要赞扬一下以表示他们很喜欢这个礼物。

B: 吃饭的时候，他们有没有对你劝吃劝喝？

A: 当然有了，他们一直都说"多吃点儿、再来点儿"，而且只要看见我的碗里有一点儿空，就马上给我添饭夹菜，所以我那天吃了4碗米饭，不知道吃了多少菜，后来撑得我都走不动路了。在美国，主人从来不劝吃劝喝，客人能吃多少就吃多少。

B: 那就是中国人对客人表示友好和欢迎的方式，他们始终觉得让客人多吃、吃好是最重要的。

A: 还有，他们明明做了一桌子的饭菜，特别丰盛，可是他们却说"没什么可吃的，准备得不太好"之类的话，这让我觉得更奇怪了，如果他们准备得好，那会有多少菜啊？

B: 哈哈，那是中国人谦虚的表现，即使他们准备得更多、更丰盛，他们也会这样说的。还有，中国的主人们通常会准备一桌子菜，如果饭菜不丰盛，主人会觉得丢面子。准备丰盛的饭菜表示对客人的尊重。

A: 哦，中国习俗这么复杂啊，你要是不说，我永远都不懂。

B: 每种文化都有特别的地方。其实，有一些西方的习俗，中国人也觉得不容易理解。

A: 我觉得我从中学到的就是，学习一门语言，必须还得了解那个民族的文化，要不然就容易产生误会，导致交际的失败。

B: 我同意。

Background Reading 背景阅读

Different Diet Customs 不同的饮食习俗

Many people say that China is a food culture, that is, one that really emphasizes and pays a lot of attention to the customs surrounding eating and food. Chinese people, then, sometimes mistake the lack of similar customs in America for coldness or lack of hospitality. However, it only indicates that Americans show hospitality and caring in other ways. American Southerners are famous for their hospitality. Many of their customs surrounding eating are similar to those of China. The host will often urge the guest to eat and drink more, and apologize for the inadequacy of the dishes served. Chinese and American hosts may serve different dishes, but they practice many of the same customs for many of the same reasons—to express warmth and kindness.

很多人都说中国是一个饮食文化，就是中国人太强调和重视和吃饭及食物有关系的习俗了。因此，有时候中国人会因为中国和美国习俗的差异而误解美国人，认为他们待人冷漠、不够好客。然而，这只表明了美国人以不同的方式表现他们的好客和关心。美国南方人也以好客而闻名。他们的很多和吃有关的习俗和中国很相似。主人会经常劝客人多吃多喝，并且还会为饭菜准备得不周到而道歉。中国和美国的主人准备的饭菜可能不一样，但他们遵从不同的习俗都是出于同一个原因——为了表达热情和好意。

Customs surrounding dining vary throughout the United States like they vary in China. America is a nation of diverse cultural backgrounds, so customs vary from person to person, household to household. For example, many people in the southwest and in big cities in the US are of Mexican descent, and they follow customs that are sometimes very different from the customs of Americans of European descent. Sometimes inviting a person to dinner can be a very casual affair, and sometimes it can be very formal. A good rule of thumb is to ask the host before the dinner about the level of formality and if you should bring anything. Instead of bringing a gift, a good guest usually brings something to contribute to the meal, like a bottle of wine.

就像在中国一样，美国各地的饮食习俗也不尽相同。美国是一个有着多种文化背景的国家，所以人和人之间、家庭和家庭之间的习惯都不一样。比如说，美国西南部和一些大城市的很多人都是墨西哥后裔，他们的风俗和欧洲裔美国人的风俗就不一样。请一个人来吃晚饭有时候是件很随便的事情，有时候也可能很正式。一个人人都说好的办法是在去吃饭以前问问主人这顿饭的正式程度以及需不需要带什么东西。一个好客人通常会为这顿饭准备些东西，比方说带一瓶酒，而不是礼物。

There are many differences in drinking culture between China and the US. Bars and pubs have been part of Western culture in some form or another for hundreds and hundreds of years, but they are a very recent phenomenon in China. In China, alcohol is consumed mostly at restaurants while eating dinner, and rather than sipping a little at a time like Americans usually do, there will be a series of toasts in which everyone is expected to drain their glass. Still, Western-style bars and clubs are becoming more common in China, although mostly in the biggest cities, like Beijing and Shanghai. In addition to foreigners, their customers include an increasing number of young Chinese.

在喝酒文化方面，中国和美国有很多的不同。几百年来，酒吧和小酒馆在某些方面一直都是西方文化的一部分，但是在中国是最近才有的现象。在中国，大部分人是在饭馆吃饭的时候喝酒，而且不像美国人那样小口小口地喝，他们会不断地敬酒，每个人都得干杯。然而，西式的酒吧和俱乐部在中国越来越普遍了，虽然大部分在大城市里，比如北京和上海。酒吧的客人除了外国人以外，还有越来越多的中国年轻人。

In many American restaurants, there are free refills for many drinks, such as soda, coffee and iced tea. It is the waiter's job to make sure patrons' glasses stay filled. Because it is customary in America to tip waiters or waitresses in restaurants, they have an incentive to make sure restaurant patrons are never without their drinks. But at home, when Americans have guests over for dinner, it is more common for people to serve themselves, though it varies from person to person and depends on the situation.

在很多美国饭馆，很多饮料比如说苏打水、咖啡和冰茶都可以免费续杯。确定客人们的杯子是满的是服务员的工作。因为在美国饭馆，客人通常都会给服务员小费，所以他们有动力确保客人们的杯子总是有喝的。但是美国人在家里请客的时候，客人们自己动手是更常见的，当然人和人不一样，每次的具体情况也不一样。

168

Exercises 练习

Answer these questions.
1. Have you ever experienced culture shock?
2. What do Chinese usually do when they accept gifts?
3. What do Westerners usually do when they accept gifts?

Translate these sentences into English.
1. 美国南方人以好客而闻名。
2. 各个地方的餐桌礼仪和饮食习俗都不一样，但是有一些东西是普遍的。
3. 中国人常常在自己吃之前先给别人加菜，这是为了表示对别人的尊重和关心。
4. 许多主人都会劝客人多吃、多喝以表示他们的好客。
5. 中国人喝酒时会不断地敬酒，每个人都得干杯。
6. 请一个人来吃晚饭有时候是件很随便的事情，有时候也可能很正式。

Complete the following paragraph with these words or phrases.

| display situations especially universal compliment |
| interact stressful |

There are certain __1__ in which going to someone's house for dinner can be a __2__ affair, __3__ if one is unsure of the host's customs and how to __4__ with him or her. But your best bet is to sit back and relax—dinner should be fun! Most customs are __5__ : the host will find a way to __6__ warmth and hospitality while the guest should find a way to __7__ the food and atmosphere.

 Answers 答案

Translate these sentences into English.
1. Americans from the south are famous for their hospitality.
2. Dining etiquette and customs surrounding eating vary from place to place, but some things are universal.
3. Chinese people often serve others before themselves to show respect and concern for others.
4. Many hosts will express their hospitality by urging their guests to eat and drink more.
5. When Chinese people are drinking, there is usually a series of toasts in which everyone is expected to drain their glass.
6. Sometimes inviting a person to dinner can be a very casual affair, and sometimes it can be very formal.

Complete the following paragraph with these words or phrases.
1. situations 2. stressful 3. especially 4. interact
5. universal 6. display 7. compliment

词 汇 表

culture shock
      文化碰撞
originally
      本来
occasion
      时刻
misunderstand
      误会
incredibly
      难以相信地
abundant
      丰盛的；充裕的
modesty
      谦虚
surrounding
      周围的
lack
      缺少
hospitality
      好客
urge
      劝；激励
inadequacy
      不够；不充足
warmth
      热情
decent
      子孙；后裔
diverse
      各种各样的
household
      一家人
casual
      随意的
sip
      小口地喝
toast
      敬酒
drain
      使…干涸
refill
      续杯；再添满
patron
      客人；主顾
customary
      习惯的
incentive
      动力

43. To Tip or not to Tip?

小费，给还是不给？

Dialogue

A: I've been in China for a month now, but I'm still not used to not tipping at restaurants.

B: I don't really understand the point of tipping, I mean, don't restaurants in the US pay their servers?

A: Of course they do, but the legal minimum wage for servers and bartenders is much lower than for everyone else, so most of their income actually comes from tips, not from their paycheck. It's a chicken-and-egg situation, though: the minimum wage is lower because the government assumes that servers earn money from tips.

B: Then why don't they just raise the minimum wage and then people wouldn't have to tip anymore?

A: The reason people tip isn't really because they know their waitress is badly paid, it's more like a way of saying thank you to her for doing a good job.

B: Do you tip more or less depending on how good of a waitress she is?

A: Well, the standard is 15 − 20%. Some people are jerks and they always tip less, no matter how good the service was. I've worked as a waitress, so I always tip more. Even if the service was bad I'll still tip 20%. There's only one time I've ever tipped less than 15%, and that time the service was so bad I actually asked to speak to the manager.

B: Having lived in both China and the US, which do you like better, tipping or not tipping?

A: I guess it makes it a little bit cheaper to go out to eat if you don't have to tip, but also I know how hard servers work so I like to be able to express my appreciation by leaving a tip.

B: What about as a server: would you rather work for tips, or have a higher hourly wage?

A: Working for tips is definitely less stable, but usually in the end you earn more than the restaurant could afford to pay you. Also, working a Friday or Saturday night shift kind of sucks for your social life, but those are usually the busiest shifts, so you make the most money. It's a tradeoff.

B: It's probably better for the customer, too, because the waiter has an incentive to give good service.

A: Definitely, but whether you'll get rewarded for working hard is unpredictable. You have good nights and you have bad nights, but when someone leaves you a really great tip it really makes you feel good, like they liked you and really appreciated how hard you're working.

B: Ok, if I go to America I'll be sure to remember to tip well!

对 话

A: 我来中国已经一个月了，但是我还是不习惯在饭馆里不给小费。

B: 我不太明白为什么要给小费，我的意思是难道在美国，饭馆不给服务员工资吗？

A: 当然给，但是法律规定的服务员和酒吧侍者的底薪比其它的工作低很多，所以他们大部分的收入要靠小费，而不是薪水。这好比先有鸡还是先有蛋的情况，服务员的底薪很低是因为政府认为他们可以从小费中得到收入。

B: 那为什么政府不提高底薪，这样人们就不用再付小费了。

A: 其实人们付小费的真正原因并不是他们觉得服务员的待遇不好，付小费其实是对她的优质服务表达谢意的一种方式。

B: 那小费的多少是取决于服务的好坏吗？

A: 嗯，一般是 15% 到 20%。但也有一些"奇怪"的人不管服务多好，总是给很少的小费。我以前做过服务员，所以我给小费给得比较多。即使有时候服务不太好，我也会付 20%。只有一次我付了不到 15%，那次的服务太差了以至于我不得不向经理投诉。

B: 在中国和美国生活过以后，给小费和不给小费你更喜欢哪种？

A: 我觉得如果去外面吃饭不用付小费的话会更便宜，但是我也知道服务员的工作很辛苦，所以我想用付小费的方式来表达对他们的谢意。

B: 那站在服务员的角度：你更愿意靠小费赚钱还是拿更高的小时薪金？

A: 靠小费赚钱不稳定，但是赚得通常会比饭馆能给你的多。另外，在星期五或星期六上晚班你可能就没有时间进行社交活动，但通常那是最忙碌的时间，所以最赚钱。有得必有失。

B: 付小费对消费者来说也比较好，因为这会刺激服务员给顾客更好的服务。

A: 当然，但是你服务得好是不是就能真的得到回报是不可预测的。有的晚上你可能收入不错，有的晚上则可能收入很少，但是当有人给你一大笔小费的时候那种感觉真的很好，那表示他们喜欢你，而且十分感谢你的辛苦工作。

B: 好的，如果我去美国的话我一定会记得要多给小费。

Background Reading　背景阅读

Tipping in the US：Restaurants　在美国付小费：饭馆

There are many different situations in the US where a tip is expected, and the same rules don't always apply. In restaurants, tipping 15 −20% is the norm. Most restaurants reserve the right to add a mandatory 15 −20% gratuity on the bill for parties of 8 or more people. If it is a restaurant where you order at the counter, there is often a tip jar, but tipping is optional. If you tip in this situation or when ordering takeout, you usually leave just a dollar or two, rather than a percentage of the bill. However, if you get food delivered to your house it's customary to tip the delivery person.

在美国，付小费有很多不同的情况，而且一样的原则并不适用于所有的情况。在饭馆，通常付15% 到 20% 的小费。当一起就餐的人数是8 人或多于8 人的时候，大多数餐厅会保留强制性地多加15% 到 20% 小费的权利。如果是在你自己在柜台点餐的餐厅，他们常常在柜台有一个小费瓶，你可以选择付或不付。在这种情况下，如果是点餐带走，你可以只留一两美元作小费，而不是根据账单的百分比付。但是，如果你要外卖送到家里，通常就要给送餐的人小费。

Tipping in the US：Bars and Coffee Shops　在美国付小费：酒吧和咖啡馆

The standard tip in bars and clubs is ＄1. 00 per drink, but will often be less if you order more than one drink at a time (＄2. 00 for three drinks, for example). You can also run up a tab on your credit card and then tip 15% on the final amount. Coffee shops often have tip jars on the counter. Tipping is optional and the amount varies; many people will just put their coin change in the tip jar.

在酒吧和俱乐部付小费的标准是每份饮品1 美元，但是如果你一次点超过一份饮品时，常常会给得少一些（比如三份饮料给2 美元）。你也可以在你的信用卡上记账，然后付账单的15% 作小费。在咖啡馆的柜台上常常有一个小费瓶。你可以选择付不付小费，以及付多少；很多人只是在小费瓶里放一些零钱。

Tipping in the US：Other Situations　在美国付小费：其它情况

Taxi drivers in the US usually expect a tip of about 15% , but tipping isn't mandatory like it is in restaurants. It is also polite, but not mandatory, to tip barbers and hairdressers. Upscale hotels have bellboys who will help you with your luggage; it is customary to give them a few dollars' tip, and often they will wait in your room for a few extra minutes if you do not tip them right away. Many people also give a yearly tip or "Christmas bonus" to certain people during the holiday season. This can include maids, newspaper and mail carriers, or building superintendents and doormen for people who live in a large apartment building.

在美国出租车司机通常会收15% 的小费，但是并不像在饭馆里一样有强制性的。同样，给理发师小费也是出于礼貌而不是必须的。较好的宾馆会有门童，他们帮你提行李；我们习惯付给他们几美元的小费，而且如果你不立刻付小费的话他们通常会在你的房间多等几分钟。很多人也会每年在节日期间给一些人小费，或者"圣诞节奖金"，包括女佣、报童、邮差、公寓大楼的物业管理员和门卫。

Tipping in Europe　在欧洲付小费

The customs related to tipping in Europe vary from country to country. In France, restaurants always include a service charge in the bill, although people will sometimes tip a little extra on top. Tipping is not the custom in Spain and it is almost never done. Service workers in Germany don't depend on tips for their income as they do in the US, but it is still customary to tip 5 −10% for satisfactory service. Tipping throughout the UK is strictly optional. Tipping restaurant employees, hairdressers and taxi drivers is polite, but not expected. Some restaurants add a 10% service charge, and in bars and pubs the patron will sometimes offer to buy the bartender a drink instead of giving a cash tip.

在欧洲，各个国家付小费的习惯不一样。在法国，饭馆的账单里常常包含服务费，但是有时候人们除了服务费以外还会再多付一些小费。在西班牙没有付小费的习惯，人们几乎从来不付小费。德国的服务员不像美国的服务员一样靠小费赚钱，但是人们如果对服务满意的话通常会付5% 到10% 的小费。在英国，付不付小费是完全随意的。给餐厅服务员、理发师和出租车司机小费是对他们的尊重，但不是必须的。一些餐馆会加收10% 的服务费，但是在酒吧和小酒馆，人们有时候会给酒吧侍者买一份饮品来代替给他们现金小费。

Exercises 练习

Answer these questions.

1. Do you think tipping is reasonable? Why or why not?
2. If you're a server, would you rather work for tips, or have a higher hourly wage?

Translate these sentences into English.

1. 付小费其实是对服务员的优质服务表达谢意的一种方式。
2. 在美国，大部分服务员和酒吧侍者的收入来自小费，而非薪水。
3. 付小费在中国并不常见，但是在美国几乎所有的饭馆里都得付。
4. 法律允许服务员的底薪很低因为政府认为他们能从小费中赚钱。
5. 付小费对消费者来说也比较好，因为这会刺激服务员给顾客更好的服务。
6. 在有的国家，饭馆的账单里常常包含服务费。

Complete the following paragraph with these words or phrases.

> customs   considered   implies   example   rude   extra
> all over

In the US, failing to leave a tip at a restaurant is __1__ extremely __2__. However, this is not the case __3__ the world. In Japan, the opposite is true: leaving a tip is considered rude, because it __4__ that servers must be paid __5__ to ensure they do their job. This is a good __6__ of why it's important to learn about the __7__ of another country before you visit!

 Answers 答案

Translate these sentences into English.

1. Leaving a tip is like a way of saying thank you to your server for doing a good job.
2. In the US, for most servers and bartenders, their income actually comes from tips, not from their paycheck.
3. Tipping is not customary in China, but is expected in almost all American restaurants.
4. The law allows servers' minimum wage to be very low because the government assumes that they earn money from tips.
5. Tipping is probably better for the customer, too, because the waiter has an incentive to give good service.
6. In some countries, restaurants always include a service charge in the bill.

Complete the following paragraph with these words or phrases.

1. considered   2. rude   3. all over   4. implies
5. extra   6. example   7. customs

词 汇 表

tip	（给）小费
legal	合法的
minimum	最低限度
wage	工资
assume	设想；假定
depending on	取决于
shift	值班；轮班工作
reward	奖赏
reserve	保留；预定
mandatory	强制性的
gratuity	赏金；小费
counter	柜台
jar	瓶子；罐子
optional	可选择的
takeout	打包带走
run up	增加
tab	账单
amount	数量；总额
barbers	理发师
hairdressers	美发师
bonus	奖金
maid	女佣人
superintendent	管理员
on top	除…以外
patron	老主顾；赞助人

44. Friendship and Family

友情和家庭

A: I've noticed a lot of differences between Chinese society and American society, but I think they're all based on one core difference: Chinese is a society of collectivism while America is a society of individualism.

B: For the most part I agree with you, but China and America are both changing, and I wouldn't say that either country is purely collectivist or individualistic. Neither Chinese nor Americans completely rely on other people or do things one hundred percent on their own.

A: It seems like in China, families are very close and friends seem to go out of their way to help each other all the time. In America it's a little different. Families are still close, but parents play less of a role in their children's lives once they grow up and move out.

B: I think that's right. In America, when children turn 18 they usually move out—either to go to college or straight into "the real world." There aren't many children who will let their parents tell them what to do once they're officially adults.

A: I think that's because in America more emphasis is put on independence, individualism, and self-reliance. Most American parents expect their children to become independent adults, make their own decisions, and lead their own lives. Even though you may care about someone a lot, in order to show respect you have to let them go their own way.

B: But to me that seems kind of lonely. In China, where children tend to live with their parents even after they graduate and start working, families are closer. Sure, parents might meddle in their children's lives more, but everyone can rely on one another.

A: Well of course Americans love their families too, they just express it differently. Parents in the US take pride in their children's independence. It's hard to let go, but it's also rewarding to see that your children are strong enough to make it on their own. In China, they say "If you don't listen to your elders, you'll wish you had." There isn't really an American saying with exactly that meaning.

B: Yeah, the closest I can think of in English would have to be "those who cannot learn from history are doomed to repeat it," but that doesn't quite mean the same thing as the Chinese saying. So these two cultures are very different, but each has its own good points and bad points, strengths and weaknesses.

A: I agree. But the fact that we're all different means that we can all learn from each other. As Confucius said, "When three men are walking together, there is one who can be my teacher."

对 话

A: 我发现了中国社会和美国社会的许多不同，但是我觉得这都是因为一个核心的不同：中国是一个集体主义的社会，而美国是一个个人主义的社会。

B: 我基本上同意你的看法，但是，中国和美国都在变化，所以我不能说哪个国家是纯粹的集体主义或个人主义。中国人和美国人做事情都不是完全依靠别人也不是百分之百靠自己。

A: 看起来，在中国，家人之间的关系非常近，而且朋友之间不惜一切也一直要互相帮忙。在美国情况有点儿不一样，家人之间仍然很近，但是一旦孩子们长大了、搬出去了，父母在孩子生活中的作用就小了。

B: 我觉得是那样的。在美国，通常孩子满18岁以后就会搬出去——或者上大学、或者直接步入社会。一旦他们成了法定的成年人，就没有孩子会让父母告诉他们该做什么了。

A: 我觉得那是因为美国人更重视独立、个人主义和自力更生。大多数美国父母都期望他们的孩子成为独立的成年人，自己做决定，独立生活。即使你可能特别担心他，但是为了表示你对他的尊重，你得让他自己做决定，过自己的生活。

B: 但是对我来说，那有些孤独。在中国，有些孩子在毕业、开始工作以后还跟父母一起住，家人的关系非常亲近。当然，父母可能会干涉孩子的生活，但是他们都可以互相依靠。

A: 美国人也很爱他们的家人，只是表达方式不同。在美国，父母们以孩子的独立为骄傲。虽然他们也舍不得让孩子离开，但是能看到孩子可以自己养活自己了也是值得的。在中国，他们说"不听老人言，吃亏在眼前"，在美国真的没有这样的说法。

B: 对，我觉得最接近的话可能是"不吸取教训的人一定会再吃亏"，但是和中国的那句话并不完全一样。所以这两种文化很不同。但是它们各有优缺，长处和短处。

A: 对，我同意。因为我们的文化不同，所以我们可以互相学习。就像孔子说的"三人行必有我师焉"。

Friendship in China and the West 中式友谊与西式友谊

Chinese expect friendships to be lasting. For Chinese a true friendship endures throughout life changes. Chinese people will consider someone a friend even if they haven't spoken for 20 years. If you shared something at one time, then all your life you are friends. This is the basis of *guanxi*（关系）, the intricate network that connects Chinese through time and space. Chinese invented the world wide web long before anyone had ever dreamt of a computer.

In America, even close relationships may not survive life changes such as moving to another city, graduation from a university, a change in economic circumstances, or marriage. If the people do not see each other regularly, it is much more difficult to maintain the relationship.

中国人希望友谊可以长长久久。对中国人来说，真正的友谊能经受一生中各种各样的变故。即使20年没说过话，也还是朋友。如果你们曾经一起做过某件事，那你们就是一辈子的朋友。这就是"关系"，即跨越时空将中国人维系在一起的错综复杂的网络。中国人早在有人梦想有电脑之前很久就已发明了"互联网"。

在美国，尽管是感觉很近的朋友一旦要是搬到了别的城市、从大学毕业了、经济状况发生了改变或结了婚，他们的友谊就都不复存在了。如果人们不能有规律的见面，他们的关系也很难维持。

Different Foundations for Friendships 友谊的不同基础

Chinese friends share "things in common": a job, a class, a hometown. Friendships are formed by people who work or go to school together. You may or may not like the person, but if he or she can do something for you because of his position or job, you can be friends.

But in America, although people are often friends with their coworkers, business and friendship are kept separate. As in China, Americans' friends are often their colleagues or their classmates, or people who grew up in the same town. In the West, friendship is based on equality, so friends tend to have similar financial circumstances. If one can afford to treat the other to a meal at an expensive restaurant and the other does not have enough money to do the same, it can cause tension in the relationship.

中国的朋友之间享有共同之处：工作、课程、家乡。一起工作或学习的人自然地成为朋友。你可能喜欢或不喜欢这个人，但是如果他或她能利用他的职位或工作为你做事情，你们就能成为朋友。

在美国，虽然人们也和同事做朋友，但是，工作和友谊是两回事。和中国人一样，美国人的朋友也通常是他们的同事、同学，或在老家一起长大的人。在西方，友谊是建立在平等的基础上的。所以朋友之间往往有相似的经济状况。如果一个人可以请得起另一个人在昂贵的饭馆吃饭，而对方却没有足够的钱来做同样的事情，他们的关系可能就会紧张。

Westerners Don't Like to Be Dependent on Their Friends 西方人不喜欢依靠朋友

Westerners place a high value on self-sufficiency, so they usually do not feel comfortable in a relationship in which one person is giving more and the other is in a dependent position. Their friendship is mostly a matter of providing emotional support and spending time together. When their friend has a problem, a Westerner will respond by asking "what do you want to do?" Their role as a friend is to help think out the problem and find a solution, and then to support the other person's choice.

Chinese friends give each other more concrete help. A Chinese person will use their own connections to help a friend get something they wouldn't be able to obtain on their own, such as a job or an appointment with a good doctor. It is not unusual for Chinese friends to give each other money; they might even help out financially over a long period of time.

西方人很重视自给自足，所以如果一个人给予很多，而另一个依靠朋友的给予，他们就会觉得很不舒服。他们的友谊主要是待在一起提供情感上的支持。如果朋友有了麻烦，一个西方人会问"你打算怎么做?"他们的角色是帮助朋友彻底想清楚问题并找到解决办法，然后支持朋友的选择。

中国朋友之间互相给予更多具体的帮助。一个中国人会用自己的关系帮助朋友得到靠自己很难得到的东西，比如说找工作、或者与一个好医生的约诊。中国朋友之间也互相借钱，而且可能借很长时间以帮助朋友度过经济上的难关。

Exercises 练习

Answer these questions.

1. In what ways are Chinese and Americans' expectations of friendship different?
2. Why do Americans move out of their parents' houses after they graduate from college or begin their first job?

Translate these sentences into English.

1. 在中国，家人之间的关系非常近，而且朋友之间也会一直帮忙。
2. 在美国，通常孩子满 18 岁以后就会搬出去——或者上大学、或者直接步入社会。
3. 在中国，有些孩子在毕业开始工作以后还跟父母一起住。
4. 在美国，父母们以孩子的独立为骄傲。
5. 对中国人来说，真正的友谊能经受一生中各种各样的变故。
6. 在美国，工作和友谊是两回事。

Complete the following paragraph with these words or phrases.

> however elections legally members purchase
> in a sense decisions

When Americans turn 18 they are ___1___ adults. It is at this age that they are allowed to vote in local, state, and national ___2___. At 18 they are also old enough to join the army. ___3___, this is when Americans are expected to become ___4___ of civil society. ___5___, in America it is not permitted to ___6___ alcohol until you are 21 years old. So in the eyes of the law, Americans are not truly considered to be capable of making all of their own ___7___ until they are 21.

 Answers 答案

Translate these sentences into English.

1. In China, families are very close and friends seem to help each other all the time.
2. In America, when children turn 18 they usually move out either to go to college or straight into "the real world."
3. In China, children tend to live with their parents even after they graduate and start working.
4. In America, parents take pride in their children's independence.
5. For Chinese a true friendship endures throughout life changes.
6. In America, business and friendship are kept separate.

Complete the following paragraph with these words or phrases.

1. legally 2. elections 3. In a sense 4. members
5. However 6. purchase 7. decisions

purely
完全；纯粹地
rely on
依赖
grow up
长大
officially
官方地；法定地
self-reliance
自力更生
meddle
干涉
rewarding
值得做的
doom
注定
endure
经受
throughout
贯穿；始终
invent
发明
survive
幸存
circumstance
情况；形势
regularly
有规律地
position
职位；位置
leisure
休闲
tend to
倾向于…；往往
dependent
依靠的；从属的
respond
回应；反应
think out
彻底想一想
solution
措施；办法
concrete
具体的
obtain
获得

45. Getting Around

出　行

Dialogue

A： I was talking to another one of my American friends today, and we agreed that one of the things we miss the most about America is driving.

B： I don't know how to drive. Is it fun?

A： I like driving, but I don't like having to drive. I much prefer to live someplace where I can ride my bike or take the bus or the subway wherever I need to go. I think driving your own car for everyday stuff like going to school or work or the grocery store is kind of annoying. And besides, between gas, parking fees, repairs and car insurance having a car can be really expensive.

B： Does everyone in the US have a car?

A： Not everyone, of course, but most people. The interesting thing is that in China it's mostly people in cities who own cars, but in America people in cities are less likely to own a car than people who live in smaller towns and rural areas.

B： Why?

A： Well it's not true in all cities, but in the bigger and denser cities like New York, Chicago and Boston, they have good public transportation systems on the one hand, and on the other hand having a car is more trouble than it's worth because parking is really expensive and traffic is terrible.

B： In Beijing, everyone I know takes the bus wherever they need to go. Is it the same way in American cities?

A： Yes and no. Low-income people use public buses much more than anyone else. In New York City, everyone takes the subway, no matter how wealthy they are. But in other cities like L. A. , anyone who can afford to ·has a car.

B： I think it has to do with American culture. America was founded on the principle of individual freedom, so the freedom and flexibility of having your own car is almost ingrained in American society.

A： That's definitely true. But for me personally, I think depending on where you live you can have just as much freedom riding a bike. Riding a bike is often much faster than driving if there's traffic, and you never have to worry about finding a parking space!

B： It's good exercise, too.

A： Yeah, but in the US people don't ride bikes nearly as much as they do here in China. I wish Americans would take a lesson from the Chinese and ride bikes more often!

B： Haha, don't hold your breath!

对 话

A： 今天我和我的另一个美国朋友聊天，我们一致认为我们最怀念在美国的一件事情是开车。

B： 我不会开车。好玩儿吗?

A： 我喜欢开车，但是不喜欢强迫自己开车。我更喜欢住在一个不管去哪儿都可以骑自行车、坐公共汽车或者坐地铁去的地方。我觉得开着自己的车过日常生活，像上学、上班或是去杂货商店很让人厌烦。除此之外，油费、停车费、维修以及保险费，养车的开销很大。

B： 在美国每个人都有车吗?

A： 当然不是每个人，但是大多数人都有。有意思的是在中国，有车的大多是城里人，而在美国有车的城里人比有车的小城镇和郊区的人少。

B： 为什么?

A： 当然也不是所有的城市都这样。但是在比较大的、人口比较密集的城市，像纽约、芝加哥和波士顿就是这种情况。一方面因为它们拥有比较完善的公交系统，另一方面在这些城市中有车会更麻烦，因为停车费很贵并且交通也很混乱。

B： 在北京，我认识的人出行时都会乘坐公共汽车。在美国的城市里也是这样吗?

A： 也是也不是。低收入阶层的人们比其他阶层更多地乘坐公交车。在纽约，不管有多少钱，人们都愿意搭乘地铁。但是在其它城市，像洛杉矶，人们都有私家车。

B： 我觉得这和美国的文化有关。美国是建立在个人自由的基础上的。因此，有私家车的自由感和随意感在美国社会深入人心。

A： 没错。但是就我个人来说，我觉得取决于你住在那里。骑车也可以带给你同样的自由感。而且堵车的时候，骑车常常比开车快得多，而且你不用为找停车位而担心!

B： 骑车也是很好的锻炼。

A： 是啊，但是美国人不像中国人那样常常骑车。我希望美国人能像中国人学习，常常骑自行车!

B： 哈哈，有劲就使出来吧!

Background Reading 背景阅读

Different Types of Transportation 不同的交通方式

The way a country develops has a huge effect on the types of transportation used by its citizens. The most important period of economic development in the US started after WWII and lasted through the 1960s. Two of the most important changes that took place during these decades were the growth of suburbs and the construction of the interstate highway system. Both of these changes greatly encouraged the tendency for Americans to use private automobiles as the most popular form of both local and long-distance transportation.

一个国家的发展方式对其国民所采用的交通方式有着非常大的影响。美国经济发展最重要的一段时期始于二战后，并持续到60年代末。在这几十年间，最重要的两个变化就是郊区的增加以及州际高速系统的建设。这两个变化极大地推动了私人汽车在美国的地方和长途运输中成为最受欢迎的交通工具的趋势。

Not many people in China own their own car, but everyone still gets where they need to go. China's excellent rail system provides the bulk of long-distance travel. Unlike the US, where passenger trains are few and far between, in China it's very easy to get all around the country on the trains. Urban residents in China also have lots of options for getting around. Many Chinese cities have very good public bus systems, with buses running frequently and stopping in many different parts of the city. City governments have also made it easy for people to ride a bicycle as their main mode of transportation, by creating bike lanes on busy roads and providing safe places for people to park their bikes.

在中国有私家车的人不是很多，但是每个人都能到达他们想去的地方。中国发达的铁路系统承担了大部分的长途运输。在中国，可以乘火车去国内的任何地方，不像在美国，客运列车很少而且间隔时间很长。中国的城市居民出行时也有很多选择。中国的很多城市有发达的公交系统，公共汽车频繁地运行停靠于城市中的很多地方。市政府也为人们把自行车作为主要交通工具提供了方便，如在繁忙路段开辟自行车道以及为人们停放自行车提供安全的地方。

Americans themselves aren't totally to blame for being addicted to driving, however. Almost all Americans live in areas that were built with the assumption that most people would have their own car. In rural areas everything is very spread out; and while suburbs are concentrated residential areas, most people still have to drive to go to work, or school, or to go shopping. Even in some cities, especially in the Midwest and West, getting around is very inconvenient if you don't have a car. In China, on the other hand, both cities and rural areas tend to be much denser than in America. Of course this is partly because the overall population density is far higher in China. However, it is also important that cities and towns were built in a culture that was not based around private car ownership.

美国人开车上瘾，这并不完全是美国人自身的原因，因为，几乎所有美国人居住的地方都是在假设人们都有私家车这样的情况下修建起来的。在乡下，每个地方都是分散的，郊区是集中的居住区，大多数人还是要开车上班、上学或购物。甚至在一些城市，特别是中西部或西部，如果你没有汽车，出行会很不方便。而在中国，城市和郊区都显得比美国拥挤。当然部分原因是中国的人口密度很大，但中国的城市和城镇并不是建立在拥有私家车的文化基础上也是很重要的原因。

While cultural values and national history play important roles in determining how people get from place to place, there is another crucial factor that cannot be overlooked. Simply put, car ownership is far more widespread in the US than it is in China because the US is a wealthier country. As China develops, more and more people will be able to afford to buy a car, and many already have. However, letting this trend continue unabated would have disastrous effects for the global climate crisis. China faces the challenge of finding a more environmentally responsible way to develop.

文化价值和国家历史固然对决定人们怎样从一个地方到另一个地方起着重要的作用，还有一个不容忽视的关键性因素。简单地说，在美国，有车的人比中国多是因为美国是一个更富裕的国家。随着中国经济的发展，越来越多的人有能力买车，而且很多人已经有车了。但是，让这种趋势持续发展下去会对全球气候危机造成灾难性的影响。中国面临的挑战是寻找更为环保的发展方式。

Exercises 练习

Answer these questions.

1. What is one reason that most Americans own a car?
2. How do people who live in New York City usually get around?
3. What kind of transportation do you use most often? Why?

Translate these sentences into English.

1. 在美国有车的城里人比有车的小城镇和郊区的人少。
2. 比较大的、人口比较密集的城市通常拥有完善的公交系统。
3. 在纽约，不管有多少钱，人们都愿意搭乘地铁。
4. 堵车的时候，骑车常常比开车快得多，而且你不用为找停车位而担心。
5. 中国发达的铁路系统承担了大部分的长途运输。
6. 中国的城市居民出行时也有很多选择。

Complete the following paragraph with these words or phrases.

picked up funded across dropped off riding public

The US does have one kind of __1__ transportation that is extremely successful __2__ the entire country: school buses. Any child that goes to public school in the US but lives too far away to walk will get __3__ in the morning and __4__ in the afternoon by the school bus. Furthermore, school buses are __5__ by the taxpayer, so __6__ the bus doesn't cost the student a penny.

 Answers 答案

Translate these sentences into English.

1. In America people in cities are less likely to own a car than people who live in smaller towns and rural areas.
2. The bigger and denser cities usually have good public ransportation systems.
3. In New York City, everyone takes the subway, no matter how wealthy they are.
4. Riding a bike is often much faster than driving if there's traffic, and you never have to worry about finding a parking space.
5. China's excellent rail system provides the bulk of long-distance travel.
6. Urban residents in China also have lots of options for getting around.

Complete the following paragraph with these words or phrases.

1. public 2. across 3. picked up 4. dropped off
5. funded 6. riding

grocery	杂货店；食品店
annoying	令人心烦的
parking fees	停车费
rural	农村的
dense	密集的；稠密的
afford	付得起
found	建立
principle	原则
ingrained	根深蒂固的
citizen	市民
suburb	郊区
tendency	趋势；倾向
global	全球的
urgent	紧急的；急迫的
bulk	大部分；主要部分
urban	城市的
lane	车道
blame for	承担责任
be addicted to	对…上瘾
assumption	假设
concentrate	集中
overall	全面的
unabated	不减弱的
disastrous	灾难性的
crisis	危机

46. Volunteering

志愿活动

A: I've been doing a lot of volunteer work lately, and I've come to realize that being a volunteer is not only meaningful, it's also really fun.

B: Really? What kind of work have you done?

A: I was a volunteer tour guide at a museum, so I explained the origins and historical background of the different artworks to the people who visited the museum. I learned so much doing that job.

B: That's a really important point: even though volunteer work is unpaid, you definitely get something out of it. Have you done any other volunteering?

A: I also taught English at an orphanage. That class was kind of special—the children weren't orphans, but all of them had parents currently serving prison sentences, so they needed even more care and attention.

B: Teaching that kind of class isn't easy.

A: It was difficult at first. But as time went on, the kids and I became more familiar with each other and it went much more smoothly. Now they really like me, and my class.

B: My brother is very passionate about volunteer work. He's a medical student, and last year he went to Africa to volunteer with local AIDS patients.

A: Really? That's incredible! It must have been really difficult working there, huh?

B: I think so, but whenever he talked to us he never mentioned anything bad, he just told us that he was doing well.

A: He's really an idealist!

B: That he is. As a medical student who's planning to look for a job in the US, his future is very bright. But he's always thought that the greatest happiness comes from helping

182

others.

A: That kind of person really is a hero; we should all learn from him!

B: I've never done any volunteering, and although I'm going back to the US next month, I want to come back to China for the 2008 Beijing Olympics. I'm going to be a volunteer for the Games, to be a guide for foreign tourists and give them an introduction to Beijing.

A: What a great idea! I was thinking of doing something like that too.

B: Let's go sign up together then!

对 话

A: 我最近参加了很多志愿活动，我觉得做一个志愿者不仅很有意义，而且很有意思。

B: 是吗? 你做的是什么工作?

A: 我在一家博物馆当导游，给来参观博物馆的游客讲解一些艺术品的来源和相关的历史故事。通过做这个工作，我增长了很多知识。

B: 这一点非常重要: 做志愿工作虽然没有报酬，但你一定会有收获。你还做过其它的志愿活动吗?

A: 我还去了一个儿童村当英文老师。那个儿童村比较特别，那儿的孩子并不是孤儿，他们的父母都在监狱服刑，所以这样的孩子更需要关怀和照顾。

B: 当这样的老师很不容易吧。

A: 一开始是这样。但时间长了，我和他们熟悉了，就很顺利了。现在他们很喜欢我，也喜欢上我的课。

B: 我哥哥特别热中于参加志愿活动，他是一个医科学生，去年他去非洲做过志愿者，帮助当地的艾滋病人。

A: 是吗? 他太伟大了! 他在那儿工作的时候一定有很多困难吧?

B: 我觉得是，但他跟我们联系的时候，从来都不说他的困难，只是告诉我们他很好。

A: 他真是一个理想主义者!

B: 是的，因为他是学医的，所以在美国找工作，前途也是一片光明，但是，他总是觉得能帮助别人就是最快乐的事。

A: 这样的人才是真正的英雄，我们都应该向他学习!

B: 我还没做过志愿者，虽然下个月我就要回美国了，但我打算 2008 年北京开奥运会的时候再来中国，当一个奥运会的志愿者，向那些外国游客介绍北京，给他们当向导。

A: 好主意! 我也是这么想的。

B: 那我们一起去报名吧!

Volunteer Service 志愿服务

Volunteer service has its origins in the 19th century, in the religious tradition of charitable service that had already existed in Western nations and developed over more than a hundred years. Volunteer work is characterized by being self-motivated, for the benefit of others, and unpaid.

志愿服务起源于19世纪，在西方国家，宗教传统的慈善服务已经存在和发展了一百多年。志愿工作以自愿、利他、不计报酬为特征。

Volunteers are people who devote their own time and energy in order to better society, and they are motivated by their moral beliefs, empathy and a sense of responsibility rather than by their own material benefit. "Volunteer service in general uses one's own time, one's own abilities, one's own resources, and one's own kindness, and using non-profit, non-professionalized action to benefit your neighbors, your community, and society as a whole." ——Kofi A. Annan

志愿者是指在不为物质报酬的情况下，基于道义、信念、良知、同情心和责任，为改进社会而提供服务，贡献个人的时间及精力的人和人群。"志愿服务泛指利用自己的时间、自己的技能、自己的资源、自己的善心为邻居、社区、社会提供非盈利、非职业化援助的行为。"——科菲·安南

America has long history of volunteerism and civil organizations. Some argue that the volunteer tradition has its origins in the Christian spirit of helping others; others say that America's unique status as a country of immigrants that formed a society before they formed a nation led to a societal emphasis on helping others rather than depending on the government to do it. The US has the world's highest rate of volunteerism, with a participation rate of 50%. Public awareness of and participation in volunteer activities are extremely widespread: more than 80% of people identify themselves as a member of some sort of organization. Adults spend on average 4.2 hours each week volunteering.

美国有悠久的志愿活动和公民社会组织历史。关于其志愿服务的文化传统，一些人认为来自基督教助人给予的精神；另一些人则认为美国是移民国家，先有社会再有国家，所以人们更习惯于相互帮助，而不是依靠政府。美国是世界上志愿服务率最高的国家，参与率为50%。公众意识和公民参与都非常普遍，80%以上的人承认自己是某种组织的成员。成年人平均每周从事4.2小时的志愿服务。

What are people's motivations for becoming a volunteer? For some, it's because an organization asked for help; for others it's a way of acting on their principles. Some people volunteer in order to broaden their own experience; still others simply believe that it's important to help other people. The "motivation question" is the hardest thing for those who research volunteerism to explain, but most likely it's a combination of a desire to help others, a sense of responsibility to contribute to society, and simple personal enjoyment.

人们做志愿者的动机是什么？有的是"组织要求去做"，有的是为实现自己的理念，还有的是为锻炼自己增长经验，还有人认为帮助别人很重要。"动机问题"是有关志愿者的研究中最难讲清楚的问题，但是大多数人的动机是想帮助别人的愿望、社会责任感和简单的个人满足这三方面的结合。

Exercises 练习

Answer these questions.

1. Have you ever been a volunteer?
2. What are some possible motivations for becoming a volunteer?
3. What are some examples of volunteer activities?

Translate these sentences into English.

1. 做一个志愿者不仅很有意义，而且很有意思。
2. 做志愿工作虽然没有报酬，但你一定会有收获。
3. 我哥哥特别热中于参加志愿活动。
4. 我打算做 2008 年北京奥运会的志愿者。
5. 美国是移民国家，先有社会再有国家。
6. 一些人参加志愿活动是出于一种想做一些对社会有益的事情的责任感。
7. 你从中得到的和你付出的一样多。

Complete the following paragraph with these words or phrases.

> experience volunteer self-confidence independence
> social circle workforce increase

In addition to helping others as a ___1___ , you also reap personal benefits and enhance your personal growth. You can ___2___ social awareness, learn through service, gain ___3___ , discover your strengths and talents, build a sense of ___4___ , and expand your ___5___ . Volunteering can help you develop skills you will use in the ___6___ . By volunteering you can also gain work ___7___ , explore career options, and develop a job-finding network.

Answers 答案

Translate these sentences into English.

1. Being a volunteer is not only meaningful, it's also really fun.
2. Even though volunteer work is unpaid, you definitely get something out of it.
3. My brother is very passionate about volunteer work.
4. I'm going to be a volunteer for the 2008 Beijing Olympics.
5. America is a country of immigrants that formed a society before they formed a nation.
6. Some people volunteer out of a sense of responsibility to do something to benefit society.
7. You can get as much out of it as you put into it.

Complete the following paragraph with these words or phrases.

1. volunteer 2. increase 3. self-confidence 4. independence
5. social circle 6. workforce 7. experience

词 汇 表

meaningful	有重要意义的
tour guide	导游
museum	博物馆
origin	起源
artwork	艺术品
unpaid	无报酬的
orphanage	儿童村
smoothly	顺利地
passionate	充满激情的
medical	医学的；医科的
AIDS	艾滋病
mention	提到
idealist	理想主义者
hero	英雄
sign up	报名参加
religious	宗教的
charitable	慈善的
self-motivation	自愿
morality	道德
sympathy	同情心
devote	把…奉献给
civil	公民的；民用的
immigrant	移民
broaden	拓宽；开阔

185

47. Free Huggers

抱抱团

Dialogue

A: Guess what? I was walking down the street today when this stranger came up and hugged me—they were part of a group of young people called "Free Huggers."

B: What's a "free hugger"?

A: Their activities are organized spontaneously over the internet. They hope that by hugging strangers, they can bring people closer, and get a little bit of warmth into the interpersonal relationships that are often too cold and detached.

B: Oh, I know, there are people who do that in the US and Australia too. But in China when you meet someone, aren't you supposed to shake hands? Are there times when it's customary to hug someone?

A: Shaking hands is a formal type of greeting; hugging is only between friends and family. The "Free Hugs" philosophy holds that hugging can empower people, and make them vividly feel that someone cares about them. When I got hugged by them, I had an intense feeling of warmth and happiness. And what's more, I really wanted to pass this feeling onto other people.

B: That's great! It seems like you could call what the "free huggers" do an important public service!

A: Totally! More and more in modern society people only pay attention to their own interests, and so interpersonal relationships get more distant every day. "Free huggers" have appeared in order to change this kind of situation, to say no to the cold, detached nature of interpersonal relationships and call on society for more caring between people.

B: So have "free huggers" in China received any sort of widespread recognition and support?

A: I think a considerable number of people have a supportive attitude: they think that this

186

kind of activity is noble and well-intentioned. There are also people who support the idea behind the "free huggers" but they don't support what the "free huggers" do; they think that if you want to spread friendliness, a smile is enough; you don't necessarily need to hug someone. Because just like you said, hugging isn't really in line with what Chinese people are accustomed to. Hugs between strangers of the opposite sex in particular draw criticism from some people.

B: I think those concerns make sense. After all, Chinese history is thousands of years old, and some traditions can't be changed that easily. Not to mention, Americans don't randomly hug strangers either. Actually, "free hugging" is more like a type of performance art, using a specific action to convey an idea.

A: Good point. People can be distant or they can be close, but coming closer is what everyone wants. Hugging is only one way of fulfilling this desire; it's the means to an end.

对 话

A: 你知道吗？今天我走在街上，被陌生人拥抱了。拥抱我的是一些被叫做"抱抱团"的年轻人。

B: "抱抱团"是什么？

A: 这是一个通过网络自发形成的组织。他们希望通过与陌生人的拥抱，传递彼此的温暖，从而拉近人与人之间的距离，驱走人际关系中的冷漠。

B: 噢，我知道，在美国和澳大利亚也有人这样做。但是中国人见面的时候不是应该握手吗？你们什么时候也习惯拥抱了？

A: 握手只是一种礼节上的问候，拥抱只存在于家人和朋友之间。而"自由拥抱"的理念是拥抱给人以力量，让人真切的感觉到来自他人的关怀。当我被他们拥抱的时候，我有一种很强烈的温暖和幸福的感觉。同时，我也很渴望把这种感觉再传递给别人。

B: 真不错！看来"抱抱团"所做的事情称得上是一项伟大的公益事业了！

A: 当然是！现代社会中的人们越来越看重利益，所以人与人之间的关系日渐疏远。"抱抱团"的出现就是要改变这种现状，向冷漠的人心说"不"，向社会呼唤人与人之间的关爱。

B: 那么"抱抱团"在中国得到人们的普遍承认和支持了吗？

A: 我觉得相当多的人是持支持态度的，他们认为这种行为是善意的、高尚的。也有的人支持"抱抱团"的想法，但并不支持"抱抱团"的做法，这些人觉得想要传递友好，一个微笑就够了，不见得一定要拥抱，因为就像你说的，拥抱不符合中国人的习惯，尤其是陌生的异性之间的拥抱还会招来一些人的非议。

B: 我觉得后一种人的担心也是有道理的，毕竟中国有几千年的历史了，一些传统不是那么容易就能改变的。再说，美国人也不是随便拥抱陌生人的。其实，"抱抱团"算是一种行为艺术，通过某种行为传达某种理念。

A: 你说的对！人与人之间的距离，可以近也可以远，拉近彼此的距离是所有人的愿望。拥抱，只是满足这种愿望的一种方式。拥抱不是目的，是方式。

Background Reading 背景阅读

The Origin of Free Hugs 抱抱团的由来

The person who first brought this idea into the world was an American named Jason Hunter. The inspiration came from his late mother. Five years earlier at his mother's funeral, Jason was incredibly moved when he heard so many people speak about how she had cared for them with such warmth and love. Jason knew he had to rely on the warmth provided by others in order to deal with the grief of losing his mother, so he made a sign saying "Free Hugs" and walked up and down the main street in his hometown. The first person to hug him was a woman passing by; she stopped, looked at the sign, and without hesitating for a moment opened her arms to Hunter. From that day on, "Free Hugs" started to spread throughout the United States.

最早向世界推行这个活动的是美国人贾森·亨特。活动的灵感来自于他去世的母亲。5 年前，在母亲的葬礼上，贾森听到了许多关于母亲的事迹，得到过亨特母亲帮助关心过的人，回忆从她那里得到的温暖。他感觉自己需要借助他人提供的温暖，来克服丧母的悲痛，于是做了一个写着"真情拥抱"的纸牌走上家乡的大街。第一个与他"真情拥抱"的人是一个路过的姑娘，她停了下来，看了看纸板，毫不犹豫地向亨特张开了双臂。从这一天起，"FREEHUGS" 开始在全美国蔓延。

In 2006 an Australian man named Juan Mann stood at a busy intersection in Sydney, holding up a sign that said "Free Hugs" and giving hugs to strangers, spreading a kind of "caring among strangers." Mann says that this is one way to make everyone break into a grin, "because all it takes is one person to hug me, and there will be smiles on the faces of five more people passing by." He has taken this spirit to the whole world through his website: www. free-hugs. com

2006 年澳大利亚一个名叫胡安·曼的男子在悉尼闹市街头手举"自由拥抱"的牌子，发起与陌生人拥抱活动，传达一种"来自陌生人的关怀"。曼说，这是让大家笑容绽开的一种方式，"因为只要有一个人跟我拥抱，就会带动从旁经过的五个路人脸上绽开微笑"。他通过他的网站：www. free-hugs. com 将这种精神推向了整个世界。

"Hug Corps" was launched in China by an advertising professional named Cai Zihao. He was inspired to start a new branch of the movement when he saw a video online that showed a foreigner holding a Free Hug activity at a busy intersection. Their actions were a way of promoting human caring and saying "no" to people's ever more disengaged nature. After the "Hug Corps" had been active for a while in Changsha, chapters began to be established one by one in Beijing, Nanjing, Guangzhou, Tianjin and other cities. Members find each other through the internet, with the goal of "making people begin to sincerely smile at perfect strangers—the people they would normally brush right past—thanks to the influence of the group's activities."

中国"抱抱团"活动的发起人是一名叫才子豪的广告从业人员，他发起这次活动缘于在网上看到的一个视频，内容为某国外男子在繁华街头进行的免费拥抱活动，以此向日益冷漠的人心说"不"，倡导一种人文关怀。在长沙抱抱团成功举行了多次活动后，北京、南京、广州、天津等地也纷纷成立抱抱团，成员通过网络相识，目的是"让那些原本擦肩而过的人们，因为这样的活动影响，开始对素不相识的陌生人真心微笑。"

Exercises 练习

Answer these questions.

1. Why do "free huggers" hug complete strangers?
2. What's your opinion of "free hugging"?
3. Would you like to be a "free hugger"?

Translate these sentences into English.

1. "抱抱团"是通过网络自发形成的组织。
2. 他们希望通过与陌生人的拥抱，拉近人与人之间的距离。
3. 他们认为现代社会中人与人之间的关系日渐疏远。
4. 拥抱不符合中国人的习惯。
5. "抱抱团"是一种行为艺术，通过某种行为传达某种理念。
6. "抱抱团"的出现就是要向社会呼唤人与人之间的关爱。
7. "抱抱团"在中国还没有得到人们的普遍承认和支持。

Complete the following paragraph with these words or phrases.

Internet organized take on certain coldness warm
slogan

In China, Free Hugs groups were __1__ with members recruited through the __2__. In some cities like Beijing, Shanghai, Changsha, etc., a __3__ group of people decided to __4__ what they see as the __5__ and apathy of human relations in the big city by giving out free hugs. They raised a big sign with their __6__, "Free Hugs", on the street. Whenever anyone who would like to hug came over, they would receive a __7__ hug from the Free Huggers.

Answers 答案

Translate these sentences into English.

1. "Free huggers" are organized spontaneously over the internet.
2. They hope that by hugging strangers, they can bring people closer.
3. They believe that interpersonal relationships are getting more distant every day.
4. Hugging isn't really in line with what Chinese people are accustomed to.
5. "Free hugging" is more like a type of performance art, using a specific action to convey an idea.
6. The "Free Hugs" movement calls on society for more caring between people.
7. "Free huggers" haven't received widespread recognition and support in China.

Complete the following paragraph with these words or phrases.

1. organized 2. Internet 3. certain 4. take on
5. coldness 6. slogan 7. warm

189

48. Philanthropy

慈善事业

Dialogue

A: Recently I've been seeing stories all over the media about this one Chinese celebrity couple whose daughter was born with a cleft lip. They founded a Children's Fund in order to help children from poor families suffering from the same affliction as their daughter to afford surgery. Have you heard about this?

B: I have, actually. Their fund has already received donations from tons of people, including many donations from other stars and celebrities, and even former President George H. W. Bush!

A: They've devoted themselves to philanthropy, and they are also calling others' attention to these issues. It's a really praiseworthy way of using their wealth and fame for a good purpose.

B: I agree. It seems like more and more people are paying attention to philanthropy, which not only enables those people faced with hardship to receive assistance, but also contributes to the progress of society as a whole.

A: And it's not just the rich and famous who care about philanthropy: everyday people, even those who don't have much of their own, are also doing what they can to help others. I saw a story in the newspaper about an elderly man in Beijing who, even though he had no income of his own and was living off the money he earned collecting trash, donated what little he had to help more than a dozen students pay for college.

B: That's so moving. After I graduate college and get a job, I'm definitely going to take out part of my paycheck to help kids who can't afford to go to school. For many people education is the only opportunity to change their lot in life.

A: That kind of attitude is very admirable. In the US, some of the wealthiest people donate almost their entire fortunes to charity, like Andrew Carnegie, the famous railroad tycoon from the 19th century, and contemporary multibillionaires like Warren Buffett and Bill Gates.

B: But in reality everyone earns their fortune from society, so when people donate their money to charity it's really just a way of giving back what society gave them in the first place.

A: To look at it from another angle, charity is two kinds of giving in one: at the same time as we're helping others, it can also be personally fulfilling. Philanthropy can be a way to cleanse your own spirit too.

B: I agree. In a way, charity is like love, and you can't love others until you love yourself.

对 话

A: 最近我在很多媒体上看到，中国的一对明星夫妇因为自己的女儿患有先天性唇裂而出资筹建了一个儿童基金会，专门资助那些来自贫困家庭的、和他们的女儿有同样病症的儿童进行手术，你听说了吗？

B: 是的，目前，他们的基金会已经得到了很多人的捐款，其中大部分来自明星和名人，还有美国前总统老布什的个人捐款呢！

A: 他们自己为慈善事业做出了贡献，还能号召其他人来共同关注慈善事业，他们用自己的财富和名声来做善事的做法真值得称赞！

B: 的确，关注慈善事业的人越来越多，不仅能使那些有困难的人得到帮助，而且也会给整个社会带来很大的进步。

A: 其实关注慈善事业的不只是那些名人和富人，一些普通人甚至是不太富裕的人也在尽自己的努力帮助别人。我在报纸上看到，在北京，有一位老人，他自己根本没有收入，靠捡垃圾养活自己，可是他却用捡垃圾的钱资助了十几个大学生。

B: 他的行为太让人感动了！等我大学毕业以后有了工作，我也想从我的收入中拿出一部分去帮助那些上不起学的孩子，我觉得让他们接受教育才是改变他们命运的唯一途径。

A: 你有这样的想法就很让人佩服！在美国，很多富人都把自己的几乎全部财富捐献给了慈善事业，比如说，一百多年前的钢铁巨头卡耐基和现代社会的美国亿万富翁巴菲特和盖茨。

B: 其实每个人的财富都来自社会，人们把财富捐赠给慈善事业，这实际上是回报社会的一条途径。

A: 从另一方面讲，慈善是一种给予，既能给予别人，也能给予自己，我们在帮助别人的同时也充实了自己，使自己的心灵得到了净化。

B: 我同意，其实，慈善就是爱，爱别人就等于爱自己。

Background Reading　背景阅读

Philanthropic Activities and NGO　慈善活动与非政府组织

The word "philanthropy" is of Greek origin and means "to love all of humanity." There are two general types of philanthropy: first, individual expressions of this "love for humanity" through charitable acts or donating money for the purpose of advancing human welfare and quality of life. And second, to provide a service or participate in volunteer activities in order to decrease human suffering and change people's lives for the better. Organized philanthropic activities tend to be more widespread in developed countries. In 1999, 70% of American families donated to philanthropic organizations, on average contributing $1,075 per family, or 2.1% of their family income.

"慈善"（Philanthropy）一词源于希腊语，意为"爱全人类"。它具有两层含义，一是爱全人类，这种爱通过个人的善举或通过捐献钱物来促进人类的福利、提高生活质量，另外一个意思是指通过捐赠、提供服务或其他志愿活动来减轻人类的痛苦和灾难，改善人类的生活质量。有组织的慈善活动在发达国家比较普遍。1999年，70%的美国家庭对慈善组织进行捐献，平均每个家庭的捐献为1 075美元，占他们家庭收入的2.1%。

Non-governmental organizations, or NGOs, can include associations, social groups, charitable funds, philanthropic trusts, and non-profit corporations. They are not considered government agencies, and they are often under special legal jurisdiction. NGOs are not part of the government, and as such they are not motivated by a pursuit for power; they're not part of the private economy, so they do not rely on economic profit for motivation. NGOs' strength comes from the energy of their volunteers, and their finances come from individuals' donations and, via state funding, the contributions of the entire society. In the US there are many large and powerful private funds that support all kinds of American and international NGOs. Many countries also encourage private donations by reducing taxes on income donated to charity.

NGO，英文"non-government organization"一词的缩写，中文翻译为非政府组织，是指在特定法律系统下，不被视为政府部门的协会、社团、基金会、慈善信托、非营利公司或其他法人。NGO 不是政府组成机构，不靠权力驱动；它不是经济体，所以也不靠经济利益驱动。NGO 的原动力是志愿精神。非政府组织的经济来源主要是社会及私人的捐赠。美国有众多大型而有效的私人基金会支撑着各种本国及国际化的NGO。国家从税收上确立捐赠部分可以抵税的制度，鼓励捐赠。

The global scope of interest in NGOs dates to the 1980s. As global population, poverty and environmental issues became deeper day by day, people realized that it was not enough to rely on traditional governmental or market forces to attempt to resolve these continually developing problems. In response, NGOs rapidly came to form a new sector of society, which is now seen as a crucial part of a developed, modern society.

NGO 在全球范围的兴起始于20世纪80年代。随着全球人口、贫困和环境问题的日益突出，人们发现仅仅依靠传统的政府和市场两级还无法解决人类的可持续发展问题。作为一种回应，NGO 迅速成长为社会新的一级。一个发达的现代社会需要发达的非政府组织。

Exercises 练习

Answer these questions.

1. Why should a person donate to charity?
2. What are the two general types of philanthropy?
3. What is an NGO?

Translate these sentences into English.

1. 中国的一对明星夫妇出资筹建了一个儿童基金会。
2. 他们的基金会已经得到了很多人的捐款。
3. 关注慈善事业的人越来越多会给整个社会带来很大的进步。
4. 我想从我的收入中拿出一小部分去帮助那些上不起学的孩子。
5. 在美国，很多富人都把自己的几乎全部财富捐献给了慈善事业。
6. 人们把财富捐赠给慈善事业，这实际上是回报社会的一条途径。
7. 我们在帮助别人的同时也充实了自己。

Complete the following paragraph with these words or phrases.

in a way   reportedly   fits   related   notion   mutual

There are __1__ more than 2 million American NGOs, with more than
9 million workers. __2__, the large and vibrant NGO scene in the US
__3__ with the American __4__ of "big society, small government."
This system is __5__ to America's history as a nation of immigrants
with a strong tradition of __6__ assistance.

 Answers 答案

Translate these sentences into English.

1. A Chinese celebrity couple founded a Children's Fund.
2. Their fund has already received donations from tons of people.
3. More and more people are paying attention to philanthropy; this
   contributes to the progress of society as a whole.
4. I'm going to take out part of my paycheck to help kids who can't
   afford to go to school.
5. In the US, some of the wealthiest people donate almost their
   entire fortunes to charity.
6. When people donate their money to charity it's really just a way of
   giving back what society gave them in the first place.
7. At the same time as we're helping others, we can also gain
   personal fulfillment.

Complete the following paragraph with these words or phrases.

1. reportedly   2. In a way   3. fits   4. notion   5. related   6. mutual

---

词 汇 表

cleft lip	兔唇
suffer	遭受
affliction	痛苦；折磨
surgery	外科手术
donation	捐助
praiseworthy	值得赞扬的
as a whole	作为整体
live off	靠…生活
moving	令人感动的
trash	垃圾
a dozen	十几个
admirable	令人佩服的
fortune	财富
charity	博爱；慈善团体
tycoon	巨头；大亨
contemporary	当代的
multibillionaire	亿万富翁
in the first place	原先
angle	角度；观点
cleanse	净化
non-profit	非盈利的
jurisdiction	司法权
via	经由；经过
scope	范围
resolve	解决；消除

49. Protecting the Environment

保护环境

Dialogue

A: Now that you've lived in Beijing for six months already, what do you think? Do you like it here?

B: Of course I like it! Everything about Beijing is great, the only exception is that the environment is kind of a mess. When I first arrived I really wasn't used to the air in Beijing.

A: Yeah, Beijing is growing so fast, and every day there are more and more cars, so traffic jams are becoming a problem and the air is getting worse and worse.

B: But in 2008 there will be millions more people coming to Beijing for the Olympics, so if the air quality then is the same as it is now, I'm not very optimistic about what will happen.

A: You're right, lots of Chinese people are worried about that too, so the government is putting a really strong emphasis on environmental protection.

B: But not only the government, every urban resident should also be conscious of the need for environmental protection. In fact, there are a lot of little things you can do in your everyday life to contribute to environmental protection.

A: Like what?

B: Well for starters, people should use public transportation as much as possible. That will reduce air pollution from cars, and make it easier for us all to breathe.

A: But there are already so many people who own cars, it might be hard to get them to use public transportation if they could drive their own car instead.

B: There are plenty of other things people can do too. For example, if you're eating out you shouldn't use disposable chopsticks, paper cups, that kind of thing. If we conserve paper we won't cut down as many trees, and the more trees there are, the better the air is.

A: That's a good idea, it's also really easy to do.

B： Also, if you separate your trash, some things can be recycled and used over again, and at the same time it will reduce overall waste.

A： I've always been diligent about recycling, but even when I separate the trash, the trash collectors just put it all back together when they take it away!

B： That's too bad. There are still some things that need to be worked out on the government level too, of course. But there's one more thing individuals can do: when you go to the market, it's best to think ahead of time and bring your own bag. That way you will use fewer plastic bags, which will cut down on another serious source of pollution.

A： That's true, there are always plastic bags littered on the streets. All of the things you mentioned are great ways to reduce pollution, I'm going to tell all of my friends and family about your suggestions.

B： Great! If we can just get everyone to put a little effort into protecting the environment, the world will be a more beautiful place!

对 话

A： 你已经在北京住了 6 个月了，你喜欢北京吗？

B： 当然喜欢了，北京什么都好，美中不足的一点就是北京的环境有点儿糟糕，我刚来的时候，真的很不适应北京的空气。

A： 是的，北京发展得特别快，汽车的数量每天都在增加，所以交通拥挤成了问题，空气也越来越差。

B： 2008 年的时候，一定会有很多人来北京看奥运会，如果那时候北京的空气质量和现在一样，我真是觉得不太乐观。

A： 是的，这也是很多中国人担心的问题，所以现在中国政府非常重视保护环境。

B： 不仅是政府，普通市民也应该有环保意识。其实在生活中的很多小细节上，你都可以为环保事业做出贡献。

A： 你有什么好的建议？

B： 比如说人们出行的时候应该尽量选择公共交通。那样的话，汽车废气的排放会减少，我们呼吸也就更舒畅。

A： 可是现在有车的人已经很多了，他们应该不会在自己有车的情况下去坐公共汽车，这一点很难做到。

B： 还有很多事情可以做啊，比如，外出就餐的时候尽量不使用一次性筷子、纸杯等一次性产品；还应该节约用纸，这样我们能少砍伐一些树木，树越多，空气就越好。

A： 这是个好办法，而且很容易做到。

B： 还有，把垃圾分类，这也有利于垃圾的回收，也能减少污染。

A： 我一直在坚持把垃圾分类，可是虽然我把垃圾分开了，收垃圾的人却一起都收走了。

B： 那太糟糕了。政府方面也应该采取一些相应的措施。还有，去市场买东西的时候，最好自己准备袋子，少用塑料袋，塑料袋也是很严重的污染源。

A： 是的，现在大街上都是乱扔的塑料袋。你的办法都不错，我要在我的朋友和家人中推广你的办法。

B： 太好了！如果我们都能为保护环境尽一份力，世界就会更美好！

Background Reading 背景阅读

Traffic Pollution 交通污染

If the cigarettes don't get you the traffic pollution will. Up to a fifth of all lung cancer deaths in cities are caused by tiny particles of pollution, most of them from vehicle exhausts. That's the conclusion of the biggest study into city pollution to date, which tracked half a million Americans for 16 years. It suggests the impact is far greater than previously feared.

According to a recent report by the UNEP, if car numbers keep increasing at the present rate, there will be more than a billion on the road by 2025. Today, motor vehicles put out 900 million tons of carbon dioxide a year—about 15 percent of our total output. More vehicles will mean more global warming. Also by 2025, two thirds of the world's people will live in cities. So traffic jams and pollution will loom large in most people's lives.

如果香烟没有置你于死地的话，那么交通污染将成为你的杀手。城市里五分之一的肺癌死亡病例都是由细微污染颗粒物所致，而颗粒物的主要来源就是机动车排放的废气。这是迄今为止一项规模最大的关于城市污染的研究所得出的结论。这项研究长达 16 年，对 50 万美国人进行了跟踪调查。研究表明，交通污染影响的严重性远远超过人们之前所担忧的。

根据联合国环境规划署最近的一次报告，如果汽车数量保持现在的增长速度，到 2025 年，汽车总数将超过 10 亿辆。现在，机动车每年排放 9 亿吨二氧化碳，约占二氧化碳总排放量的 15%。更多的车辆将意味着更严重的全球变暖。同样到 2025 年，世界三分之二的人口将在城市居住，因此交通拥挤和环境污染问题将日益突出，并影响大多数人的生活。

What Can We Do? 我们能做什么?

There are many things we can do in our everyday lives to help protect the environment. The three main things we can do are Reduce, Reuse, and Recycle. First, we can reduce the amount we consume and cut down on the water and energy we use in our homes. Second, we can reuse. Using reusable utensils and containers and getting out of the habit of using everything only once will help decrease waste. Third, we can recycle items like cans and bottles. Recycling cuts down on the overall amount of resources we use, and rather than wasting them puts those resources to use a second time.

日常生活中，我们可以做很多有利于保护环境的事情。最主要的三件事是：节约、重复使用和回收。首先，我们应该减少我们的消费量，在家里节约用水和其它能源。第二，我们可以重复利用。使用可以重复利用的用具和容器并改掉东西只用一次的坏习惯，有利于减少浪费。第三，我们可以回收像易拉罐和瓶子一样的东西。回收有利于减少我们所用资源的总量，而且再用一次也比浪费了好。

What Is Global Warming? 什么是全球变暖?

The US National Resources Defense Council says it is when, "higher temperatures threaten dangerous consequences: drought, disease, floods, lost ecosystems. And from sweltering heat to rising seas, global warming's effects have already begun. But solutions are in sight. We know where most heat-trapping gases come from: power plants and vehicles. And we know how to curb their emissions: modern technologies and stronger laws." There is an ongoing debate as to whether the responsibility should rest with the government or the individual, but a strong majority of Americans feel the government should take more action to prevent global warming.

美国国家资源保护委员会说它是"高温带来的危险的后果：干旱、疾病、洪水、失去生态平衡。从天气酷热到海平面上升，全球变暖已经开始起作用了。但是解决措施也就在我们眼前。我们知道这些热气体是从哪儿来的：能源厂和机动车。我们也知道如何控制他们的排放：现代科技和强有力的法律。"保护环境的责任应该在于政府还是在于个人，这个问题一直在争论，但是绝大多数美国人觉得政府应该采取更多的行动来防止全球变暖。

Exercises 练习

Answer these questions.
1. What are the positive and negative consequences of owning a vehicle?
2. What can we do in our everyday lives to help protect the environment?
3. What is global warming?

Translate these sentences into English.
1. 我刚来的时候，真的很不适应北京的空气。
2. 这个城市的汽车数量每天都在增加，所以交通拥挤成了问题，空气也越来越差。
3. 不仅是政府，每个市民也应该有环保意识。
4. 使用公共交通，不开车，是很易行的保护环境的办法。
5. 日常生活中，我们可以做很多有利于保护环境的事情。
6. 汽车排放的尾气不仅对你的健康有害，而且对环境也不好。
7. 更多的车辆将意味着更严重的全球变暖。

Complete the following paragraph with these words or phrases.

cut down emission action recycle laws vehicles

Global warming is caused largely by the __1__ of greenhouse gasses from __2__, factories, and power plants. There are many things we can do during our everyday lives to __3__ on this kind of pollution, like reduce, reuse, and __4__ the items we use. Governments can also take __5__ by passing stricter environmental protection __6__.

 Answers 答案

Translate these sentences into English.
1. When I first arrived I really wasn't used to the air in Beijing.
2. The number of cars in this city is climbing every day, so traffic jams are becoming a problem and the air is getting worse and worse.
3. Not only the government, every urban resident should also be conscious of the need for environmental protection.
4. Taking public transportation instead of driving a car is one small way to help protect the environment.
5. There are many things we can do during our everyday lives to help protect the environment.
6. Car exhaust is not only bad for your health; it is also bad for the environment.
7. More vehicles will mean more global warming.

Complete the following paragraph with these words or phrases.
1. emission 2. vehicles 3. cut down 4. recycle
5. action 6. laws

词 汇 表

exception
　　　　例外
mess
　　混乱；肮脏
traffic jam
　　　　堵车
quality
　　　　质量
optimistic
　　　乐观的
conscious
　　　　意识
disposable
　　　一次性的
conserve
　　节约；保存
diligent
　勤奋的；勤勉的
plastic
　　　塑料的
litter
　　　　乱扔
particle
　　微粒；粒子
vehicle
　　　机动车
exhaust
　　　　废气
track
　　追踪；跟踪
loom
　　　　逼近
utensil
　　　　器皿
council
　　　委员会
drought
　　　　旱灾
sweltering
　　　酷热的
power plant
　　　能源厂
curb
　　　　控制
emission
　　释放；排放

50. Lei Feng Spirit

雷锋精神

Dialogue

A: I've seen slogans on the street that say "Learn from Comrade Lei Feng". I also saw a picture of his head on a few T-shirts. Who is Lei Feng?

B: Lei Feng was an ordinary member of the Chinese army who lived during the 1960s. Mao Zedong called for all Chinese people to "Learn from Comrade Lei Feng."

A: So what kind of a person was Lei Feng?

B: He was born to a poverty-stricken home and later became an orphan. He grew up under the care of the government and neighbors, and in order to thank those who helped him, he lived only to "serve the people." He was always actively serving others; for instance, he escorted elderly people home, gave his hard-earned money to his fellow officers' mothers to help with medical expenses, and so on.

A: I think that's just average stuff, lots of people can do those things! So why should we study Lei Feng?

B: Right: actually you, I, and I dare say almost everyone has helped someone in the past, but Lei Feng didn't just do this every once in a while; he sought out people to help, even sacrificing his own needs. This is exactly what many people can't do and that's Lei Feng spirit.

A: Wow, if Lei Feng was that way, then that kind of spirit is really hard to come by. Besides helping people, what other things did he do that we should learn from?

B: He once compared himself to a screw. He would go wherever there was need and work there. He wasn't afraid of hardship and he wasn't picky. Many young people in today's society lack this kind of spirit.

A: Then how do Chinese people study Lei Feng? Was Mao Zedong's slogan effective?

B: Of course! Till today, Lei Feng spirit has influenced at least three generations of people. When we are kids, we read Lei Feng's diary, and we learn songs about him. We often go outside of school to do good deeds as well; for instance, helping widowed elderly people and cleaning public parks. We also learn from Lei Feng how to be thrifty instead of wasteful.

A: Lei Feng lived during one of the hardest periods of Chinese history, but nowadays China is developing very quickly. People have become wealthier, and they care more and more about personal comfort. Do you think the Lei Feng spirit has gone out of style?

B: In truth, people don't study Lei Feng with the enthusiasm they once did. But there are still many people who look to Lei Feng as a role model and are committed to following his example.

对 话

A: 我在街上看到过"向雷锋同志学习"的标语，还在一些T恤衫上看到过雷锋的头像。雷锋是谁?

B: 雷锋是一个普通的中国军人，他生活在上世纪60年代。"向雷锋同志学习"是毛泽东向所有中国人发出的号召。

A: 雷锋是个什么样的人呢?

B: 他出生在一个贫苦家庭，不久之后成为孤儿，在政府和邻居的照顾下长大，为了感谢帮助过他的人，他把为人民服务当成自己的全部，他总是积极主动地帮助别人，比如说，送不认识的老人回家和把自己辛辛苦苦存下来的钱拿去给战友的母亲治病等等。

A: 我觉得这些是很普通的小事，很多人都能做到啊! 为什么要学雷锋呢?

B: 是的，其实你和我，我敢说几乎所有人都曾经帮助过别人，但是雷锋不是偶尔或者顺便这样做，他是专门去帮助别人，甚至牺牲自己的利益，这恰恰是很多人做不到的，这就是雷锋精神。

A: 是的，如果雷锋是这样做的，这种精神真的是很难得。他除了帮助别人以外，还有什么别的值得学习的地方吗?

B: 他还把自己比喻成一颗螺丝钉，哪里有需要，他就去哪儿工作，不怕困难，不挑剔。这也是很多现代的年轻人普遍缺乏的精神。

A: 那么中国人是怎么学雷锋的呢? 毛泽东的那句口号起作用了吗?

B: 当然了，到现在，雷锋精神已经影响了至少三代人。我们小的时候，要读雷锋写的日记，学唱和雷锋有关的歌，还常常到学校外面去做好事，比如说去帮助孤寡老人、打扫公园等等;我们还要向雷锋学习勤俭节约、不浪费的精神。

A: 雷锋生活的年代是中国最困难的时期，可是现在中国的经济发展得很快，人们的生活富裕了，也越来越在乎自我享受，你觉得雷锋精神过时了吗?

B: 的确，现在人学雷锋的热情不如从前了。但是，还有很多人把雷锋当成偶像并继续向他学习!

Background Reading 背景阅读

Who Is Lei Feng? 谁是雷锋?

Born in 1940 in Changsha, Hunan Province, Lei Feng lost his parents when he was seven. At 20, he joined the People's Liberation Army and spent all his spare time and money helping the needy. He died in an accident on August 15, 1962 at the age of 22. Lei Feng became a household name on March 5, 1963 when the late Chinese leader Mao Zedong called on the Chinese people to "Learn from Comrade Lei Feng." March 5 has been designated "Learning from Lei Feng Day," so on March 5 of every year, millions of young people throughout China participate in volunteer activities to honor the memory of Lei Feng.

雷锋，1940 年出生于湖南省长沙，他在 7 岁时失去了父母，20 岁时，他加入了中国人民解放军，从那时起，他就把他所有的积蓄和闲暇时间都用来帮助那些贫困的人。1962 年 8 月 15 日，22 岁的他因一场意外事故而去世。1963 年 3 月 5 日，已故的中国领导人毛泽东号召全体中国人"向雷锋同志学习"，雷锋成了一个家喻户晓的名字，3 月 5 日也因此被指定为"学雷锋日"。每年的 3 月 5 日，全中国上百万的年轻人都会以参加志愿活动的形式来纪念雷锋。

The Spirit of Lei Feng 雷锋精神

There are some voices claiming Lei Feng's spirit has been forgotten by today's society. They argue that a capitalist economic system leads people to place more emphasis on pursuing fame, money, and the commodities that represent the comfortable life. Despite many people's opinion that this has become the dominant view of the present generation, there are some other voices claiming that the spirit of Lei Feng still has an enormous impact on millions of Chinese people. The great soldier's story has such a strong influence on people's ideas, values and ways of life that in every field of society there arise countless "Living Lei Fengs", who follow the example of Lei Feng and serve the people, heart and soul. The spirit of Lei Feng and his unselfish actions will always encourage us to go forward.

有些人认为雷锋精神已经被当今社会遗忘了。他们认为商品经济制度使人们更重视追求声望、钱财和以奢侈品为代表的舒适生活。尽管很多现代人都有这样的看法，但也有一些人认为，雷锋精神在上百万的中国人中仍然有着巨大的影响。这个伟大的战士的故事对人们的思想、价值观和生活方式都有着巨大的影响，以至于社会中的每个领域都有层出不穷的"活雷锋"，他们以雷锋为榜样，全心全意地为人民服务。雷锋精神和他无私的行动将会激励我们永远向前。

In Lei Feng's Words 雷锋语录

"A person's life is limited, but to serve the people is unlimited. I want to devote my limited life to serving the people endlessly."

"In the entire world, the most honorable thing is work, and the most honorable people are workers."

"Make others' hardships your own and take fulfillment from your comrades' happiness."

"人的生命是有限的，可是，为人民服务是无限的，我要把有限的生命，投入到无限的为人民服务之中去。"

"世界上最光荣的事——劳动。
世界上最体面的人——劳动者。"

"把别人的困难当成自己的困难，把同志的愉快看成自己的幸福。"

Exercises 练习

Answer these questions.

1. Why did Lei Feng devote his life to serving the people?
2. What are Lei Feng's admirable qualities?
3. What are a few ways you can be more like Lei Feng?

Translate these sentences into English.

1. 雷锋是一个普通的中国军人。
2. 毛泽东号召全体中国人"向雷锋同志学习"。
3. 雷锋活着的目的就是为人民服务。
4. 雷锋精神至少影响了三代中国人。
5. 社会中的每个领域都有层出不穷的"活雷锋"，他们以雷锋为榜样，为人民服务。
6. 很多中国人仍然把雷锋当成偶像。
7. 雷锋████████████将会激励我们永远向前。

Complete the following paragraph with these words or phrases.

textbooks   generations   inspired   preschoolers   ordinary   boyish

Lei Feng is probably the only __1__ Chinese to be remembered by the whole nation, and his selflessness and devotion have __2__ at least three __3__ of people over the past 40 years. His __4__ smile still beams today from posters, newspapers, television and children's __5__, and his name is known even to __6__.

 Answers 答案

Translate these sentences into English.

1. Lei Feng was an ordinary member of the Chinese army.
2. Mao Zedong called for all Chinese people to "Learn from Comrade Lei Feng."
3. Lei Feng lived only to serve the people.
4. Lei Feng's example has influenced three generations of Chinese people.
5. In every field of society there arise countless "Living Lei Fengs", who follow the example of Lei Feng and serve the people.
6. Many Chinese still think of Lei Feng as a role model.
7. The spirit of Lei Feng and his unselfish actions will always encourage us to go forward.

Complete the following paragraph with these words or phrases.

1. ordinary   2. inspired   3. generations   4. boyish
5. textbooks   6. preschoolers

词 汇 表	
slogan	口号；标语
army	军队
called for	号召
orphan	孤儿
escort	护送；陪同
fellow	同伴
seek out	寻求
come by	得到；获得
screw	螺丝钉
hardship	困难，苦难
picky	挑剔的
deed	事迹；功绩
thrifty	节俭的；节约的
commit to	致力于；献身
needy	贫困的人
late	已故的
designate	指定
commodity	商品
fame	声誉；名望
enormous	巨大的
field	领域
arise	出现；涌现
unselfish	无私的
devote	把…贡献给

201

图书在版编目（CIP）数据

英语畅谈青春文化50主题：英汉对照/刘佳静，（美）罗伯逊（Robertson，J.），
（美）卡特（Carter，L.）著.
北京：外文出版社，2007（英语国际人）
ISBN 978-7-119-04828-4

Ⅰ. 英… Ⅱ. ①刘… ②罗… ③卡… Ⅲ. 英语—汉语—对照读物 Ⅳ. H319.4

中国版本图书馆 CIP 数据核字（2007）第 069115 号

英语国际人
英语畅谈青春文化50主题

作　　者　刘佳静　　Jessica Robertson（美）　　Liz Carter（美）
选题策划　蔡　箐
责任编辑　李　溇
封面设计　红十月设计室
印刷监制　冯　浩

ⓒ外文出版社
出版发行　外文出版社
地　　址　中国北京西城区百万庄大街24号　　　邮政编码　100037
网　　址　http：//www.flp.com.cn
电　　话　（010）68995964/68995883（编辑部）
　　　　　（010）68995844/68995852（发行部/门市邮购）
　　　　　（010）68320579/68996067（总编室）
电子信箱　info@flp.com.cn/sales@flp.com.cn
印　　制　北京佳信达艺术印刷有限公司
经　　销　新华书店/外文书店
开　　本　小16开　　　　　　　　　　　印　　张　13
印　　数　0001—8000 册　　　　　　　字　　数　230千字
装　　别　平
版　　次　2007年6月第1版第1次印刷
书　　号　ISBN 978-7-119-04828-4
定　　价　25.00元

外文社图书　版权所有　侵权必究
外文社图书　有印装错误可随时退换